READING AND WRITING DISABILITY DIFFERENTLY: THE TEXTURED LIFE OF EMBODIMENT

What is the meaning of disability, and how are our conceptions of disability formed in contemporary society? In this book, Tanya Titchkosky challenges us to read and write disability differently than we ordinarily do in daily life. Through the examination of everyday texts about disability, this unique and detailed study explores how disability is put into text, narrated, and made present in readers' lives. Using interpretive social theory, *Reading and Writing Disability Differently* engages news media and policy texts that depict disability as a clear-cut problem in need of clear-cut solutions. These texts become opportunities to reveal dominant Western ways of constituting the meaning of people, and the meaning of problems, as they relate to contemporary understandings of our embodied selves.

Releasing disability's power as something more than a problem, and other than positive or negative, this study demonstrates the imaginative potential of regarding texts on disability as sites to examine neoliberal culture. Given that media and policy texts on disability are informed by tacit cultural assumptions, these texts serve as a social scene worthy of critical inquiry. We are shown how we can pursue a self-reflexive analysis of ordinary ways of reading and writing as they constitute embodiment as a problem, and how we might escape the confines of a collective imagination dedicated only to solving troubles. The rigorous mixing of social theory and concrete analysis allows for the possibility of a radical new approach to disability. Titchkosky holds that through an exploration of the potential that lies behind limited representations of disability, we can relate to disability as a meaningful form of resistance to the restricted normative order of contemporary embodiment.

Tanya Titchkosky is a disability studies professor in the Department of Sociology and Equity Studies at the Ontario Institute for Studies in Education, University of Toronto, and author of *Disability, Self, and Society* (2003).

TANYA TITCHKOSKY

Reading and Writing Disability Differently

The Textured Life of Embodiment

UNIVERSITY OF TORONTO PRESS
Toronto Buffalo London

© University of Toronto Press Incorporated 2007
Toronto Buffalo London
Printed in Canada

Reprinted 2008

ISBN 978-0-8020-9236-6 (cloth)
ISBN 978-0-8020-9506-0 (paper)

Printed on acid-free paper

Library and Archives Canada Cataloguing in Publication

Titchkosky, Tanya, 1966–
Reading and writing disability differently : the textured life of
embodiment / Tanya Titchkosky.

Includes bibliographical references and index.
ISBN 978-0-8020-9236-6 (bound)
ISBN 978-0-8020-9506-0 (pbk.)

1. People with disabilities in mass media.   2. Sociology of
disability.   I. Title.

HV 1568.T583 2007   302.23'2087   C2006-906615-9

This book has been published with the help of a grant from the
Canadian Federation for the Humanities and Social Sciences,
through the Aid to Scholarly Publications Programme, using
funds provided by the Social Sciences and Humanities Research
Council of Canada.

University of Toronto Press acknowledges the financial assistance
to its publishing program of the Canada Council for the Arts and
the Ontario Arts Council.

University of Toronto Press acknowledges the financial support
for its publishing activities of the Government of Canada through
the Book Publishing Industry Development Program (BPIDP).

For Sydney

In particular, because speech acts are bodily performed, the body is a rhetorical instrument that contributes to the 'force' of those speech acts ... The question is: How might disabled individuals speak with our own authority against this psychically internalized authorization only to cite able-bodied norms?

– Susan Stocker, 'Problem of Embodiment and Problematic Embodiment,' 35

... how to think, write, and read otherwise ...

– Elizabeth Grosz, 'Histories of the Present and Future,' 22

It is no easy matter to attend to qualities that are not given, but which make the given possible, lace its emergence, hover at its boundaries.

– Judith Butler, 'Foreword' to *The Erotic Bird*, by Maurice Natanson, xiii

Contents

Acknowledgments   xi

Introduction   3

1 Text and the Life of Disability   11

PART ONE: PROBLEMS

2 Totally a Problem: Government Survey Texts   45

3 Metamorphosis: Making Disability a Medical Matter   79

4 Reading and Recognition: Un-doing Disability's Deadly
  Status   108

PART TWO: DIS-SOLUTIONS

5 Governing Embodiment: Technologies of Constituting
  Citizens with Disabilities   145

6 Overcoming: Abled-Disabled and Other Acts of Normative
  Violence   177

Afterword   209

Notes   213

References   219

Index   237

Acknowledgments

Many organizations and people have influenced this book and made it possible. I would like to thank St Francis Xavier University, the Social Sciences and Humanities Research Council, the Aid to Scholarly Publications Programme, and Human Resources Development Canada for financial support. Dr Ron Johnson and Dr Mary McGillivray, respective past and present academic vice-president and provost of St Francis Xavier University, have provided financial and other sorts of support that have helped bring this project to fruition. The comments of the anonymous reviewers for University of Toronto Press (UTP) were most helpful. Virgil Duff, UTP's executive acquisition editor, provided consistent, warm, and methodic engagement throughout the publication process of this book. All these efforts are much appreciated.

There are too many undergraduate students from St Francis Xavier University for me to name who have helped with this book; many students have brought me newspaper articles as well as other texts and images of disability. A special word of thanks is due to the students of 'Interpretive Methods of Social Inquiry.' In this course, many of the theoretical issues regarding reading and text were carefully engaged. Through our course work together, I was provided with the opportunity to clarify my own commitments and enrich my analysis of the active social character of reading and writing.

Terri Pitts, past student and now patient teacher, has lent her patience to my text as she helped to put my dyslexic words into order. The 'I've Had It!' reading group, and all the other student reading groups over the past years, were especially engaging and provocative. So thanks to Katie Aubrecht, Jonathan Francis, Colleen Wall, Patrick McLane, Erin Hynes, Allison MacDonald, Carly MacDonald, and Rod Michalko. Katie Aubrecht, in particular, has been a most enjoyable friend, and a great research assistant. Her own graduate work has already fulfilled the promise to rewrite and reread disability again and again. Katie not only helped to gather resources for this book but has opened me up to thinking my own words in new ways.

The publication of this book also marks my leaving St FX and the Department of Sociology and Anthropology in Antigonish, Nova Scotia, where I learned how to teach and make my writing responsive to my teaching. I would like to thank many of my colleagues at St FX and people in the town of Antigonish. Special thanks for supportive poignant conversations are owed to Dan and Annette Ahern, Agnes Calliste, Heather Carson, Patricia Cormack, Robert Kennedy, Jeanette and David Lynes, Will Sweet, and Judy and Dan MacInnes. The entire MacInnes' family, Dan, Judy, Colin, Catherine, and Iain, has offered me unwavering support through detailed incisive conversation on many aspects of this work and did so whether we gathered in Antigonish, Cape Breton, or elsewhere. Carla Haley Baxter, administrative assistant par excellence, has befriended me in all my dyslexic ways and made teaching, writing, learning, and technical matters like completing forms much easier for me, and she will always have my gratitude. Carla also provided impeccable editing and proofreading. To all those who provided music, dance, and conversation at the Ceilidh's, this book is undoubtedly the better for your lively energy, thank you.

I thank Lilith Finkler, who sent me scores of articles and always spurred me on with her unbounded enthusiasm for the project. Thanks, too, to Donna Smith for sending me news articles and for critical, sociologically informed engagement. Len Barton has been most supportive and friendly toward this project, thank you. Penni Stewart's unwavering interest, belief, and ironic wit have constantly encouraged me. I thank Lori Beaman and Bev Matthews for providing me with the opportunity to think about the term 'intersectionality' anew. I thank also the Institute on Race and Disability at the 2006 Society for Disability Studies (SDS) for helping me return again to the issue of intersectionality and improving the Introduction to this book. I am particularly indebted to Nirmala Erevelles' incisive engagement, alongside the friendly provocation of the many people whom I have met and engaged with through SDS conferences and online Listserv. SDS's organizational commitment to practices of inclusion, as well as its commitment to keep rethinking the shape and social significance of inclusive practices, have been most inspiring to me. Even as many other organizations have not yet begun to think about practices of radical inclusion of embodied difference, SDS is serving as a lively testimony of the need to theorize inclusion as it translates embodiment and serves as a productive force of constituting the meaning of being together. I completed some of the final edits on this book after attending the 2006 SDS conference in Washington, DC. It is my hope that this book has something to offer both the new and established scholars and activists whom I met there, since all of you offered so much to me and enhanced my commitment to sociologically theorizing embodiment.

This book carries the influence of all of these people. All of you will remain with me as I begin my new life and work in the Department of Sociology and Equity Studies in Education at the Ontario Institute for Studies in Education of the University of Toronto (OISE/UT). What remains constant in my teaching, reading groups, conference going, theorizing, politicizing, and living with disability is Rod Michalko's provocative support. Rod has listened to every word of this book, often many times over, and has edited it from the point of view of his blindness. Rod has discussed many of the ideas and issues in this book with me. For all the different ways of living and working in disability that you continue to share with me, I thank you.

Early versions of some parts of chapters have been published elsewhere. Thanks to the journals, organizations, and people who have allowed me to return to my early writing and rework it here. A version of the Introduction has appeared as 'Pausing at the Intersections of Difference,' in *Gender in Canada: A Multi-Dimensional Approach*, edited by Beverly Matthews and Lori G. Beaman (Toronto: Pearson, 2006). Yet another version of the Introduction was presented at the 2006 SDS conference and titled, 'Re-imagine Disability Representation as a Paradoxical Provocation.' A version of chapter 3 appeared as 'Clenched Subjectivity: Disability, Women and Medical Discourse,' in a special issue of *Disability Studies Quarterly* (25.3 [2005]) on technology, edited by Gerard Goggin and Christopher Newell (www.dsq-sds.org). Some parts of chapter 4 appeared in 2005 as 'Disability in the News: A Reconsideration of Reading,' *Disability & Society* (20.6: 653–66). Finally, a version of chapter 5, 'Governing Embodiment,' appeared under the same title in the *Canadian Journal of Sociology* (28.4 [2003]: 517–42).

READING AND WRITING DISABILITY DIFFERENTLY:
THE TEXTURED LIFE OF EMBODIMENT

Introduction

It was the late summer of 2005. I watched television coverage and read newspaper accounts about the poor and black people in the midst of the U.S. gulf coast devastation that followed hurricane Katrina. Black people were described as looting; white people, as securing provisions. A white male senator said that the behaviour of the people of New Orleans is 'shaming America'; a white female *New York Times* writer spoke of 'United States of Shame,' given the government's lethal lack of response (Dowd, *New York Times*, 3 Sept. 2005). I watched this human degradation unfold during a gentle summer in Eastern Canada. From the Scottish Highlands of rural Nova Scotia in a small university town, I watched the CNN coverage; I watched in all my middle-class whiteness; I watched black, poor women and men suffering and dying in New Orleans.

In our attention to such images and words, we find the making of the meaning of people. It is not just that we 'all have our differences'; it is, instead, that we attend to differences differently, making them *intersect* in particular ways. One form of attention can lead to compelling news stories for some. Another form of attention leads to reviling trauma for others. Our identities are forged, in part, by how we attend to these intersecting differences. Among all our identifications, of both ourselves and of others, lies the possibility of uncovering how we constitute a sense of the world. The concept of 'intersectionality' can be read, then, as a call to watch our watching, to read our readings, and to uncover a few of the ways we identify differences, including those differences that are today identified as disability.

Responses to the storm represent identifications of disability – disabled people are present everywhere, and disability is one thing that all cultural endeavours always bring into being. Many wheelchair users appear in the media coverage of Katrina, blankets draped over them; some people are entirely covered, blanketing signs of gender and race, but not of death. Through images and words, disabled people are depicted as stuck outside of the big sports dome or stuck inside some attic awaiting transfer to a habitable environment. These people are referred to as the 'special needs' people, the 'elderly,' the 'infirmed,' and the 'weak,' or simply as the 'vulnerable.'

Vulnerable is a term that can allow blackness, poorness, and disablement to intermingle as if these differences are merely individual fates. *Vulnerable* can be used so that people do not have to imagine how the intersections of some social differences are made to appear as if natural, like unwanted storms. But keeping close to the concept of intersectionality, we could ask what it means to interpret the intermingling of some social differences as 'the vulnerable' and who is thus constituted as 'the strong'? From this more social perspective, *vulnerable* can draw attention to daily life as it is tied up with collective ways of interpreting embodiment. A very deep vulnerability lies in the ease with which we can forget that embodiment is always a mediated social phenomenon. Embodiment appears through intersecting interests of self and of others. During the aftermath of Katrina, it seems that people try to remember this; some say, 'Just because they were vulnerable, doesn't mean they deserved to die.' More than identity politics is at stake here, since people are never in their bodies alone.

Disability appears in other ways too. I read in the newspaper, 'Why does this self-styled "can do" president always lapse into such lame "who could have known?" excuses.' Or, '... they were deaf for so long to the horrific misery and cries for help of the victims in New Orleans – most of them poor and black' (Dowd, ibid.). *Blind* to the levee issue, *deaf* to the anguished calls, *lame* in

their responses, and needing to *stand up and run* with some courageous leadership. This disability discourse serves something
other than the interests of disabled people. Disability is made
viable as a metaphor to express only that which is unwanted and
that which is devastatingly inept. What might be made of the
intersection between disability as a taken-for-granted metaphor
for 'big problem' and disability as a blanketed dead body
slumped in a wheelchair outside the sports dome?

The point of pausing at such contradictory intersections of the
meaning of people is not just to find more positive images or
more accurate expressions. As Sharon Snyder's and David
Mitchell's work suggests, in the midst of cultural representations, disability studies scholars and/or activists might instead
'destabilize our dominant ways of knowing disability' (2006: 4).
Critical attention to how disability is and is not read and written
today is one way to participate in the disability studies project of
destabilization. Such attention can lead us toward reading and
writing disability differently, and provide for the possibility of
developing new relations to the cultural values that ground the
various appearances and disappearances of disability in everyday life.

Disability appears in the everyday life of text in a host of seemingly contradictory ways. In a single newspaper there are representations of disability as a dead body outside the sports dome
and as a viable metaphor of choice to express inadequate
responses to the storm. A deep provocation lies in the fact that
the very ways that disability is included in everyday life are,
also, part of that which structures the continued manifestation of
disabled people as a non-viable type. It is, for example, provocative to think about how disability is both excluded *and* included
simultaneously in the interstices of our lives, or included as an
excludable type. It is essential to think about how we do and do
not notice these forms of exclusion *and* inclusion. The different
expressions of disability found in media accounts of Katrina
demonstrate that the meaning of embodiment is made by people
(and this is another way that we are never in our bodies alone).
One meaning constituted today is that disability is the metaphor

of choice to express problems, while often disappearing from the social landscape as a form of human existence. The meaning of disability is composed of conflicts of inclusion and exclusion as this intersects with our ordinary ways of recognizing people ... or not.

Attending to print and images about the intersections of difference in our daily lives is a way to understand that we are active participants in making up the meaning of people. Differences are never merely noted, since we always notice from a particular context and we are always guided by interests. Noticing differences, we actually *produce* a depiction of storms and their aftermath; we note differences and make the story of what happened to and for other people. We perform the meaning of our embodied existence by the *way we narrate* the intersections of human diversity in the midst of which our bodies appear and in the ways that we 'sell' those stories to others. *Reading and Writing Disability Differently* requires relating to disability as it appears in powerfully paradoxical ways, and going on to regard this lived interpretive complexity as the prime space to rethink our culture in new ways. Disability, made by culture, is the prime space to reread and rewrite culture's makings.

The expressions of disability, seemingly everywhere in the mass media, are provocative, not because I disagree with the critique levelled against the U.S. federal government, and not because I want to clean up the English language; but, rather, because viable status is not granted to disability. In *Undoing Gender* (2004: 2), Judith Butler theorizes the social act of *recognition*, in which some people are recognized as less than human and produced as non-viable. Media *reports* about such activities and phenomena as storms, war, genetic testing, accidents, physician-assisted suicide, unsafe work environments, and mass ultrasound projects are some of the key discursive practices including, surrounding, and constituting disability today. These narratives make for a restricted imagination since they do not include the possibility of claiming disability as a desired status, as Simi Linton (2006, 1998) suggests we should do; nor do they include disability as a difference that the collective needs, which

Rod Michalko's work (2002, 1998) invites us to imagine. In the ordinary goings-on of daily life, we commonly talk about the tragic character and negative consequences of impairment; there is also a lot of talk that uses disparaging disability-metaphors; however, it is possible and, I think, necessary to reflect on what disability talk *does*. *Reading and Writing Disability Differently* is dedicated to an analysis of the here-and-now talk about disability, by asking, 'How does our current discursive action organize and assert the meaning of embodied existence?' As disability is written into texts for mass consumption, all involved are participating in making up the meaning of people; uncovering such meaning-making is a way to read and write disability differently. I hope this book exemplifies more viable and imaginative ways to live with the social fact that our embodiment is text mediated.

Much of this book was written prior to the gulf coast disaster. Still, that disaster has confirmed for me the necessity of uncovering what sort of world we are making when we *do* typical and expected disability talk in ordinary daily life. By dealing with such ordinary expressions, perhaps we might be better prepared to understand the horrific and extraordinary stuff that happens to disabled people. Throughout this book, I operate on the principle that it is both possible and desirable to investigate our everyday expressions of embodiment as they construct an immediate sense of self and world. I conduct my investigation without moving off elsewhere, to some more distant place of, for example, what should or might have been done, or ought to have been known; or to how disability might be better modelled or programmatically managed. The already written is my realm of interest. Words on disability are themselves a doing, are themselves a way of knowing; such words reside among us and help to make our fate as embodied beings. From this comes the need to stay in touch with common and ordinary expressions of disability, and to uncover the type of people and type of world those expressions presuppose.

Such a project entails escaping from the demand that disability simply get added to the oft-cited trilogy of gender, race, and class. Disability is certainly gendered, raced, and classed through

everyday talk, and disability also intersects with sexuality, ethnicity, age, family status, and all other forms of difference. But
citing and adding difference to difference will not necessarily
reveal how daily existence needs and makes these differences;
how it needs and makes some differences notable some of the
time, in some places, and other differences neither noticed nor
viable. Let us return again to Butler's reminder: 'Certain humans
are recognized as less than human, and that form of qualified
recognition does not lead to a viable life. Certain humans are not
recognized as human at all ...' (2004: 2). Disability, often defined
through inability, lack, and loss, receives recognition of this
negating sort. Since disability has typically been left out of the
politics and theorizing of gender, race, and class, it can serve as a
prime discursive field where the meaning of alterity under contemporary conditions can be considered. Disability is not merely
the Other to normalcy, but is rather an irreducible productive
force, a kind of alterity to any interest we have developed in
identity and difference. From here identity politics might move
on to address the powerfully political process of recognizing
how identities have and have not been recognized, formed, and
narrated by everyday life.

In the welter of differences, my aim is to uncover how we might
encounter disability in new ways, or at least read disability differently, by attending to how we already do and do not notice
embodied existence. This is not adding disability to existing
senses of difference. This is, as Anna Mollow's work demonstrates, questioning the idea that all that needs to be done is the
'installation of disability as another identity category' (2004: 269).
Such questioning is also a way to reconcile ourselves to the current play of absences and presences that disability has been made
to be so as to think new relations to alterity. Speaking about difference in feminist projects, Elizabeth Grosz puts the issue this
way: '... how to think, write, or read *not* as a woman, but more
complexly and less clearly, how to think, write and read otherwise ... how to accommodate issues, qualities, concepts that have
not had their time before' (2003: 22). How to notice, read, and
write disability otherwise than the dominant modalities of daily

life would have us encounter disability, is my aim. Such an aim requires that we face and interrogate those dominant modalities that already, in the here and now, give us disability as a clear-cut problem in need of a solution. Considering disability as something different from undesired difference, as something other than an add-on, and as more than a problem can allow us to understand how embodiment is organized and made manifest. So, I do not treat disability as an empirical problem; I do not ask how often does disability appear in the news, and I do not ask how often is disability depicted positively or negatively. Instead, I always treat disability as an interpretive issue. This book continually asks: what do we make of disability such that it makes an appearance in everyday life as a problem? Once disability is understood as a problem, what solutions arise? Finally, as a dissolved problem, what becomes of embodiment? My guiding assumption is that this interrogation of the daily textual appearance of disability will allow for the possibility of thinking, reading, and writing disability otherwise. I also assume that most people live with textual representations of disability, but that we all do so in very different ways. My dyslexia, teaching disability studies, and sharing my life and work with a blind person are disability experiences which have undoubtedly given me access to the desire to read and write disability differently. I hope that readers' embodied differences will also provide for such access too.

This book attempts to reveal how the life of disability is textured by the ordinary ways that print media enunciates both the problem of disability and its (dis)solutions. Daily, print media depicts disability as a troublesome difference, a problem, as a way to refer to other problems, or as a problem that has been undergone, overcome, managed, or dissolved. Texturing the life of disability as a problem leads me to wonder just what sort of problem disability has been imagined to be for and by the contemporary minority world. As, for example, a blanketed dead body in a wheelchair and as a derogatory metaphor to express inadequate responses to a storm, disability is made present as the space of provocation where we might begin to reread how culture puts our embodiment to text and textures all of our lives. Attend-

ing to our taken-for-granted lives as embodied beings by analysing how disability is put into text in ordinary ways can begin to
disrupt the seemingly natural conflation of disability with undesired vulnerability and ineptitude. In this way, perhaps embodied
existence can be lived and imagined a little differently.

1 Text and the Life of Disability

Still the risk must be taken. A reformulation must be attempted if the life world is not to be dashed to linguistic bits. *Someone* must take responsibility for the English language. Whatever presents itself in perceptual awareness is a candidate for phenomenological scrutiny.

– Maurice Natanson,
The Erotic Bird: Phenomenology in Literature, 22

My project here is to analyse the achieved social significance of disability in everyday life, especially the everyday life of print. As a way to pursue this project, this chapter lays out the conceptual and interpretive affiliations necessary for bringing to awareness the ways in which the meaning of disability is enacted in everyday texts. This chapter represents the risk of believing that our on-going textual encounters with disability are interactive scenes where we can engage and scrutinize the contemporary cultural organization of embodiment. Through an introductory discussion of what such engagement entails, I seek to narrate the necessity of developing self-reflective and critical responses to textual constructions of disability.

Disability and Embodiment

This book grows out of an interest in unpacking the social significance of disability by engaging its meaning as it appears and is enacted in everyday life. 'Disability,' for my purposes, is a process of meaning-making that takes place somewhere and is done by somebody. Whenever disability is perceived, spoken, or even thought about, people mean it in some way. The ways that disability comes to have meaning have something to teach us about our life-worlds. Understanding disability as a site where meaning is enacted not only requires conceptualizing disability as a social accomplishment, it also means developing an animated sense of that which enacts these meanings. Again, disability, made by culture, is a prime location to reread and rewrite culture's makings.

My aim is to open an inquiry that develops a desire to uncover the meanings of disability within contemporary Western culture, while resisting the temptation to simplify by rendering disability into a definable objectified *thing*.

All sorts of people and institutions aim to concretize the definitional parameters of disability, and all sorts of definitions abound. Definition is one form of meaning-making; definition, like any other talk about disability, has, following W.I. Thomas (1971), 'real consequences' for the ways in which disability can be read, written, thought about, lived. Rather than create more definitions, I orient to disability as an arena of already existing talk and conduct. Such talk and conduct actively make what counts as disability, while relying on and producing the meanings of embodied existence. As something said and done by people, disability becomes a site where it is possible to uncover how the use of this meaningful concept is simultaneously the accomplishment of culture.

I hold that the problematic of 'embodiment,' of fleshy life, of our being embodied beings, can be grasped through an analysis of how we give meaning to disability within everyday life (Titchkosky 2003a). Disability is made meaningful by the ways we say it to be and live its being. Annemarie Mol and John Law remind us of the importance of conceptualizing embodiment as a relation to the social fact that 'we all *have* and *are* a body. But there is a way out of this dichotomous twosome. As part of our daily practices, *we also do (our) bodies*. In practice we enact them' (2004: 45).

Embodiment is all the many and various ways that we (self and other) accomplish relations to being in possession of the bodies that we are. The concept of embodiment brings to attention the sorts of relations we develop to the body-object (e.g., impairment) and the body-subject (e.g., disability) (Radley 2002). Whether experienced as warring sides or as a harmonious whole, subject and object are brought to consciousness relationally through the concept of embodiment. This is why Mol and Law are correct to assert that keeping ourselves together, that is, *embodiment* is 'one of the tasks of life' (2004: 57). This is also why disability, in whatever way it is defined, narrated, and lived, serves as an occasion when we might critically examine the cultural provision of dominant ways of keeping ourselves together.

Embodiment as the complexity of relations we develop to having and being bodies is, then, allied to the constitution of the meaning of persons. Understanding this, everyday talk and conduct surrounding disability can become an opportunity to examine the dominant ways that we have of constituting the meaning of people, and the meaning of problems, and the ways that we have to live with our embodied selves in the face of both. To speak of embodiment is to form some knowledge of it, and how we know our embodied reality acts upon how we orient toward disability. Thus, I remain committed throughout this book to an analysis of what might be called the 'now' of disability. Such a critical focus allows me to continually ask, How does disability appear in our here-and-now existence? What values and assumptions does this appearance serve? Written text is, of course, one moment when some people confront embodied existence in the here and now of everyday life, but I will say more on text later.

For a variety of reasons, I am attached to the project of uncovering how, and to what ends, disability is made meaningful, and some of my reasons can be regarded as quite personal. For example, my life is tied to a host of different experiences of disability: I teach disability studies; I teach some disabled students; I am dyslexic; I share my life and my scholarly work with a blind person, Rod Michalko, who is also a sociologist; and we both read and write about disability and culture. Moreover, like everyone else, I live in a culture that daily produces and displays texts that have something to say about, and to do to, disability. So, my particular life is intimately bound up with a variety of disability-words and disability-deeds, as well as a variety of ways of knowing disability: sociologically, historically, bureaucratically, juridically, medically, personally – in a word, *typically*. All of these various appearances of disability, while incredibly diverse, share in common the fact that any one of them, and all of them, can and do appear in *text*.

Textual Enactment of Disability

Let us begin simply: through the mass media and seemingly effortlessly, we become aware of disability. In the face of the advent of this awareness, we may say, 'What a shame' or 'It's no different' or 'Why that's just like me' or 'They have a lot to deal with' or 'That's hardly disabled!' or ... A host of conceptions can organize our experience of disability even as our fleshly life might be helping us rethink our perception of embodiment. But notice that becoming aware of disability is simultaneously the noticing of a shift, a change, or a difference that, even as it is being evaluated as 'not so bad' or as 'not different really,' is already positioned as unwanted, undesirable, or, at least, unusual. Could disability be noticed outside of this basic understanding of its undesirability? Perhaps. Nonetheless, now is the time to attend to how that which is typically regarded as an undesired difference at the level of embodiment is actually acted on and lived with – enacted – within everyday life *as* disability. It is in this way that our here-and-now awareness of disability in everyday life can come under scrutiny.

Attending to everyday life can begin to make us sensitive to the fact that texts on disability abound. The West's bureaucratized-consumeristic-information age, steeped in literacy as it is, has also made me certain that most people have some sort of textual encounter with disability on a daily basis. Entering a government office, I see a poster of two white men in suits; one is a wheelchair user. The poster reads: 'One of these men is a burden to society. The other is disabled.' (The intention of this poster is to show that non-disabled persons' attitudes are a burden to society.) I pick up the Sunday edition of the *Toronto Star* (10 June 2001: F4) and read: 'Tragedy turned into hope for millions: Louis Braille's accident in his Father's saddle shop became a turning point for the blind around the world.' The news ticker on my computer screen tells me about a connection between genes and depression, while a different story is told on drug labels and product inserts. Reading about world politics in the *Chronicle Herald* (16 January 2005: A10), I find: 'It's a robbery of retirees: Elderly, disabled stage mass protests in Russia over loss of social programs like free medicine.' While waiting in the dentist office, I flip through a variety of magazines; all sorts of articles abound on the promises of genetic research to eliminate or cure disability at some future time. Then, of course, there are advertisements for food, supplements, and other products making claims to stave off this or that impairment. Buying some wine, I see the charity box; the sign above the box indicates that this week the money will be given to the MS society. If memory serves, last week it was for the Coalition of Injured Workers, which puts me in mind of the poster of a severed hand that I saw on the public washroom stall door that tells me to 'work safe.' Be it related to body, mind, or senses, depictions of impairments abound in texts of everyday life, intersecting with age, gender, sexuality, race, class, location, and all the other desires and differences that help to constitute our selves in relation to others.

Experiencing a plethora of textual renderings of disability can be provocative. They can make us want to understand embodiment as a social phenomenon, since clearly disability is never one objective thing but is better understood as an interactive scene. Moreover, text gives us a place where we can organize an encounter between our embodied selves reading in time and space, and the time of the text with the spaces it delineates, as all of this orders our consciousness (Smith 1999). The hope of such an encounter is that, upon interrogation, it can lead to understanding, where understanding means neither acquiescing nor accepting, but rather discerning, how our culture already lives through us and how we might better live through it. I am suggesting that various and even conflicting textual renderings of disability as hope, burden, charity, promise, etc., are occasions to question how we make bodies mean and to evaluate the sorts of relations people can and do establish with the meaning of disability. I am not suggesting that disability merely needs to be added in to the identity politics debates. Instead, given that all identities, as well as the way that we politicize them, are accomplished by embodied beings, disability is an occasion to reconsider the meaning of identity politics and all the other ways we have of relating to ourselves and to others.[1]

The colossal prevalence of our ongoing textual interaction with disability is not due strictly to the fact that so many of us are disabled or becoming so. It is also due to the fact that the cultural spaces amenable to providing an occasion for a textual engagement with disability are expansive: textual renderings of disability occur daily in newspapers, medical and government pamphlets and posters, magazines, online, in the yellow pages of phone books, company advertisements, and even in lines at the grocery store where we consider whether or not we should drop our change into a particular donation box for the care or cure of some type of impairment or another. How we live with and in disability is an inter-textual phenomenon. And even if there is a reader of this book who believes that they do not have an intimate connection to disability, most surely even he or she will still experience disability through text. Insofar as the meaning of disability is actively being produced from our daily relations with texts, there are ethical, political, and practical reasons for the analysis of this phenomenon.

The examination of the textual enactment of disability is a fascinating process whereby we can come to understand the constitution of the meaning of persons, or at least what is governing our relations to our embodied existence. Moreover, we can pursue this encounter through an analysis of the here and now of our social acts of reading and writing. 'Scrutinizing,' as Natanson (1998) puts it, how disability is brought to awareness through textual products is a way to attend to the *textured life of disability.* The term 'textured' refers not merely to the fact that disability abounds in texts. Textured also refers to the fact that the weight, substance, and sense of disability are put together by texts that are woven into readers' lives in a variety of ways. Attending to this texturing is to uncover how disability is made meaningful through its enactment in our daily lives. In scrutinizing our textured lives resides the possibility of responding to disability as something more complex than an undesired-embodied-difference. Pursuing such scrutiny takes responsibility for attending to how the presence of disability is being made manifest.

In order to further this project of analysing the achieved social significance of disability, this chapter now lays out the conceptions and interpretive axis necessary for pursuing a form of social inquiry that treats the meaning of disability as an enactment and, in particular, a textual enactment.

Appearance as Enactment

In the midst of appearances – someone or something making itself apparent to us or us to them – lies an 'enactment.' Appearances are enactments in a reflexive sense insofar as they are an enactment of social life and take place within that realm. Whatever appears does so conditioned by the possibility of its appearance. This conditioning is represented in the socio-cultural ground organizing the appearance, as well as in the observing subject located on, and ready to read an appearance from, this ground. Thus, appearances reflexively organize them(our)selves through the social processes of an *enactment.*

I make use of the concept of enactment to pursue the possibility of scrutinizing what we *are doing* to make disability, and thus our lived-embodiment, present and apparent to ourselves and to others in the here and now. Attending to enactment allows for the question: 'When we read something about disability, how is the meaning of disability being enacted in our lives?' This question grows out of my need to resist the dominant cultural demand to get at the 'truth' of disability, the real definition, the authentic experience, the facts of the case, or some other isolated originating objective place of disability. The question I propose here allows me to continue to develop my commitment to the principle that the meaning of disability lies 'between' people and not merely in people (Titchkosky 2003a, 2000). The question of how the meaning of disability is being enacted will not provide answers to where the meaning of disability originates, but will hold open the possibility of addressing that which is readily apparent in our daily lives. What is readily apparent is that textual renderings of disability confront me and you in a variety of different contexts and give shape to the meaning of persons both included and excluded by those contexts. How we come to imagine disability has everything to do with how we forge relations between ourselves and others. As different as these contexts of disability are, they still reflect something about our modern-capitalist, bureaucratically ordered, and consumeristically driven literate background.

While analytically efficacious, the concept of enactment is neither rare nor new to social thought.[2] For example, Judith Butler's deployment of the concept 'performativity' is currently having much influence on how we think about the enacted character of identity and the achievement of daily reality. Her work, especially *Bodies That Matter* (1993), *Undoing Gender* (2004), and *Giving an Account of Oneself* (2005), has certainly influenced me here. All of this work demonstrates an understanding that in the opacity of being neither radically free nor strictly determined, people make relations with what has made them and thereby enact some sense of who they are.

Enactment has even gained a kind of popular usage, and debates about the concept's political and theoretical efficacy are cropping up (Beck-Gernsheim, Butler, and Puigvert 2001; Fenstermaker and West 2002: 189–216). In some cultural studies and feminist theory circles, for example, arguments are arising regarding the place and power of this concept, especially as it pertains to performing our political agendas with, and analyses of, differences and identities on the margins and in the mainstreams (see, especially, Benhabib et al. 1995; Butler 2004; Parker and Sedgwick 1995; McRuer and Wilkerson 2003; Sandahl and Auslander 2005). These arguments are stimulating and have provoked me in many ways. However, deciding on whether we enact our identities, or whether these identities are given materially, or whether either argument leads to a more efficacious politics or analysis, is not my agenda. It is not my agenda since origin stories, portrayals of what we are all about, or narrations of our needed end-point are already instances of enacting what it means to be human, or feminist, or politically efficacious.

My aim is to proceed by uncovering what meanings have already been accomplished by various descriptions, definitions, and other narrative renderings of disability that appear in text. Borrowing from Henri-Jacques Stiker 'At most my goal is to enlarge the understanding that we already have' (1999: 18), *enlarge* here does not mean to progressively improve. Instead, I mean to interrogate how we already comprehend disability and thus enlarge our understanding of our understandings. Limiting my work to the aim of enlarging understandings of disability allows me to make use of a variety of social theorists. I sport no exegetical commitment to any one theorist but instead rely on anyone who can help enlarge the understandings of disability that are already in circulation in daily life.

Others have also taken an interest in the fact that we are enacting our existence and that what appears can thus be recognized as ripe for analysis since the appearance reflects what has made it possible to appear in the first place. In discussing Husserl's work, Gail Weiss suggests, 'When I perceive an object ... [it] is situated within a perceptual field that itself serves as a kind of background or horizon against which, and by means of which, the object is perceived' (2003: 26). Between this ground and the observing subject lies the enactment of an appearance. According to Aaron Cicourel (1970: 148), the normal form of this appearance is that which we employ in order to 'assign sense' to everyday existence, and what seems sensible is *normed*. However, more than sensibility or intelligibility is at stake here.

Between the perceiver and the perceived, *meaning* is released ambiguously since neither fully determines the other, while both act upon each other. This is one way to understand Max Weber's concept of oriented action: 'Action is social in so far as, by virtue of the subjective meaning attached to it by the acting individual (or individuals), it takes account the behavior of others and is thereby oriented in its course' (1947: 88). My action, say, of reading a newspaper article on disability, is social insofar as it takes into account the subjective meaning attached to disability by others, for example, the words and genre of the text and our shared and differing contexts. So, my reading of disability 'is thereby oriented in its course'; it is oriented to understanding the understandings others have and make of disability. As the phenomenologist Maurice Merleau-Ponty says, '... word is a gesture, and its meaning, a world' (1958: 214). What is written on and read about disability acts to gesture the type of world that grounds the possibility of disability having the meanings that it does. Any reading is filled with something well beyond an individual's 'take' on disability, since reading is made up of the words of others which, ironically, include an individual reader's words on these words as they are enacted into our existence. Following Dorothy Smith I emphatically hold that 'to speak or write is thus always essentially dialogic' (1999: 136), and so this book represents a study of the textual enactment of disability within this understanding.

While there are many differences among all the theorists just mentioned, they can all provoke us to consider the act, power, and products of interpretation and move the analysis of understanding disability along. They also share in common an ability to disrupt the taken for granted relations of embodiment and rouse the need for an exploration of disability as something that is made meaningful through the activity of writing and reading its appearance into existence. Sharon Snyder and David Mitchell argue that 'since texts provide us access to perspectives that inevitably filter disability through the reigning ideologies of their day, their analysis proves tantamount to turning social beliefs into an object of investigation' (2006: 201). What is essential here is not whether readers or writers are in possession of impairment or identify as disabled. Instead, what is essential is that the appearance of disability in text comes under a radical interpretive scrutiny, where how we regard the embodied existence of self and other is reconsidered and we remake these relations anew.

Meaning-Making

The making of meaning resides in the enactment of an appearance. In *The Psychic Life of Power,* Judith Butler develops the matter in this way:

> Power acts on the subject, an acting that is an enacting; an irresolvable ambiguity arises when one attempts to distinguish between the power that (transitively) enacts the subject, and the power enacted by the subject, that is, between the power that forms the subject and the subject's 'own' power. (1997: 15)

Appearance is an act of mediation conducted in the liminal space between subject and ground, between power that forms the subject and the subject's own power of being in the world. This between-ness is what generates *both* the clarity and the ambiguity of appearances. It is this between-ness that allows me to regard the appearance of text as something much more significant than a 'communication about' embodied selves.

Texts never just get it right or get it wrong insofar as they are also a 'doing' – right or wrong, texts are always *oriented social action*, producing meaning. Texts do not just talk about the world, even though that might be their self-proclaimed intention. Texts, insofar as they appear, are our world. That is, for any word on disability to make sense, it needs to gesture at a whole world that allows for such sensibility. Thus texts act on us and help constitute our social contexts. Even when the text strikes me as 'getting it all wrong,' I, reading that text, am 'activating' (Smith 1999: 5, 146ff) a relation between text, myself, and that which it speaks about. All this is part of power relations, and so, as Butler suggests, an 'irresolvable ambiguity arises.' 'It' appears. Yet, it appears in some way, for example, wrongly. The reader appears to be making a judgment that the text makes its subject appear wrongly. Still, it appears, but so does the fact of reading, the experience of reading something, something which can be judged, judged *as* something not-correct. In the act of reading, disability appears through me, so I am in my reading, I am in disability. All of these appearances – of author, of reader, of judgment – participate in the enactment of disability.

The enactment of an appearance relies on the sensible and intelligible production of meaning, the meaning which enables us to enact our responsiveness through and to it. This is why Merleau-Ponty (1958: xi, 171) suggests that we understand the perception of anything as a 'closely woven fabric' since our perception is not based on an objective science, nor on a subject's single deliberate act, but instead perception is '... the background from which all acts stand out, and is presupposed by them.' This is why perception is both *of* and destined *for* the world. Perceiving the appearance of disability in text *is* to texture embodied existence. Understanding how the perception of bodies is bringing to awareness 'disability' is to find a way to position inquiry between the extremes of objectivism and subjectivism.

The goal of understanding the complexity of the daily life of reading about disability is not to say that there is not a hard brute reality to all the stuff that appears in and as disability. I am not putting forth an anti-materialist argument. Rather, I am following an essential point made by phenomenologists and interpretive sociologists, namely, that the appearance of anyone and anything is *done in the midst of people situated in the midst of other people*. We are at least a 'consciousness among consciousness' (Merleau-Ponty 1958: xiv). We are, moreover, possessed by a 'perceptual sensitivity of the second degree' (Natanson 1970: 70) and thus aware of the ways in which we are aware of our common realities. While strikingly obvious, it is nonetheless complex to realize that whatever appears does so only for someone in particular, whether individual or collective, who is now in relation to this appearance. The world we are born into, all appearances, and even the word 'appearance,' says Hannah Arendt, 'would make no sense, if recipients of appearances did not exist – living creatures able to acknowledge, recognize, and react to ... what is not merely there but appears to them and is meant for their perception' (1971: 19). Appearances are meant for people, and it is people who endow them with or, better, *as* meaning. For example, when we shudder or look away, we reveal the 'complicity of the observer in the situation of the sufferer' (Radley 2002: 5). Any bodily manifestation is no different in the universal sense that embodiment *is an appearance 'to' some one* and never only 'of' some thing. I do not want to forget *this* material fact.

People enact appearance and thereby make something appear, not as just sheer arbitrary stuff, but as meaningful stuff. We can, and often must, act as if something 'has' meaning in itself; that is, we act as if meaning inheres within a material reality (Tausigg 1993: xviii). Still, it is a 'we,' and not anything else that is interpreting, orienting, and acting as if meaning is given off by some thing. A well-practised refusal to contemplate the matter of meaning-making is part of that which grants much power to current ways of organizing and treating social differences and social identities, such as disability.[3] Competent comprehensive reading is a practice which helps accomplish this refusal, since reading competence is achieved through a dis-attention to the activity of reading and a focus on that which is read or, more precisely, that-which-is-read-about.

Understanding the identification of an appearance, such as a text on disability, as an enactment allows us to follow Joan Scott's recommendation that identity can be treated as '... the effect of an enunciation of difference that constitutes hierarchies and asymmetries of power' (1995: 5). Identity, or even identification, can be regarded as an enactment accomplished through, as Scott suggests, enunciation. *Treating* identity as such enables us to attune ourselves to what we are making of others and of ourselves. However, this is not the same as simply insisting that 'discourse determines.' Attending to or treating the subject of disability as the effect of discourse is not the same as asserting that discursive regimes are the beginning and the end of identity. Enunciation, of any sort, including texts, is both the effect of discourse and an agentive moment, and this is why much of what is said *about* disability is much more revelatory of dominant discourses organizing able-ist subjectivity than it is of our lived fleshly actuality of differential embodiment. And, still, it is people, interpretive beings, who live *with* the discourses that make an appearance in our world and make us appear as certain types of some-bodies.

In relation to disability, an emphasis on enunciation means not taking for granted the appearance of disability and not then moving on to evaluate whether it is granted a correct or incorrect depiction, or a positive or negative value. Image-evaluation deploys cultural conceptions of disability, but this is not the same as analysing that which grounds the possibility of and desire for these conceptions of disability as they come to appear in our lives in the first place. Judging an image, text, comment, or practice as 'negative,' 'untoward,' or 'unwanted' are undoubtedly part of the ongoing flow of everyday life. However, such judgments do not necessarily reckon with the productive forces organizing the appearance of, as well as the various ways that we can acknowledge, conform to, question, and resist, such images, thereby influencing what they mean. A critical emphasis on how the stuff of life is enunciated means treating any act of noticing disability as, indeed, a social act, which has the effect of constituting the meaning of the difference so identified, as this difference interacts and acts upon our perception of it. This is how disability as an enactment can and will be engaged here. The appearance of disability is tied to a complicated circumlocution worthy of analysis. As Joan Scott (1995) reminds us, we do not discriminate because we have noticed a difference. Rather, within a hierarchicalized techno-bureaucratic capitalist culture, we discriminate and thereby enact difference. This book attends to those discriminations, forms of perception, which are grounded in and destined for our world (Merleau-Ponty 1958: xi, xii).

Thus there is no need here to pursue arguments about whether or not disability is a difference that all cultures throughout all time have noticed and degraded or valorized. Nor is there any need here to argue whether disability is nothing but the effect of discourse, nor whether different experiences of embodiment might give rise to different forms of discourse. What matters for my project is *how* the given meanings surrounding disability are noticed in the here and now of everyday life. What matters is *how* disability is spoken about, narrated, and thereby made present in our lives. How disability is said to be is made possible by (and represents) the '... conceptual forms which we inherit as our ways of apprehending and orienting' (Blum 1993: 87) to the matter of embodiment.

'Most of all,' say Gail Weiss and Honi Haber, '... we must keep our focus on the present, the temporal dimension that alone allows us to incorporate both the lessons of the past and the hopes we have for the future' (1999: xvii). Paying critical attention to how disability is made manifest in this presentist fashion also means inserting a different take on disability. This difference lies in the fact that critical analysis can bring to attention how disability appears, the grounds of that appearance, as well as the various interpretive slants, such as acceptance or critique, of the current appearance of disability in our lives. Such engagement with disability as a pluralistic rather than singular phenomenon allows for the problematizing of embodiment. It is this kind of engagement that resists the totalizing of disability and allows for the possibility of accepting, even inserting, alterity into our world. A commitment to awakening a desire for alterity is also, for me, practising a politics that aims to shrink the types of lives that are normally dismissed, devalued, or treated as better off dead.

My discussion of the textured life of embodiment has aimed to show some of the key concepts employed in this book that will aid me in the work of uncovering the ways in which disability is made to appear. Conceiving of disability as that which is *enacted* through text allows me to keep this analysis focused on the socially oriented activity of accomplishing meaning. In the face of disability oriented to the effect of the enunciation of embodied difference, it is important to locate a particular form of enactment that is amenable to social inquiry. Elsewhere, I have shown how disability is enacted through social interaction in everyday life, including academic culture (Titchkosky 2005b, c; 2003a, b). Here, I turn to 'text' as the primary site for this inquiry.

Text

'Text' is a broad and inclusive concept. For some theorists, text is a metaphor for society; for example: 'Societies then are specific texts – created by and creative of – human beings' (Taborsky 1997: 200). For others, text is the 'structure of meaning that is obvious and inescapable from the perspective of whatever interpretive assumptions happen to be in force' (Fish 1980: vii). For this book, text is embodied in popular texts readily available to literate consumers of the mass media, that is, mainstream newspapers, magazines, and government documents generated for general public use or consumption. Still, these concrete texts are treated here as opportunities to get at the social significance, the structures of meanings, that provide for the possibility of disability appearing as it does in daily life.

We live in a time that assumes literacy as one of its normative conditions, making text a key form of socio-cultural ground organizing the appearances of disability within western(ized) societies. Texts are more than outcomes or products of literate social action. Texts *are* forms of action: textualizing is something we do to issues of concern; texts organize those issues, enter our lives; and some things we live only through text. Finally, texts also provoke readers. Under the normative conditions of literacy, all people must develop a relation to text, even if only in the negative; for example, 'I did not read that' or 'I cannot read.' Texts, then, are a tricky matter inasmuch as they are produced things, are forms of social action, and are occasions or sites for self-regulation and, even, self-assertion.

To describe text as I have just done is to say with M.M. Bakhtin that 'the text lives only by coming into contact with another text (with context). Only at the point of this contact between texts does a light flash, illuminating both the posterior and anterior, joining a given text to a dialogue' (1986: 162). Texts appear to people, and with real consequences texts enter our lives. In the context of our lives, texts come to life. This life reflects, if only in a flash, the meaning of the being of that which the text speaks, since it speaks to us about (lives in) the context of its appearance as meaningful. In reading, we commit ourselves to the promise of meaning that every text actualizes in some fashion.

Conceptualizing text *as if* it is only a simple object to which readers respond does not address texts in their full sociality. Texts are more than mere mediators of pre-existing messages. Text is a social location and organizer for the accomplishment of meaning, making text count as a form of social action. I wish to explore the concept of 'text' in its most inclusive or metaphoric sense so as to demonstrate its significance for my particular inquiry bent on engaging disability as an enactment.

I proceed from Dorothy Smith's assertion that the social world, and all that makes an appearance in it, including text, is a result of *'the ongoing concerting and coordinating of individual's activities'* (1999: 6, italics her own). In a variety of ways, in both academic and everyday life, disability is made to appear as a textual phenomenon. This appearance is produced by individual activity, coordinated by the ongoing production of social beliefs and practices, and is part of the ongoing concerted action that continues to organize the appearance and meaning of, the reading and writing of, disability. Smith's *Writing the Social* (1999) demonstrates that texts are an important site for the examination of power relations and their productive force. How people put disability into text, disability's ordinary and expected appearance in the texts of daily life, can thus be examined so as to reveal the organized enactment of disability, and thus of embodiment in general.

As with the birth, life, and death of all members of this technocratic and bureaucratic culture, a textual rendering of the 'characteristic movements of life' (Foucault 1978: 25) supersedes, organizes, and thereby enacts what counts as birth, death, and all the other characteristic movements of life that lie between. Inasmuch as it is possible to recognize that, say, illness, injury, wounding, or accident is sometimes conflated with and sometimes antithetical to disability, or that disability in one culture or historical moment is not disability in another place or time, it is also possible to regard embodied difference as a characteristic movement of life that is, at some times and in some fashion, rendered into a particular shape and form and, thereby, enacted as 'disability' (Davis 1995; Stiker 1999; Corker 2002, 2001, 2000).

Textuality is one way to accomplish the rendering of disability. To design a disability verification tax credit form; to report a story; to write an account, case, or file; to develop a policy on embodied differences: these practices enact the meaning of disability through text. In cultures that assume literacy as a normative value, text becomes a method and a location for the organization, reproduction, and, thereby, enactment, of disability's meanings. As a way to begin to explicate the concept of 'text' so as to examine disability in a way that will reveal some of the specific problematics of embodiment, I turn for a moment to the example of birth.

Textual Enactment of Birth

Consider the plethora of possible texts enacting and circumscribing the social significance of birth. The recognition of pregnancy begins with the reading of texts: from the colours of the pregnancy testing wand, where the pink or blue may move one on to the doctor's office; to the reading of pregnancy and parenting magazines in the waiting room of that office; to the reading of texts produced by a doctor in the form of charts and measurements, ultrasound images (much more on this in chapter 3), heart-rate print-outs, blood-work readings, amniocentesis findings. All of these textual renderings of a potential birth become part of the case file, with notes added regarding what the pregnancy appears like from a medical gaze (Foucault, 1975: 107ff). Between medically ordered texts of and on the woman's body and those people involved in the rendering and reading of such texts, the phenomenon of birth is in the process of enactment. This enactment is accomplished in relation to a host of other institutionally organized texts, such as discussions of health-care costs, the production and reading of medical journals, or advertisements about current technical and pharmacological products.

The texts that mediate and organize pregnancy are then reified, (e.g., as test results) and are now separate from the pregnant woman.[4] They may be sent to a specialist or to a hospital before, at the same time as, or after a particular woman herself is sent to a specialist or to a hospital. Difficult, anomalous, and even ordinary births are surrounded by a further proliferation of text used to document complications and normal or abnormal births. The lived actuality of birthing is organized by these texts and interpretations of birth as wanted/unwanted, hard, painful, surprising, disappointing, devastating, happy, and more. A plethora of relations can be held in relation to birth, yet most are made possible in relation to these texts. While a woman may find herself in a conflictual, resistant, or conforming relation to these various texts, they are undoubtedly enunciations of her birthing experience. Still, none of these texts is birth, even though all become ways that birth is delivered in literate contexts.

In the midst of these reified pregnancy and birth texts, further texts are produced. The state issues a birth certificate indicating the officially registered, named, and gendered being located in the time (month/year) and place (town/city/province) of interest to bureaucratically organized notions of time and space. This is an official enactment of birth. Birth is organized in such a way that it feeds further textual proliferation in the form of birth rate statistics and other demographic counts, social welfare surveys and forms, taxation forms, child protection acts, etc. It almost seems as if babies are born through text or, at least, give rise to an amazing amount of textual production.

In the course of this textual enactment of birth, a 'personal text' is also enacted. Only some birth texts count as, or serve the genre of, the 'personal,' even though many texts may happen to a person. It is in the realm of 'personal experience,' as Kay Cook (1996: 68, 65) suggests, that the various medical ways that the body has been authored 'collide' with cultural and political ways of mediating bodily experience. The personal is mediated through a host of texts delivered via the reading of images, printed words, signs, and verbal messages. There are prenatal classes with their films, pamphlets, and diagrams, comparisons of bodily sensations against pregnancy book depictions of pregnancy, television documentaries, parking spaces designated for 'Moms to be,' shopping at the maternity store, and, of course, the guesses: will it be a boy or a girl? Then there is the personal birth announcement produced in the midst of the texts already produced by the medical and state bureaucracy. Birth announcements, in the shape of cards, letters, or e-mails, are thus also accomplished through, and simultaneously organized by, text. For example, birth is surrounded by a myriad, yet restricted, set of texts readily available within a consumeristic culture. The card, the letter, the balloon with either words or images announcing a newborn; the outfits, text messaging, digital camera pictures, Internet websites, e-mails (attachment included), the flowers delivered in baby-print paper; or meetings with agents of social services along with their institutionally organized forms and guidelines: all this is part of the textual organization of birthing.

The medical and state organization of birthing is the authoritative context within which the personal message of birth is enacted. Not knowing if her premature baby will survive, a mother may wait until a particular medical text is delivered to her before sending out her own birth announcements. The official birth certificate of the infant who dies may be kept forever. The technological variability of possible responses to birth is at the ready for the organization and production of an expression of birth, and the relation between state, medicine, and the woman who gave birth can easily lead to an astounding accumulation of texts that further organize the meaning of birth even as these texts express it. A woman's letter of complaint regarding the doctor's management of the birth may lead to a proliferation of juridical text. Social scientists publish articles and books on various aspects of birth, including the relation between personal integrity and bodily examination; doctor/patient negotiation of time and voice; the use and interpretation of prenatal testing; etc. Statisticians, working in state registration offices, compile birth rates and correlate these rates with issues such as mortality, state medical policy and funding issues, as well as infant health issues such as rates of illness and impairment. These texts, too, help enact the meaning of a particular birth and show that a woman's 'personal' account of pregnancy is a complicated enigmatic intertwining of a variety of discourses displaying the fact that 'we have only images and narratives through which to form bodily boundaries ...' (Cook 1996: 64).

Recalling Judith Butler, we have here a fleshy enactment of the material fact that '... an irresolvable ambiguity arises when one attempts to distinguish between ... the power that forms the subject and the subject's "own" power' (1997: 15). Moreover, women's reproductive potentiality seems thinkable only in relation to all our already established social/textual relations to women's reproductive potentiality. Where and how might reproduction appear in the absence of all the texts that are described above?

The use-value of these culturally established textual practices is part of what organizes the enactment of identifying and constituting the meaning of the birth as well as its difference or uniqueness. Undoubtedly, there are many more texts surrounding birth. Those I have mentioned demonstrate that appearances are reflexively enacted within social life. The appearance of a birth is organized and conditioned by particular genres of textual organization within and of this technological, medical, and bureaucratic consumer culture. This means that any one text does not merely represent a reality, but is a creative or productive power within the reality it helps to constitute. Complicating matters further, all textual productive power occurs in relation to other texts and in relation to a variety of readers whose lives have been entered by text. *Given all this complexity, text can be examined as a key cultural arena, and even as a constitutional force, within contemporary times.* This book does exactly that.

Many of the texts that organize and coordinate the meaning of birth also serve to enunciate the birth of disability (Michalko 2002: 113ff). Disability is just as complicated a textual matter as birth. Disability texts happen and when they do, so too does the meaning of disability. It is important now, however, to do more than note the ubiquitous presence of text in the organization of the movements of life, since we must remember that textual presence signifies, according to Smith, the 'concerting and coordinating' of our lives in relation to the meaning of that which appears within them. Text, then, needs to be read as social action – action that attaches and organizes a subjective meaning to the lives of individuals, and to individual appearances (Weber 1947: 88). In so doing, text orients all of us to its rendering of the meaning that it has inscribed as disability, thus making it appear as a certain something – texts of the body become embodied texts. Appearance is, indeed, activated. Disability is born through text. In the knowledge economy of the Enlightenment world, such activation involves texts' employing the 'god trick,' a trick worthy of some exploration.

The God Trick and Other Methodological Concerns

'God trick' is Donna Haraway's (1991: 189) way to refer to, and to turn her reader's attention to, the taken for granted practices involved in the contemporary production of knowledge found in informative texts. A text's unbiased or objective knowledge claims are activated by a variety of practices, such as making the author, and other signs of concerted human action, disappear, while making it apparent that knowledge is produced by a disembodied, even other-worldly, stance of an authority seemingly seeing everything from nowhere. 'The data shows,' 'statistics say,' 'research reveals' only insofar as the social beliefs and practices that organize knowledge are hidden and repressed. If one is to produce knowledge under modern conditions, the trick is to make claims to truth that simultaneously cover over any sense of their own grounding in human activity and organization.

   This trick includes practices that help reader and writer to forget those involved in the production of the text; thus knowledge producers should 'deny their responsibility for the things they survey and construct' (Warner 2001: 118). Part of being a normal reader is forgetting that we know how to dis-attend to 'fact' as an accomplished social activity. Knowledge can appear to be simply *about* human activity and organization, but only if such knowledge does not itself reveal much of its own human activity and organization. Knowledge made to appear as if it is objectively given from above results in making knowledge appear as if it is unencumbered by any touch of the mundane reality of the place and people of its making. One consequence of all this is that our *desire for* knowledge and certainty often does not come under scrutiny, as this desire is replaced/repressed by a false security that we 'have' a certain bit of knowledge and the facts of the case. (So, 'desire' is not merely a response to a lack, such as a lack of knowledge, but is also a productive force, for example, rendering knowledge as something one could lack and that one should gain.)

Employing the god trick, authors make it seem as if the meaning of appearance described in the text actually resides within an appearance itself, as if it is not we, people, actively making stuff appear as a meaningful something. Through the god trick, it seems as if the text has nothing to do with organizing the ground upon which an appearance appears, and as if the text has nothing to do with mediating and orienting our observations, as if the text is not a power which forms the subject, a subject with which readers must reckon. Under the influence of the god trick, it seems reasonable to encounter knowledge without knowers, as well as facts, statements, and descriptions that are radically estranged from their own social organization. In these ways, texts make absent their own ongoing participation in the reproduction of the discursive regimes that support their knowledge claims. As a consequence, such texts, as well as our relations to them, often reproduce our taken for granted sense that 'true' knowledge is not a product of the concerted and coordinated activity of people. Through our ordinary orientations to text, it seems to provide facts, statements, and descriptions about the world, all the while repressing the cogency of its production.

This ordering of our relation to knowledge, and thereby to text, urges us to neglect the question of how the appearance of the text is a social action: text acts upon appearance, so that it coordinates our relations to these appearances. Writers and readers empower the text's knowledge claims by ignoring how a variety of factors are animating its appearance in the world. For example, it is relatively easy to ignore how writers, readers, and discursive regimes are brought into relation to one another. Of this, Dorothy

Smith says:

> Texts are the mediators and bases of discourses and ruling rela-
> tions that regulate and coordinate beyond the particular local set-
> ting of their reading or writing. But they are always occurrences in
> time and space: they happen; they are activated at a particular
> moment of reading in the time it takes to do that reading and in a
> particular place. The act of reading is very deceitful in this respect;
> it conceals its particularity, its being in time and place ... The mate-
> riality of the text is key to investigating the ruling relations as the
> local and ongoing concerting of people's activities. (1999: 80)

Under contemporary conditions, we are encouraged by our
taken for granted ways of knowing to come to the text as if the
only truth of interest lies in the text's truth claims. We are encouraged to read as if the truth is in the text and that this truth 'stands
alone,' isolated from, and even bereft of, any social organization.
But the hard brute reality remains – texts are produced and read
by people. As a happening or an achievement, and not as a final
and totalizing objectively given statement of what is, texts enact
the appearance of that which they speak, but they do so through,
between, and in the lives of people. The god trick continues to
hold power unless and until we treat the text's knowledge claims
as a form of social action and thereby 'make visible the obscured
assumptions embedded within' (Warner 2001: 118).

In this book, I attempt to understand the 'truth' of disability as
a part of the weave or sequence of oriented social action delivered
through the complex textured relations of reading and writing.
Disability is a particular enunciation of specific identifications
and revealing the assumptions behind how we take notice of the
appearance of embodiment through our reading and writing
allows us to grapple with the meaning of disability. Thus, what
has already been written, and how we read has something to
teach us about the truth of the matter of disability. Texts are thus
regarded as in need of explication but not merely as this pertains
to their coherence, validity, or their logic. Instead, I explicate
texts' knowledge claims with the understanding that they are a

concerted and coordinated doing, a doing that reflects ordinary and powerful discursive domains that organize and orient our relations to disability.

Text on Text: Self-Reflection

My text, like any other, is involved in the production of knowledge. But unlike the texts that I examine, I attempt to display the social character of this knowledge as well as the (not-so-dominant) discursive domains that I am activating in order to authorize and legitimize my analysis. Attempting to understand how truths about embodiment are claimed, I aim to reveal what sort of social relations these truth claims advance between readers and the appearance of disability. Such an analysis involves uncovering the discursive regimes and practices that are organizing writers' and readers' conceptions of, and relations to, embodiment, difference, and disability. As a way to continue to resist employing the god trick, let me expose a bit of my orientation to the writing of this book.

My form of inquiry uncovers the meaning of embodied existence inasmuch as the topic of disability allows for this. I am guided by the methodological principles of phenomenology and hermeneutics as they have been developed within various types of poststructural feminisms, cultural studies, and disability studies. In drawing upon the eclectic character of theorists that I do, I am following a sociological tradition of inquiry that holds that understanding how people interpret (live in) their world is an important arena for social inquiry. So, in texting our lives and reading those texts resides interpretive acts through which existence is made, and made meaningful. Reading and writing becomes the beginning place for our wondering (Merleau-Ponty 1958: vx). My work is guided by the understanding that the significance of humanity is essentially tied to the inescapable fact that we are meaning-makers. We are interpretive beings and this, suggests Hannah Arendt, is our 'specifically human way of being alive' (1994: 308). I study this way of being alive. Moreover, I seek out relations to interpretation that are oriented to interpretation itself as the vitality of everyday life. Social theory can be regarded as one such dynamic relation that allows us to problematize our relations to interpretation.

Disability appears in the midst of people and thus is the site of embodied interpretive relations. The appearance of disability is also the appearance of ordinary regimes of sensibility and truth upon which all interpretive acts draw. The apperception of disability provides a starting point for reflexive social inquiry. What we do and say, how we live, constitutes and reflects the ready-made stuff of meaningful life. Inquiry into the ready-made, for example, the readily apparent, the already written, the already read, or what I referred to earlier as the 'here and now,' is an opportunity to consider the organized processes of the on-going interpretation that is reflecting and making the meaning of our collective existence. Of this dynamic potential, Homi Bhabha reminds us that there is no primordial unity in the meanings and symbols of culture, so that 'even the same signs can be appropriated, translated, rehistoricized and read anew' (1994: 55). Telling or retelling the stories that lie latent in what has already been written and read on disability is the way in which this book commits itself to reading and writing disability anew.

In regard to the need to draw on a variety of theorists' work, I follow Mairian Corker, who says:

> You may have noticed that in spite of my 'self-definition' as a post-structuralist feminist, I quite readily draw on work that is *not* part of this tradition. This is because I am uncomfortable with locating myself exclusively within the 'authority' of a single epistemological tradition as, among other things, I see this to be profoundly anti-feminist. (2002: 27)

The point is not to become a master (expert manipulator) of an epistemic tradition and its particular methods, but to allow traditions to enable the inquirer to pursue an analysis of the production of social significance and, self-reflectively, to contemplate possible alternative interpretive relations to such made meanings and us as meaning-makers. One way this understanding and endeavour can be actualized is by using disability texts to examine 'how experience becomes known and how knowledge is experienced' (Warner 2001: 117–18). Kieran Bonner puts it this way: 'The problem of reflexivity for sociology concerns the ability of the inquirer to take responsibility for what one says while simultaneously being able to say something substantial about the phenomenon or object of inquiry' (2001: 267). I am attempting to pursue a form of inquiry that not only reveals how disability is made meaningful through text, but, through critical attention to all the different permutations of the relation between the knower and the known, can also help to insert into the world a kind of responsibility toward our embodied existence.

Responding in this way opens the potential of alterity. I am not aiming to fix the 'tablets of tradition' but rather, as Bhabha recommends, participate in the 'on-going negotiation that seeks to authorize cultural hybridities that emerge in moments of historical transformation' (1994: 3). One such hybridity, or emerging alternative relation that is seeking to make disability materialize differently, one that informs my work here, is represented by the field of disability studies.

Disability Studies

This book not only interrogates the textured life of disability but necessarily adds to this texture as well, since it takes its bearings from and aims to represent the growing field of disability studies. Disability studies is an interdisciplinary field inclusive of a great deal of variety since the social significance of disability, its exclusion and inclusion, can be tracked and traced in and by every discipline. Despite this variety, it is still possible to characterize some principles that animate the field of disability studies.

A disability studies perspective is one that rejects the idea that disability can be studied as an object in and of itself. It also rejects the idea that anything revolutionary can be learned from documenting, yet again, how persons with disabilities adapt to, cope with, succumb to, or overcome bodily, sensorial, or mental impairments. Instead, disability studies attempts to treat seriously one particular and inescapable fact: whenever and however disability appears, it appears in the midst of other people. Disability is, therefore, a social and political phenomenon and should be studied as such. Disability does not appear outside of our social, historical, and political relations. But, it is very easy to ignore this fact.

The ongoing constitution of disability-as-a-problem condition is accompanied by writing, reading, and otherwise acting as if embodied differences can appear purely – as if they are outside of cultural influence, untouched by political and social organization, as if dominant discourses are not organizing our past, present, and future relations to disability, to impairment, to embodiment. A defining feature of disability studies scholarship, however, is that it is establishing a tradition of inquiry that problematizes the ways in which disability is figured against an ahistorical, apolitical, and even asocial background.[5] Attending to disability as a meaningful concept built from, and enunciated within, daily life leads to a form of social inquiry that takes disability into account by examining the interrelation between conceptions of disabled and non-disabled people.

The interrelation of disability and non-disability is particularly pertinent within the realm of text. It is, for example, quite difficult to find a text, especially in the mass media, written both by and for disabled people. Even on those occasions when it is a disabled author writing about disability, the text is typically directed to a community of readers imagined as non-disabled, which, ironically, is more than likely impossible. Of course, the media excludes many writers involved in various inquiries from the margins; media texts on feminism, sexuality, and race often appear as 'writing about' rather than 'written by' people from the margins. Disability, too, joins the ranks of the 'written about' (appearing as an object about which subjects know), which again points to the socio-political character of embodiment – we are never in our bodies alone. Able-ist objectifications of disability have functioned for some scholars and activists as a call to take ownership of disability representation and to reclaim disability for disabled people. However, the fact that disability texts appear in the midst of a non-disabled presupposition serves, in my work, as a call to pursue an inquiry that can address the complex *inter*relation between readers, writers, and whom and what is written about. Instead of shoring up the differences between ability and disability, the right to representation might better serve a growing sense of ambiguity. In the space between, in the dynamics of becoming interested in how self and other might be mutually constitutive, we have the chance to read and write disability differently. The reading and writing of disability into a time and space imagined as non-disabled has much to teach us about the social organization of normal senses of embodiment required by a certain way of relating to whatever is regarded as not normal, different, out of the ordinary.

It is not easy to start to think about disability as it is constituted in relation to non-disabled others representing normative attitudes and a cultural horizon organized by the assumption of taken for granted and mythical ableness. Moreover, no one wants to appear as if they do not care about such an 'unfortunate problem' that disability is assumed to be. Indeed, people's caring and compassion toward disabled people is often beyond question – quite literally, such caring is treated as nothing that is provocative of wonder. Instead, we know that we care about disability and that caring often obliterates any further questioning. On this issue, Lennard Davis comments that

> the first assumption that has to be countered in arguing for disability studies is that the 'normal' or 'able' person is already fully up to speed on the subject ... disability seems so obvious – a missing limb, blindness, deafness. What could be simpler to understand? ... Just the addition of a liberal dose of sympathy and pity along with a generous acceptance of ramps and voice-synthesized computers allows the average person to speak with knowledge on the subject ... [However,] [t]he apparent ease of intuitive knowledge is really another aspect of discrimination against people with disabilities ... (1997: 2)

Pity, charity, and even simply caring are common practices grounded in taken for granted conceptions of disability. Still, they are practices that are not necessarily self-reflective – they are not forms of analysis, even though these practices are grounded upon all sorts of truth claims. Claiming to know disability, while not experiencing a need to reflect upon the assumptions, organization, and consequences of this knowledge is a common yet potentially oppressive social practice.

Disability studies places disability and non-disability in context by aiming to think about their interrelation in complex ways. Seeking to explicate the complex interrelation that enacts the appearance of embodiment allows for caring and other forms of treatment of disability to be opened for inquiry and questioning. Being able to read about disability need not count as an obvious possession of knowledge on the subject, but such readings are a tacit display of the dominant discourses that organize our subjective interpretive relations to disability. Texts, concretely and figuratively, represent the complex interrelation of disability and non-disability, and it is certainly high time to examine them as such. Texts on disability serve here as an opportunity for a conversation that attempts to welcome all of us to the possibility that there might be something new and different to learn about ourselves and what our responsiveness means in a social sense. This book, then, is part of an ongoing conversation regarding *how* we write and read disability and *what* it might mean.

PART ONE

Problems

I READ THAT RESEARCH ought to be a 'search for solutions to real-life, open-ended problems' (Greenwood and Levin 2003: 133). Through my experiences of disability as always already a problem, I have come to a slightly different opinion. I think that the search for solutions, a common practice, should be slowed until we develop some understanding of the problems for which we find ourselves seeking solutions. The search for solutions itself needs to be opened up to reveal the conception of the problem that the solution makes manifest. For example, the problem with disability is that it is easy not to be open to the question of how it is that we continually conceive of disability as a problem. That disability is easily, readily, unquestioningly regarded as problem *is* a problem that I want to become open to here.

In the following three chapters, I show how disability is constituted as a problem. I begin in chapter 2, 'Totally a Problem: Government Survey Texts,' with an analysis of the most common and ubiquitous appearance of disability as a strict body problem seemingly unrelated to interpretation and detached from social structures and processes. This totalizing assumption of disability as objectively a problem grounds popular representations of disability such as those found in government documents where disability is given statistical shape as, and only as, a problem population.

Having revealed this version of disability as a problem, chapter 3, 'Metamorphosis: Making Disability a Medical Matter,' shows the actual processes through which readers and writers constitute the problem of disability as a medical one. I show the process of medicalization by analysing a newspaper text which relies on a medical conception of disability. Within disability studies literature, the social and political consequences of the medicalization of disability are often mentioned. Others have made the ubiquitous *fact* of the medicalization of disability obvious; my addition to this literature is to show how medicalization actually works. That is, I seek to understand the meaning of medicalization *as* a process of enactment accomplished through reading and writing. In detail, I show *how* disability is made to appear as a medical problem and reveal how this version of disability has captured our collective consciousness. This sort of critical attention allows for the possibility of desiring the medicalization of embodied differences differently.

Chapter 4, 'Reading and Recognition: Un-doing Disability's Deadly Status,' traces the socio-political consequences of this medical formulation of disability. Taking the understanding of disability as a medical problem to its furthest and most logical conclusion, disability becomes a site where the implementation of a 'negative ontology,' a life not worth living, and even a new eugenics, occurs. Disability is thus imagined as a limit without possibilities (which is impossible). Whatever else genetic research might or might not achieve, the fact remains that ordinary discourse on problem bodies is constitutive of the meaning of disability as a questionable existence ripe for eugenic practices. Regardless of the actual technological means available to manufacture human possibilities, texts that assume that disability is a negation enact disabled people as questionable. Chapter 4 shows how texts reproduce the collective assumption that disability is a questionable life at best, and a life not worth living at worst.

Taken together, these three chapters demonstrate the tight connection between regarding disability as a medicalized object of lack and the way in which some people are configured as worthless problems. I turn now to a search for problems as a way to ascertain how we manufacture disability in such a way that generates, if not the fact, then at least the desire, to dissolve disability existence.

2 Totally a Problem: Government Survey Texts

But the child is always born into a group of people among whom all the general types of situation which may arise have already been defined and corresponding rules of conduct developed, and where he [*sic*] has not the slightest chance of making his definitions and following his wishes without interference.

– W.I. Thomas, *The Unadjusted Girl*, 41

We enter a world not of our own making. From time to time, we can take note of the 'antiquated' beliefs or 'backward' attitudes of those who have come before us. Taking note of the injustices and inadequacies of our predecessors performs a separation from them even as it demonstrates the fact that we find ourselves in a predefined world which, as Cornel West (1995: 16) says, is necessarily not of our own choosing. This suggests that we do not have the 'slightest chance of making' alternative definitions without interference. Even our need to highlight the antiquated beliefs of others might in fact be steeped in, indeed, enabled by, current ways of defining the situation that are already established by those people and discourses that came before us. That disability is generally understood as nothing but a problem of a strictly medical nature is one such powerful discourse into which we are born.

This chapter examines government definitions of disability and the corresponding rules of conduct for regarding disability as a problem, specifically, as a medical problem. Medicalization is a way of defining the body that is both totalizing and reductive, and while it will come under greater scrutiny in the following chapters, this chapter begins to recognize the powers of the medicalizing process that proceeds from the unquestioned assumption of disability as a problem. This dominant way of defining – an inheritance of Enlightenment thought – touches almost all embodied differences today. So, noticing that disability is conceived of as 'totally a problem' allows me to show how the totality of this problem is medicalized through and through.

By analysing our current dominant textual enactments of disability as a problem, we can begin to embrace the chance of interfering with the ruling definitions of the day. In this chapter, I make use of *In Unison 2000*, a key Canadian government document that sets the agenda on disability issues. I also make use of the document *A New Approach to Disability Data* (Statistics Canada 2002), which claims to improve upon the past decade of factual disability knowledge. By analysing the Canadian government's way of putting disability into text, it will become obvious that such 'fact texts' employ the god trick that I referred to in chapter 1. Alongside the process of objectifying disability, the more subtle ways in which such texts are enacting the appearance of disability in relation to key cultural values, issues, and authorities will also be made available for scrutiny. The facts on disability enact a conception of the problem-body through socially organizing what can, or should, occur between the knower (text producer and reader) and the apparently known object (disability). Understanding this also serves as a way to loosen what Smith (1999: 196ff, 214) describes as the capture of the reader by the ruling relations activated in our noticing of, and reading about, any topic of concern. This chapter will exemplify the detailed methodic analysis that is necessary for engaging disability text so as to reveal neither the text's truth nor its falsity, but rather *its activity* of meaning-making.

The government documents are used in order to interrogate the sense in which disability is organized as 'objective facts' constructed as a problem. A detailed analysis of this construction of disability facts demonstrates how embodied differences are organized under the auspices of a totalizing concept of problem, which imparts a singular unity – disability is only a functional problem at the level of the individual. How this totalizing and singular concept organizes our consciousness, providing for the existence of certain questions and obliterating other forms of questioning, are issues that I leave for later chapters. Critical attention to the ways we constitute facts about disability makes possible a reflection on what it means for readers and for writers, disabled and not, to be confronted with disability as a totalized entity; an entity framed and treated as nothing more or less than a problem of a medical nature. I end this chapter with a consideration of the life tacitly recommended by the domination of a discourse that assumes disability as totally troublesome. Disability serves as the occasion, then, to open ourselves to the consequences of acting as if anything or anyone can be grasped by a singular, unified definition.

Background to the 'Facts' on Disability

First, a few facts:

> The population of Canadians with disabilities could increase from about 3.9 million in 2001 to between 5.6 (low growth) and 6.1 million (high growth) in 2026. In 2026 approximately 54% of people with disabilities will be seniors versus 42% in 2001. (Canada, *Advancing the Inclusion of Persons with Disabilities: Executive Summary* [2005], 2)

> One in eight Canadians has a disability – a total of 3.6 million people. For Canada's Aboriginal population, the rate of disability is particularly high – more than one and a half times the rate for the non-Aboriginal population. Women are more likely than men to have a disability, regardless of age. (Canada, *Advancing the Inclusion of Persons with Disabilities: Executive Summary* [2004], 6)

> An estimated 155,000 children between five to 14 years old, living in households, had activity limitations in 2001, according to the data from the Participation and Activity Limitation Survey. This

represents about 4% of all children of this age group ... Of the
155,000 children with disabilities in 2001, about 35,000, or 23%,
received help with their daily activities because of their condition.
Of the children who received help, about 15% had mild to moderate disabilities and the remaining 85% had severe to very severe
disabilities. (Canada, *Technical Report: Advancing the Inclusion of
Persons with Disabilities* [2002], 11–13)

Whatever else disability might mean, in these facts it means a
growing yet measurable problem of varying severity and type,
which is possessed by all sorts of individuals who are nonetheless
identifiable as a distinct population. While the presentation of the
facts on disability may differ, the way the Canadian government
(and many other governments) speaks about disability as a problem does not. In Canada, for example, these facts regarding
disability have been used to develop charts, pamphlets, policy
statements, news releases, and much more. These textual renderings of disability facts also export the idea that disability is a problem into all sorts of other contexts. Thus, the multiple facts on
disability help to actualize the singular ruling 'fact' that disability
is a problem in everyday life.

Since the mid-1990s, the provincial, territorial, and federal
ministers (excluding Quebec) responsible for social services have
produced a series of documents which explicitly claim to address
the problem of disability in Canada. While I am addressing only
two key documents, these documents exist in a long lineage of
many other similar government texts on disability. In *Disability
and Social Policy in Canada*, I have characterized this long textual
lineage as follows:

Since the *Obstacles* (1981) have been charted, a *National Strategy*
(1991) announced, and the *Will to Act* (1996) established, the government of Canada has also provided a 'vision' for federal, provincial and local governments to work *In Unison* (1998) toward the full
participation of citizens with disabilities; that vision, put into the
shape of a 'blueprint' (*In Unison 2000*), has been followed-up by an
account of best practices and a *Strategic Plan 2002–2007* (Office for

Disability Issues: 2002) for its implementation. All of these textual orderings of disability (surrounded by a plethora of background documents and follow-up reports) culminate in *Advancing the Inclusion of Persons with Disabilities* (Government of Canada Report, Dec. 2002: 2) which proclaims, 'This first [*sic*] comprehensive report on disability in Canada describes where our country has made progress, how the Government of Canada has contributed, and where work remains to be done.' (Titchkosky 2006b: 87)

What remains constant in all of these documents produced by the Canadian government is the fact that disability is a problem and that many facts about disabled people having problems can be circulated to a general readership year after year.

The first fact-text I will examine here is part of a document entitled *In Unison 2000: Persons with Disabilities in Canada*. *In Unison* not only defines the contour of the problem that is disability but also provides a host of best practices oriented to fixing the problem that disability is known to be. An analysis of this way of fixing disability is provided later in chapter 4, as here I wish only to focus on how disability is circumscribed, imagined, and enacted *as* a problem. The *In Unison* document, including its facts, has been circulated widely, not only among government officials but also among all of the many community organizations which may be granted or may be seeking to secure government funding on disability issues. The document has also been used in university and college courses, and in the development of disability policy. *In Unison* explicitly claims to serve as a 'blueprint' for organizations, or for anyone wanting to work in a 'consistent and coherent' manner on disability issues in Canada. Government funding is tied to organizations being 'informed' about the government's approach to (and thereby conception of) disability issues.

In Unison, like every other government document on disability produced up to 2002, relies heavily upon the data generated from HALS, the Health and Activity Limitation Survey, a survey conducted, after the census, first in 1986 and then again in 1991. Sometime after 2002, more than a decade after the last HALS, a 'new approach' to a new set of data becomes available (e.g.,

Advancing the Inclusion of Persons with Disabilities, 2002, 2004, 2005). This claim to a new approach and to new and improved data is partially established on the basis of the belief that the conception of disability deployed in the collection of this new disability survey data is more 'social' and less individualistic. The second document that I analyse in this chapter allows me to unpack this claim and to demonstrate that disability, regardless of the new survey questions and data, is still constituted as 'totally a problem,' and still as an individualistic medical problem. This second document is called *A New Approach to Disability Data: Changes between the 1991 Health and Activity Limitation Survey (HALS) and the 2001 Participation and Activity Limitation Survey (PALS)* (Statistics Canada 2002). I draw upon a few descriptive statements regarding the 'new and improved' nature of disability data in Canada and use this document to draw out the characteristics of the problem called 'disability' that have remained consistent over time, regardless of the government documents' explicit claims of newness. As a way to begin to experience the vitality of attempting to understand the textual enactment of disability as problem, I turn now to textually proclaimed disability facts located in the widely distributed Canadian government document, *In Unison*, which is geared to a general readership.

Enacting the Fact of Disability as a Problem

The 'Executive Summary' of *In Unison 2000* begins this way:

> This report sets the stage for governments, persons with disabilities, disability advocates, communities, employers, labour and the non-profit sector to jointly focus on disability issues. (ix)

Note that groups such as disability studies scholars and disability activists are not listed as those who jointly focus on disability issues. Nonetheless, this is an expansive context for the circulation of this text. This is a text that, in the main, is geared to those people who share a focus on doing something about disability issues in Canada. The text presents itself as solving (not making) the problem of disability. *In Unison* presents the problem of disability as well as a variety of ways of how it has been, is, and should be addressed and solved. For example, it refers to past governmental efforts to address the problem of disability; it details its current 'vision,' namely, that 'persons with disabilities participate as full citizens in all aspects of Canadian society' (4); it describes current approaches to fulfilling this vision; it provides stories of individual disabled people who represent this fulfilment; and it presents brief descriptions of projects across the provinces and the territories that support people in achieving the government's vision. (How all these measures dis-solve the problem of disability as the abled-disabled citizen will be addressed in chapter 5.)

According to page 5 of *In Unison 2000* (see p. 53), we still have a 'long way' to go to actualize the goal of inclusion, which is described as a basic yet definitive Canadian value. While Canadians are committed to the inclusion of disabled people, the facts and figures serve to demonstrate that this commitment has not come to fruition. The facts suggest that there are many people with disabilities in Canada who are marginalized. The facts also suggest that people have a variety of disabilities, which the document, like the survey it relies on, characterizes as 'mild, medium and severe.' These many 'people with disabilities,' of course, embody other differences, such as age, race, and gender, or differences in education, income, and poverty levels. Yet this diverse group shares a common problematic fate: 'people with disabilities' are not full participants in Canadian society. To put this in a less bureaucratic way, disabled people, regardless of age, race, gender, and educational level and regardless of how the disability is measured, face the probability of a common fate as unemployed/underemployed and are among the poorest of the poor in Canadian society (Canada, *Advancing the Inclusion of Persons with Disabilities* [2002], 1–12). Put into the language of social justice, disabled people are an oppressed minority group facing a host of discriminatory practices, ranging from inaccessible buildings, transportation, and information and services systems, to everyday interactional degradation, denial, and dismissal. Returning to the language deployed in the government text: dis-

abled people are understood as 'not full participants' in Canadian society. Page 5 of *In Unison 2000* displays one way the
understanding of problem-people is enacted.

We have here a most common representation of disability –
namely, disability is a problem in need of a solution. As Paul
Abberley (1998: 93) suggests, disability is often only interesting as
a problem. The taken for granted sense that disability is a problem orients the reader to the immediate need to find a solution.
Solution-seeking occurs to the point of repressing any consideration of how disability-as-problem is being made to appear in the
here and now and, moreover, made to appear as a particular type
of problem. An evaluation of the efficacy of the solutions, such as
citizenship supports for individuals, will not help us to uncover
how the text enacts disability as a problem since such an evaluation would necessarily presuppose answers to questions regarding the significance of disability, and it would continue to hide
how disability is being made to appear as a meaningful something. The meaningful something that counts as disability is,
namely, an individual problem condition resulting in a lack of
participation for disabled people. What is required is an analysis
of the practical procedures by and through which disability is
manifested as a problem and is concretized as a particular kind of
problem.

The presentation of 'Disability Facts and Figures' is one
method of making disability appear as a problem. Sprinkled
throughout the *In Unison 2000* document, as well as appended to
it, are many statistical facts about disability. Much of the 'Canadian Perspective' on disability is a reiteration of facts about disability. I turn now to an analysis of the presentation and content
of the first statistical fact that appears on the page of *In Unison
2000*, displayed above.

The First Fact

Set off from, yet illustrative of, the text's 'Introduction' to 'A Canadian Perspective on Disability Issues,' a coloured box appears in
In Unison 2000. In this box, eight bullet-point sets of facts are pro-

I_N U_{NISON} 2000:
Persons with Disabilities in Canada

INTRODUCTION

A Canadian Perspective on Disability Issues

Canadians share basic values that help define us as a nation.

These include a commitment to inclusion – welcoming everyone to participate fully in society.

The vast majority of Canadians believe that persons with disabilities should be supported in their efforts to be active in their communities and society. Yet we still have a long way to go to fulfill this goal.

Disability Facts and Figures

- In 1991, 16 per cent of Canadians were considered to have a disability. That is 4.2 million people – 3.9 million living in the community, and 273,000 in institutions.
- Fifty-six per cent of people with disabilities were of working-age; nine per cent were children under 14, and 35 per cent were people over 65.
- In 1991, among working-aged women, 13 per cent were considered to have a disability.
- Slightly more than half of adults living with a disability were affected by a mild disability, one third were considered to have a moderate disability, and 14 per cent were affected by a severe disability.

- The 1991 Aboriginal Peoples Survey revealed that 31 per cent of Aboriginal adults reported some form of disability – almost twice the national average.
- The disability rate among young adults was almost three times higher for Aboriginal people than for non-Aboriginal people.
- Sixty-six per cent of Aboriginal adults with disabilities were affected by a mild disability, 22 per cent by a moderate disability and 12 per cent by severe disability.
- The likelihood of a person having a disability increases with age. As Canada's population ages, the incidence of disability is increasing.

Citizenship for people with disabilities depends on having the supports necessary to take part in work and community activities. It also depends on having access to public and private facilities and to decision-making processes.

vided under the heading 'Disability Facts and Figures.' The first fact, or set of facts, reads as follows:

- In 1991, 16 per cent of Canadians were considered to have a disability. That is 4.2 million people – 3.9 million living in the community, and 273,000 in institutions.

Boxed off from the rest of the text, labelled, coloured gold (or brown in its electronic version), and stated in bullet-point form, the reader is given many signs of the special status of this text. Such framing accomplishes the understanding that this text, while illustrative of the text preceding it, is also different from that which has come before. The difference in its appearance is symbolic of the fact-text's separate status, indicating that it is also separate from the document's explicitly stated aim of articulating how the problem of disability ought to be jointly focused on, addressed, and remedied. Instead of mapping out what to do, this text is to signify how the terrain of disability is a problem. Through signs of its uniqueness, the fact-text appears as if it is not 'doing' anything. Such differences invite us to read the fact-text as if it is not prescribing anything. It is to be read as simply the facts on disability: facts that we could photocopy or remember; facts that we might refer to or cite in a presentation, or include in a book such as this one; perhaps, these are facts that some of us might even be examined on, regurgitate, and then receive a grade on.

Framed as separate from the text as a whole, yet illustrative and supportive of the descriptive and prescriptive text that comes before and after, 'Disability Facts and Figures' appears to objectively render 'what is.' Disability is a countable thing that some known number of people within a general population possess. Most people in possession of disability live 'in the community'; some others are 'in institutions.' The distinctive features that make the text count as a fact-text, as well as the language game of appearing to simply count *what is*, achieves the sense that this special text is not an enactment of disability – it is not making anything, it is not participating in organizing the appearance of disability, and it is not part of the document's overall aim of getting people to jointly focus on doing something about the problem that is disability. Instead, this textual form encourages us to encounter it and its words as merely a mirror held up to a pre-existing reality – a clear presentation of the facts of disability. The text is to be read as a mirror reflection of the figure of disability and not read as the constitution of disability as a problem.

Yet regarding this text, like any other, as social action produced and read by people allows us to continue to engage the fact-text as *an enactment of disability as a problem*. This will become clearer as we keep the form of the fact-text in mind while turning more specifically to the content of the facts.

Again:

- In 1991, 16 per cent of Canadians were considered to have a disability. That is 4.2 million people – 3.9 million living in the community, and 273,000 in institutions.

Disability is given a location; it resides in the Canadian population. It is given a time; in the population in 1991. In Canada and in 1991, something occurred so as to ascertain how many people 'were considered to have a disability.' The production of a count of disability in Canada is reliant upon a taken for granted knowledge claim. Even though 'Canadians' refers to, among other things, those who are citizens of the country, disability is only to be located in individuals, in the particularity of some bodies, minds, and senses of some Canadians. Disability is neither depicted nor imagined as *in* the conceptual and physical social milieu that gives rise to and produces this individualized version of disability. Indeed, measuring disabling barriers (Zarb 1997), or processes of disablement, or immigration and other policies that exclude disabled people, does not seem to be an imaginative possibility here. *Disability is in Canada only insofar as it is in some Canadians.* To think about disability is to think of some individuals with some functional problem; it is not to think about how the notion 'functional' is a socially organized term with a highly contingent usage that presupposes a rather mechanical version of the body and is sometimes even used to imagine embodiment as somehow separate from the socio-politico milieu within which bodies always appear.

A thingified relation to body-function supports the generation of a disability rate for the Canadian population – in this case, 16 per cent, or one in six Canadians. At the same time, the facts lead the reader away from the idea of developing a disabling rate based on a consideration of the physical, social, and political environment of Canada with all of its built-in exclusionary features. With a thingified relation to bodily functions much remains repressed. For example, the notion that the text itself is disabling, or that the text is producing ideas of how a reader should 'normally' regard bodily anomaly, remains repressed, thus garnering its taken for granted status as merely 'Disability Facts and Figures.'

In Michel Foucault's words, this is a 'very specific "truth game" related to specific techniques that human beings use to understand themselves' (1988: 18). In order to make sense, the fact – 16 per cent of Canadians are disabled – must draw upon the reader's taken for granted knowledge that disability is understood only as an individual issue caused by individual bodies, minds, or senses that have gone wrong and do not function normally. The fact-text reactivates this taken-for-grantedness, while simultaneously reproducing the ruling relations that regulate and coordinate (Smith 1999: 74–5) disability as something individuals 'have' and can be *counted* (on) to have. In possession of disability, individual Canadians are also in possession of a problem. While this truth game is set up by the facts' focus on Canadians, it comes into full play throughout the body of the text. That is, it comes into full play both in the organization of the set of facts reproduced above, and it comes into full force within all the descriptions of the policies, programs, best practices, and individual stories of disability found throughout the entirety of *In Unison 2000*. It is important to remember that, as Smith says, texts are 'occurrences in time and space: they happen' (1999: 80). The fact that (prior to 2002) Canada had a 16 per cent disability rate is a government happening – it is a government production, it has happened for government and by it. It has happened, in part, because this is a governmental bureaucratic method for demonstrating a 'problem.' While individuals have the problem of disability, governments recognize the problem only if enough individuals have it. This fact-text relies upon the tacit understanding that a problem exists in Canada only if a statistically significant number of people have it. This statistical significance also serves to justify government action in relation to the problem, especially the action of the production of *In Unison 2000*, as well as all the other documents produced prior to this one and the many more that have been produced since *In Unison 2000*. Disabled individuals are bureaucratically transformed into rates, into a disabled population statistically worthy of government intervention (Foucault 1978: 25). Let us now consider how this truth game regarding the enactment of disability as a problem-population is supported by the god trick.

God Trick

Disability is given a time and a location but the 'considerations' that transform disability into an individualized matter of fact are not. 'In 1991, 16 per cent of Canadians were considered to have a disability.' Something did happen in 1991, but *what* considerations occurred and by *whom* are left unspoken. The fact is expressed in grammatically insufficient terms insofar as the phrase 'were considered' is missing a referent for whoever did the considering. The expression of the fact has included signs of its own production – a consideration of some sort, accomplished by someone or something – indicating only a partial deployment of the god trick.

Employing the god trick in a fuller fashion than does *In Unison 2000* results in truth claims such as the following: 'Over 12% of Canadians have a disability – that means 3.6 million people' (Canada, *Advancing the Inclusion of People with Disabilities* [2004], 8); or 'Statistics Canada found in 1999 that 3.1 million people – 12.5 per cent of the population over the age of 12 – suffered from a "long term disability or handicap" ...' (*Globe and Mail*, 16 Feb. 2002: F4). These kinds of truth claims produce a sense of certainty by securing a count of the number of individuals in possession of a problem condition. This certainty is achieved by the identification and definition of human difference understood as a condition of a lack of functionality. As a condition taken as objectively given, as a disability rate within specified populations (16%, 12.5%), and through the transformation of these rates into an ascertainable number of people (4.2 million, 3.6 million, 3.1 million), the facts as well as the procedures employed in their production appear as if they are beyond human activity and artifice.

The *Globe and Mail* fact, cited above, also gives rise to the appearance of disability as suffering – suffering is used to depict the connection between people and disability, as well as between populations and the disability rate. A stance that holds that people 'suffer' such conditions is presented as if it, too, merely reflects the obvious objective nature of disability, a condition to be suffered – clearly and obviously a big problem. So clear and obvious is the problem we call disability that, for example, anti-depressants are administered as a matter of course upon the sudden acquisition of a bodily impairment. We have made it so clear and obvious that disability is nothing other than a problem that, for example, a doctor telling a medical story in a national newspaper can assume that we would all 'know' that someone whose vision was not working as it once did, and yet laughs and tells jokes, is a patient who should have her brain examined (*Globe and Mail*, 20 Dec. 2003: F7).

The data – 'Statistics Canada found in 1999 that 3.1 million people ... suffered ...' – is enunciated as if it is simply finding what is. The factual enunciation hides the act of constituting disability as a condition readily identifiable in people in the form of rates within a population that we, individually and collectively, suffer. Thus, disability is made into a condition which, *of course,* causes suffering. Suffering is enacted and made to appear independent of the social organization of physical, mental, and sensorial differences as they exist within the symbolic order and appear always in relation to the interpretations and actions of others. As Rod Michalko says, 'Disability and suffering have been paired throughout history and remain inseparable companions to this day' (2002: 1).

Facts which fully employ the god trick are alienated from their own production and produce a version of disability alienated from its lived actuality within a social world. However, the *In Unison 2000* fact hints at its own constitution by using the phrase 'were considered,' and its truth claims are partial, even hesitant. In 1991, 16 per cent of Canadians *were considered* by an unidentified subject; this phraseology posits a missing subject who would indeed enact the consideration. But this is more than a mere insufficiency of grammar. The reader of *In Unison 2000* will discover that the text maintains a cautious relation to its many facts. For example, *In Unison 2000* stipulates that 'one of the barriers to improving supports [for persons with disabilities] is a lack of data' (xi). Despite this lack, the document includes thirty-four statistical facts in bullet-point form and appends thirteen pages of bar-graph and pie-chart depictions of disability data. In footnote form, two pages prior to the presentation of 'Disability Facts and Figures,' the following appears:

Statistics in this report come from a variety of sources, including Census data, the Survey of Labour and Income Dynamics (SLID), the 1991 Health and Activity Limitation Survey (HALS) and the 1991 Aboriginal Peoples Survey (APS). This report discusses the need for improved and timelier data. Please see Appendix A for more information on data sources, methodology and limitations.

The *In Unison 2000* document concludes its final section, 'Next Steps' [*sic*], by claiming that '... there will, in a few years, be more timely data. This will help inform our collective understanding of priorities and solutions' (62). Unlike data regarding car ownership, house ownership, or even horse ownership (data found in various government data banks and documents), possession of a disability has received minimal attention from government accounting and statistical collection agencies. For example, the 2006 short census form had no mention of disability. Since 1991, the next official count of the number of people who possess a disability in Canada occurred in 2001, and the Participation and Activity Limitation Survey (PALS) data started being made available for public consumption in 2003. The *In Unison 2000* writers know that this new data will be available in the future. The issue, however, is qualitative and not quantitative in that *In Unison 2000* is cautiously regarding the quality of its facts. For example, the data, and thereby the facts, are 'dated.' Dated facts are distanced from their own ability to make immediately present the reality of that which they enunciate. Questioning the quality of facts because of their lack of timeliness is not, however, the same as orienting to such facts as a textual enactment of the appearance of disability-as-problem, which is made to appear beyond doubt. Through the presentation of the facts, and despite the caveats surrounding them, readers are provided with an unacknowledged demonstration of how to fashion disability as problem and to do so in a normal way by locating the issue in individuals.

More timely data is data that can better achieve the sense that it is only reflecting reality and not constituting it. Still it is the nature of quantitative data that it is always out of date. Definitions of embodied differences change, significant numbers of people may count as disabled one day and not on another, and the methods of collection and codification of disability information always shift. With any one of these changes, so too does the quantity of disability shift; yet, all the while, its qualitative meaning may, despite new and improved methods, *remain unchanged and unexamined*. For example, with the advent of what the government terms a more 'inclusive' census question to screen for the possibility of disability, and by changing the questions asked to people so identified, the disability rate generated by the latest survey (PALS) is now expressed in this way: 'In 2001, 3.6 million Canadians living in households reported having activity limitations; this represents a disability rate of 12.4%' (Statistics Canada, *PALS: A Profile of Disability in Canada* [2002], 7). Or, put differently: 'One in eight Canadians has a disability – a total of 3.6 million people' (Canada, *Advancing the Inclusion of Persons with Disabilities: Executive Summary* [2004], 6). This is likely to count as the fact on disability for the next ten years.

The difference in the number of people understood (produced) as disabled by PALS (2001) as opposed to HALS (1991) results is more than a half a million. There was more than half a million fewer persons who counted as disabled in 2001 than ten years prior, and this change is charged with the power to potentially influence policy and programs. However, in the words of Statistics Canada, the changes in the number of people counted as disabled are due to a change in survey methodology, changes in the content of the survey, as well as an 'updated view of disability' (Statistics Canada, *A New Approach to Disability Data* [2002], 4, 17). Another change is that HALS (1991) took into account those living in institutions, whereas PALS (2001) did not. The normal understanding of the survey is that it provides an overview of 'what is there' and is not the producer of what is there. Again, reflective of the god trick, the power of these facts to be a constitutive influence on the lives of disabled people is glossed over by the notion that 'the two surveys cannot be compared' (*A New Approach to Disability Data*, 2).

Believing that data is void of constitutive power is reflexively supported by the stipulation that such data is not itself reliant on taken for granted collective understandings. Data that is more fully organized under the sway of the god trick gives readers facts that provide for better priorities and solutions, while making it appear as if this data has no priorities of its own. By occurring closer in time to the reader, such data also suggests that it is closer to the actuality of disability. Taking for granted the productive power of facts helps to activate the text's claim to present the actual figure of disability. However, this process glosses over the text's tacit solution to the following questions: 'What is disability?' 'What is the best way to understand disability?' 'Should disability be located only in individuals?' 'Is disability only interesting as a problem?' Good data is better able to hide what Margaret Lock refers to as the 'potent, never settled, partially disguised political contests that contribute' (1993: 331) to the way in which bodies are 'seen' and disability is made manifest. Good data hides the fact that it is part of the configuration of disability and not merely an objective presentation of the pre-existing figure of disability. Judith Butler puts the matter this way: 'If we

take the field of the human for granted, then we fail to think critically – and ethically – about the consequential ways that human
is being produced, reproduced, deproduced' (2004: 222). HALS
and PALS share in common the activity of treating the individu-
alization of disability in a taken for granted fashion.

Despite the government's concern that the facts may not adequately reflect the current reality of disability, its *In Unison 2000*
fact-text has powerfully enacted the reality of disability – it is a
problem condition attached to individuals and made measurable
by asking questions about individuals' lack of so-called normal
body functionality. Whatever else the new data reveals, it would
require a revolution of the collective consciousness for it to produce something other than this individualized conception of disability. *In Unison 2000*, as with all other government-generated
disability texts, produces disability *only* as a problem condition
that a quantifiable number of individuals possess, and this number is high enough both to establish a Canadian disability rate
and to legitimize the sense that disability requires some form of
governmental attention. The problem that disability has been
made to be also requires community awareness and collective
understanding. This latter point grounds the publication of *In
Unison 2000*, and grounds the practice of including and circulat-
ing dated facts, while also aiding in its argument for the necessity
to produce timelier data.

Concluding with Community

In 1991, 16 per cent of Canadians were considered to have a disability. That is 4.2 million people – *3.9 million living in the community, and 273,000 in institutions.*

Concluding this first fact with the statement '3.9 million living
in the community, and 273,000 in institutions' drives home the
idea that disability is an anomalous problem condition of some-
bodies who happen to exist in the collective's midst. People with
problem conditions live in one of two arenas, community or institutions. While institutions are in Canada, they are depicted as

distinct from community. Nothing more needs to be said about the shape, meaning, or actuality of community life, except simply that it does not include institutions. What life as a disabled person appears like within these communities is not at issue. Institutions have their established ways to both understand and manage the problem of disability, but do communities? Concluding the fact-text in this way enacts disability as a problem condition attached to individuals who live in community, and it suggests that the organizing of community is the solution to the problem of disability. Still, this fact produces an imagined separation between communities and disabled people. (PALS [2001] does not survey those living in institutions, on Aboriginal reservations, in the Yukon, the Northwest Territories, and Nunavut, or in Quebec, which should also make us question whose version of community is being deployed here.)

Throughout the *In Unison 2000* document, community is depicted as implementing 'best practices' to solve the problem of disability. Simultaneously, community life is depicted as if it has nothing to do with the constitution of disability as a problem – after all, community is the solution. This understanding is echoed by mainstream news stories of how a community has responded (or failed to respond) to the problem that is disability. Disability is not depicted as having anything to do with how communities establish their identities in response to their imagined outsider-others. Disability is thus made a practical problem within community, but this is done by dissociating the meaning of disability from actual community practices that organize and delimit disability as a problem.

A Community of Readers

Defining community through a negation – for example, not an institution, gives us only a hint of the complexity of the term. In the ongoing bureaucratization of everyday life, 'community' is a word that buzzes with an unexplicated social significance. Social concerns and solutions are often expressed in the language of community; for example, community policing, community renewal, community organization, community development, etc. Government texts often stipulate that they are 'responding to the needs of the community'; some newspapers are called 'community based,' while other forms of nationally distributed mass media products include sections on 'community news'; local cable stations announce community events, and magazines have special issues dedicated to unique or troublesome aspects of this or that community's life. Community need not only refer to the locales where people reside and engage in life activities. Community also refers to an imagined space where some set of values and assumptions are called upon to organize community borders, and to establish, loosely or rigidly, who belongs and who does not. Such belonging includes establishing collective orientations to the act of noticing problem-people, thus making them appear.

Within contemporary literate society, text confronts us and we confront text as a community of readers. Such a community, too, establishes its borders, for example, between literate members and illiterate outsiders, or between presumed and accomplished differences in class, race, and gender positions of both writers and readers. The taken for granted notion of a community of readers also delimits forms of membership based on cultural values and assumptions. For example: 'Did you see the article in the *National Post* about Disability?' 'No, I don't read the *Post*. It's too right-wing.' In order to textually enact a 'community issue,' it is necessary to delimit a locale where the issue resides, as well as describe (and prescribe) the shape of the issue in such a way that the imagined community can understand that this problem somehow belongs to them.

Through noticing and addressing such problems, communities are also granted a sense of who 'they' are. This 'who,' of course, is made in relation to who-it-is-not, but it is also made in relation to establishing and governing appropriate, sensible, or desirable relations to a community's problems. In these ways, communities can establish the sense of 'this is how we do things around here.' The highly complex web of organized interaction that structures collective life is glossed by the friendly sounding term 'community.' To write of a 'community issue' is, therefore, to make a recommendation as to the appropriate relation *between* the imagined community and the enunciated issue. The recommended relation also enacts a version of community via an articulation of *its* issues or problems. This is why we can say that a community 'shows what it is made of' when it responds to issues, good or bad, or why Paul Hunt says, 'The quality of the relationship the community has with its least fortunate members is a measure of its own health' (1998 [1966]: 18).

As a community issue found in texts that circulate among those concerned, disability, too, represents the radical complexity of collective life as it describes, prescribes, and evaluates a community of readers. This complexity is still present, still accomplished, still worthy of critical attention, despite the ubiquitous fact that most textual representations of disability begin, as does the government's text, by enacting disability *as a problem condition belonging to individuals*, who nonetheless reside within a variety of imagined communities. For example, consider the following typical ways of mediating disability:

Beating the Odds: Youths with Learning Disabilities Receive Awards. Gerard Warfield of Glovertown, and Jessica Flight and Beth Green of St. John's, refuse to let learning disabilities hold them back. (Jean Edwards Stacey, *The Telegram*, Friday, 25 June 2004: A4)

Glad Hatters Bring Campaign to a Close. What: H'Attire Top Hat Party. H'attire, the launch to a month-long fundraising Campaign for the Association for the Rehabilitation of the Brain Injured (ARBI), took place at the Calgary Golf and ... (Pearl Tsang, *Calgary Herald*, Sunday, 20 June 2004: D7)

Tiny Call Centre to Handle Aid to Disabled: Move Will Save Quebec $500,000 a Year. But Support Groups Say Employees Would Have Hard Time Helping People in Other Regions. The government expects to save $1 million over two years by converting a province wide network of support bureaus for the disabled into a single call centre in Drummondville with four employees ... (Mike DeSouza, *The Montreal Gazette*, Wednesday, 5 May 2004: A12)

Open a newspaper today, and you are likely to find this common expression of disability's relation to community repeated. The communities above appear to respond to disability. However, how these communities have helped to formulate disability as a problem in need of overcoming and assistance is not regarded as already a community act of making embodiment materialize in a particular fashion. Whether praised, assisted, or worried about, disability is made to appear as, and to appear interesting only as, a problem that belongs only to individuals. The news is reliant upon a set of unexamined background repetitive normative notions regarding disability.

In her book *Bodies That Matter*, Judith Butler reminds us that to speak and write of

> ... *bodies that matter* is not an idle pun, for to be material means to materialize, where the principle of that materialization is precisely what 'matters' about that body, its very intelligibility. In this sense, to know the significance of something is to know how and why it matters, where 'to matter' means at once 'to materialize' and 'to mean.' (1993: 32)

Disability is made to materialize, and is often only intelligible, as a problem located in a certain number of individuals, and this is how disability is made to matter in, and for, community. Disability matters as a problem, and this problem cannot help but re-materialize in the news, in government documents, and in the 'new and improved' post-census survey data questionnaires, such as PALS. Yet the total problem that disability has been made to be still can signify something new since we now have government-generated texts on disability entitled *A New Approach to Disability Data*. This document, and in particular its claim to newness, will be analysed next.

New and Improved Data: Translation and Comparison

As a way to address the Canadian government's claim to newness, I focus now on the document *A New Approach to Disability*

Data. Specifically, I address the document's discussion of the questions that Statistics Canada developed and used on the last census in order to generate a target population readied to be further surveyed (PALS) as 'people with disabilities.' Once a target population had been established, some of these people (43,000) were surveyed (post-census) for a variety of things, such as gender, age, difficulties with certain daily activities, disability type and severity, need and use of disability supports, educational and economic characteristics, etc. (Statistics Canada, *A New Approach to Disability Data* [2002], 17). For the purposes of this chapter, I restrict my analysis to the way a general population is questioned so as to ascertain who will and who will not count as potentially 'limited' by disability. This focus on 'who counts and how' has much to reveal about the social organization of embodied difference. Counting and measuring the characteristics of 'PWDs' in Canada is reliant on developing adequate 'filter questions,' that is, questions that can filter out disabled people from the general census population.

The importance of the census filter questions is most dramatically underscored by the document itself, as its pages, nineteen in total, are almost entirely dedicated to explicating and examining the changes in the filter questions. These filter questions are also provided verbatim. The changes to the actual post-census questionnaire content are mentioned on four pages, but this sort of questionnaire content is neither replicated nor given a concrete representation for the reader. The numbers of people who count as disabled – 4.2 million in 1991, and then 3.6 million Canadians in 2001– is not my issue. Instead, how disability is made to materialize and to mean is now the matter of concern – what sort of thing is disability made to be through the accounting procedures deployed by the filter questions? My examination will reveal something about the meaning of the quantity of people who do and do not count as disabled. It is, however, the *quality* of the change that is of utmost interest here, especially in light of the taken for granted fact that the new census filter questions are described throughout as more inclusive, precise, and/or efficient (*A New Approach to Disability Data*: 4, 8, 9, 10, 11, 12, 13, 14, 18, 19).

In introducing its reader to the changes between PALS (2001) and HALS (1991), *A New Approach to Disability Data* makes the following claim:

> Statistics Canada 2001 post-sensal [after-census] disability survey uses the ICF [International Classification of Functioning, Disability and Health (2001)] as its framework, and views disability as the interrelationship between body functions, activities and social participation, while recognizing the role of the environment as providing barriers or facilitators. The name change, from *Health and Activity Limitation Survey* to *Participation and Activity Limitation Survey*, serves to underscore this updated view of disability and the significant changes implemented in the survey. (17)

One claim being made here is that a complex version of disability is being operationalized in, and by, the new and improved methods of delimiting and then surveying the population of 'persons with disabilities.' The claim is that no longer will disability be regarded as bodily impairment, abnormality, and lack of function located simply at the level of the individual. Rather, disability is said to be reliant upon the interrelation of at least four factors:

1 bodily function
2 the activities we can and cannot do with our bodies as they currently function
3 what we can and cannot participate in given what activities we can and cannot do
4 where we find ourselves or the role of the environment

In other words, the body has functions, which when limited can limit activities that limit some people's participation in particular environments. In the activities of daily life, the 'environment' may make for participation difficulties in social arenas such as work and home, and in other activities such as travelling between work and home, or in leisure. Then, for example, *non-disability* could be one or more non-functioning body parts that have nothing to do with the normal activities of daily life. In such a case, a person's participatory power remains unchanged, and s/he would not be considered disabled.

As before, with HALS and its adherence to the 1980 World Health Organization's use of the ICIDH model (International Classification of Impairment, Disability and Handicap), lack of functionality alone does not, in and of itself, come to count as disability. Nonetheless, the claim is that something *has* changed, and this has real consequences since today there are over half a million fewer people who count as disabled. It is important to notice too that how the concept of disability is operationalized is salient for developing a sense of the target population who will then be questioned as to various survey-able aspects of life with disability.

The survey of disability in Canada has undergone a name change, and this name change 'serves to underscore this updated view of disability ...' While name changes always *do* and, therefore, *mean* something, it is not always the case that the intention behind the name change is inscribed in, and carried forth by, the changed name. A name is an interpretation and as such signifies a 'translation.' A name translates or transposes something, such as a survey, into something else, as a tag for memory, a way to indicate a difference, or a way to orient to the significance of the prior something. There is always more to a name change than the underlying supposition of an originating intention. As Wolfgang Iser contends, an act of translation, such as naming, contains a

> ... space that is opened up when something is translated into a different register ... evinced by the division between the subject matter to be interpreted and the register brought to bear ... We shall call this difference a liminal space, because it demarcates both the subject matter and the register from one another, as it does not belong to either but is opened up by interpretation itself ... Furthermore, if interpretation has to cope with the liminal space resulting from something being transposed into something else, then interpretation is primarily a performative act rather than an explanatory one ... (2000: 5–6, 7)

The government has explained that the name change on its survey and the change in the survey method itself reflect a change in the understanding of disability. I have been attempting to show that the government's way of registering disability reflects our culture's totalizing conception of disability as nothing but a problem. Let us turn to one of the documented changes, provided in *A New Approach to Disability Data*, and attempt to grasp the new register being brought to bear on the subject matter that is our embodied existence. Furthermore, let us consider how the name change does not 'explain' anything, but instead is better read as performing a translation.

Filter Questions

The target population of 'people with disabilities' is ascertained via two filter questions present in the long-form version of the Canadian Census. The Canadian Census surveys households, that is, all people living together in a particular locale. The long or short version of the Census is filled out by one member of the household being surveyed. Only the long version of the census contains the disability filter questions, which read as follows:

Health and Activity Limitation Survey, 1991

1. Is this person limited in the kind or amount of activity that he/ she can do because of a long-term physical condition, mental condition or health problem
   (a) At home?
      ○ No, not limited
      ○ Yes, limited
   (b) At school or at work?
      ○ No, not limited
      ○ Yes, limited
      ○ Not applicable
   (c) In other activities, e.g., transportation to or from work, leisure time activities
      ○ No, not limited
      ○ Yes, limited

2. Does this person have any long-term disabilities or handicaps?
   - ○ No
   - ○ Yes

The new census filter questions serving to gather the population of people who may be selected for the PALS survey read as follows:

Participation and Activity Limitation Survey, 2001

1. Does this person have any difficulty hearing, seeing, communicating, walking, climbing stairs, bending, learning or doing any similar activities?
   - ○ Yes, sometimes
   - ○ Yes, often
   - ○ No
2. Does a physical condition or mental condition or health problem reduce the amount or the kind of activity this person can do:
   (a) At home?
   - ○ Yes, sometimes
   - ○ Yes, often
   - ○ No
   (b) At work or at school?
   - ○ Yes, sometimes
   - ○ Yes, often
   - ○ No
   - ○ Not applicable
   (c) In other activities, for example, transportation or leisure?
   - ○ Yes, sometimes
   - ○ Yes, often
   - ○ No

In HALS (1991), the reader is asked to evaluate his or her household members' 'limitations.' Is a member of the household limited in the normal activities of daily life at work, home, or leisure? Further, is the limitation reasonably understood as *caused*; for example, are they limited 'because of a long-term physical condition, mental condition or health problem'? Filling out the census requires a reader able to circumscribe household members' limits in a very particular way. Household members are not limited because of others' limiting actions or expectations, nor are they limited because of social environments, family obligations, exclusions based on identity issues, or by any other form of social barriers. The census asks us to conceive of the social concept 'limit' *as if* limits are unconnected to social life and are simply the obviously recognizable result of problem conditions of the body, mind, or senses. Even while it is not stated, an operating assumption of the question is that the limiting condition belongs to the person experiencing the limits and to him or her alone. This asocial conception of limit allows for the possibility of judging a person to be limited by that which is regarded as her or his own personal, individual, asocial condition.

In the 1991 survey, disability is a thing that is explicitly stated to be a problem condition which individuals are understood to possess or not. Thus, the survey can expect a person to respond either 'yes' – a member of the household is in possession of a problem condition obviously understood as a disability or handicap – or 'no' – the person cannot be regarded as such. The respondent is to judge whether a member of the household experiences limits that can be understood as locatable exclusively at the level of individual bodily conditions, and then to record that person as 'yes,' in possession of disability or handicap. The translation of bodily limit into handicap remains a tacit act, thus, (re)constituting this *conception* of disability as if it is an unquestionable reality. Disability is not recognized as a normative act of judgment occurring between people in social and historical environments.

PALS (2001) survey does not begin with the respondent's need to ascertain nor name states of bodily limitation. Instead it asks: does this person have *difficulty* ... The difficulty, of course, is of a particular kind and needs to be located somewhere. The question achieves the sense that the type of difficulty that it seeks to survey may appear in a variety of ways: a person may have difficulty doing things, difficulty seeing things or climbing stairs, or difficulty with 'similar activities.' People could have difficulty doing such activities for a number of reasons: they may not like climbing stairs; they may not wear the proper glasses; or they may not want to communicate, or they may refuse to listen. However, the respondent is asked to imagine and to judge whether or not it is the body that is causing difficulty. 'Does a physical condition or mental condition or health problem reduce the amount or the kind of activity this person can do?' In other words, the survey suggests that anyone can, and should, evaluate whether difficulty in the doing of activities stems from a body that has difficulty doing things that thereby causes a person to experience reduced activities at home, work, or in other areas. The survey suggests that difficulties, like limits, can and should be regarded as belonging to individuals alone.

For PALS (2001), disability means having a bodily difficulty, which subjects its possessor to the problem of not doing, or to not doing sometimes, or a reduced ability to do things that are considered normal for a human being to do. Once the problem of doing is established, the respondent is asked to ascertain whether or not this difficulty with bodily doings can be reasonably called, interpreted, or translated into 'a physical condition or mental condition or health problem.' As in the earlier 1991 survey, an operating assumption is that reduced activities, like limited activity, are limits or reductions that *belong*, so to speak, only to an individual, since the survey guides the respondent to only find limits at the individual level. It is tacitly asking, 'Is the difficulty of doing things understandable to you, the census taker, or to us (Statistics Canada) as an individual's problem condition?' Unlike the 1991 survey, the respondents to the 2001 filter questions need no longer name the person as disabled or as handicapped. Now those who fill out the census need only do the tricky work of transforming and judging 'difficulty doing' into a pure body or health *condition* sometimes, often, or never experienced by the person of his or her household as a reduced ability. *Disability is thus the condition of activity reduction produced by the body.*[6]

Whereas in the HALS (1991) filter questions, one could be

imagined as in possession of a problem condition, one is now imagined as in possession of difficulties in accomplishing activities of daily living caused by the reduced functionality of one's embodied existence. According to the government, this eliminates the 'negative or severe sounding terms' (*A New Approach to Disability Data*, 12). There is, then, a change in that any sense of an identity or a status has been removed from 'disability.' Disability is presented as if it no longer names a type of self, or a way of being; it is now a name for the reduced ability to *do* resulting from a lack of functionality in one's normal bodily comportment. Disability is best located, according to the new census filter questions, in the activities of daily living that are experienced by self or by others as 'reduced,' either reduced from what the person did before or from an unexplicated imagined normal range of activities of a 'normal' human being.

With this shift from being to doing also comes a dramatic shift in our conception of the environment. Consider the question as to whether or not a person has difficulty climbing stairs. Stairs, clearly an environmental feature of contemporary life, are framed as a problem in and for bodies with difficulties. Negotiating stairs does not give certain people problems; rather, people who have problem bodies have difficulties negotiating stairs. This logic is tacitly operative throughout the survey. Consider being asked if a person has 'difficulty seeing.' Seeing is not an abstract thing. People do not merely see: they see things: they see in and from a world understood as making some of its stuff seeable for some see-ers some of the time. For example, while I may have difficulty seeing what my government or my employer is doing and planning, this is not to be regarded as difficulty with seeing. If, however, something has been made available for me to see and I am oriented to seeing it, yet I do not, then I may count as someone who has difficulty seeing. Still, the idea that disability arises between humans and the world, between bodily experience and bodily interpretation, is nowhere to be found in the questions. Instead, we find the disabled body tacitly measured against an unexamined background of normal doings accomplished by equally imagined normal beings. HALS and PALS seem to equally share a commitment to leaving this background not only unexamined but also unacknowledged as a powerful organizing force.

Disability is being constituted as an unnamed condition of difficulty that reduces activity and is to be measured against some idea of normal activity at home, work, or play. This is a conception of disability that evades and even obliterates any kind of social identity or collective politics. One can no longer, perhaps never should, 'be' a disabled person since it is assumed to be more positive to be a person, with a difficulty, or difficulties, whose activity in realms of daily life is limited. What is defined as disability is a negative condition of lack and limit, and, as such, there is no point in *being* such a person. Instead, the best that can be hoped for is that one is a person who happens to be conditioned by bodily difficulties but limited as little as possible. It is the body that is posited as the causal location of these difficulties. Recall, however, that the *New Approach* document claims that the survey is also 'recognizing the role of the environment as providing barriers or facilitators.' Despite the nod toward the 'environment' as a factor for consideration and despite the data generated, which indicates that of all the people now counted as disabled over 70 per cent have 'mobility difficulties' and pain, disability remains an individual problem found in the individual restrictions caused by bodies that make activities difficult.

It is tricky to treat 'mobility difficulties' as if they are unconnected to social life and as if they are fully locatable in bodies with difficulties. True, people move. However, people only move in and through and with or against social environments. Movement is an abstract concept when it is not located in the particularity of place. People can only move some-where.

It appears, then, that we are being guided to organize our conception of disability as removed from humanity. We are being guided into making difficulties in the 'doing' of daily life appear as if such difficulties are matters outside of social life. At the same time, the survey also represents the fact that the imagined asocial condition of disability can be responded to in and by social life: questions can be asked and answered; supports can be gathered and given; numbers and reports can be generated 'on' those people who are counted as disabled. It is curious, though, that it is we, a community of readers, and writers and researchers, people who make, ask, and answer questions on the body, who must orient to bodily difference and make it appear as if it is removed, detached, and unrelated to social life.

We work to make disability appear in this way, and yet our work does not often appear. What does appear is the unquestioned sensibility of conceiving of disability in non-social and highly objectified terms. That is, disability is being constituted as unquestionably a problem. Moreover, it is a medicalized condition of limit and lack. My intention in this chapter was to demonstrate a way to revise this conception of disability, and even to resist its power, by attending to the actual reading and writing of texts on the facts and figures of disability.

Who's Counting Now?

The vitality of an analysis of the textual enactment of disability does not only lie in uncovering the repetitive constitution of disability-as-problem. It is also necessary to grasp how and why disability matters as such. Understood as a problem in and for community, the problem of disability bears the inscription of all sorts of things that trouble, concern, worry, and animate collective life. As 'problem,' disability becomes a textualized arena. Through texts of various sorts, the problem is given shape and interpreted, solutions are posed, new problems are created; and through text, community values are articulated, and the problem of disability is re-achieved. I am not arguing that the government's way of producing knowledge on disability is determining how all others, including the mass media, conceive of and deal with disability. My work is not seeking causes for disability discrimination nor offering an origin story. Instead, I have attempted to show that to put disability into text, even in a seemingly innocuous form such as census data, is to enact its meaning. The new survey data, as well as justifications and rationalizations for the survey's design and implementation, circulate through government agencies, disability organizations, the popular press, and so on. All of this gives a community of readers a new, albeit hidden, rendering of the problem. Still, disability must already exist in a taken for granted fashion as a problem in order for such survey questions to be developed and distributed. This is why the following chapters adhere to the assumption that a community receives a sense of who it is by taking notice of what is of concern to it and that, through analysis, texts on disability can be made to reveal the texture of community life.

Analysis of the textual enactment of disability within an imagined community of readers allows for the possibility of uncovering the conceptions of disability that have captivated, indeed, captured, a collective's consciousness. Such analysis also provides an opportunity to methodically reveal the socially significant values authorizing an imagined community of writers and readers who are engaged in the act of noticing, relating to, and thus constituting disability. Such an analysis puts flesh on Henri-Jacques Stiker's suggestion that

> a society reveals itself by the way in which it treats certain significant phenomena. The problem of disability is one such phenomenon. To speak at all pertinently of disabled people discloses a society's depths ... What are societies doing when they exclude in one way or another and when they integrate in this fashion or that? What do they say about themselves in so doing? The study of everything that we could call the marginalized allows us to bring out previously ignored or neglected dimensions of that society. (1999: 14, 16)

Now that disability is included as a problem in and for a community of readers, now that disability comes to us as a textured life, what can we learn about the organizing dimensions of our current times? The matter at hand, an analysis of the textual enactment of disability as totally a problem, is of importance not only for coming to an understanding of the meaning of disability but also for coming to an understanding of the organization of this meaning. Such organization is accomplished through a community of readers within which the textured life of disability is made to appear. The exclusion of any understanding of disability except as a problem condition has something to teach us about what our society is doing when it includes, and thereby enacts, disability in its mass media texts. The next chapters serve as my attempt to reveal the organization of the societal depths that makes possible exclusion and inclusion within mainstream textual accounts of disability. Simply put, each of the upcoming chapters attempts to reveal how the problem of disability is made to appear and to interrogate the social consequences of the ongoing textual enactment of disability as it pertains to us, its community of readers. This reflexive attention to the intertwined relation between readers and writers is part of the growing interest in studying disability as a social and political phenomenon revelatory of what we are as a society.

3 Metamorphosis: Making Disability a Medical Matter

The *clinical description* or its lay analogue can be understood as a set of instructions for how to select and form an account of someone 'suffering' from this condition ... I'm not arguing that there ... are no states ... that go beyond our capacities to deal with and lead us to seek help from powers beyond ours. But we need not be mystified by the medicalization of these powers.
          – Dorothy Smith, *The Conceptual Practices of Power*, 128, 132–3.

This chapter examines the textual enactment of disability as a medical problem in a single newspaper account which begins with a story of a woman who knowingly remains pregnant with a fetus depicted as possessing abnormalities. The newspaper article goes on to describe similar cases and provides an exposé on how parents typically suffer their children's disabilities. I will read this account for its set of instructions as to how to make disability matter only as an object of medicine. As a medicalized object, disability is some-thing the ordinary reader can take interest in. However, like any other version of the scientific object, the subjectivity of the knower is treated as if it has absolutely nothing to do with the appearance of that which is known. Through an analysis of this newspaper article, I aim to show *how* disability is made to appear as a medical issue and to grasp the textured life of disability as it is formulated under a medicalized discursive regime. I seek to uncover the actual practical interpretive work involved in making disability appear as a medical problem

OF HUMAN BONDAGE: HOW THE SYSTEM MARTYRS PARENTS OF DISABLED KIDS

VICTIMS OF LOVE

The first clue appeared on the ultrasound, a hint in the microscopic clenched fists' awkward inward curl and in the umbilical cord's missing artery that something was amiss.

The doctor called. It could be Down syndrome or some other genetic fluke, the simple biological mistake of a spare chromosome that can render a child mentally or physically short-changed. Only amniocentesis – examining a sample of fluid from the womb – could solve the mystery.

Adela Crossley searched her soul. Her first child, Jason, was a strapping boy who seldom fell ill. If her second child turned out to be cursed with a debilitating genetic defect, would she opt for an abortion?

No, she decided, 'Francine was conceived in love.' Adela, 34, now says, 'and we loved her with all our hearts even before she was born. The fact she was born disabled, didn't make her any less of a child.' She refused the amnio, leaving the doctors to shake their heads as successive ultrasounds revealed ever more starkly the subtle deformities of a fetus with a severe chromosomal disorder.

Francine Crossley was born with an enormous bump on the side of her head and a floppy rag doll of a body weighing little more than four pounds. In seconds, she was in the intensive-care ward, where three days later she was diagnosed with Trisomy-18, which medical texts describe as 'incompatible with life.' Most babies die before their first birthdays, the victims of heart failure or an infection their faulty immune systems are helpless to fight.

'The pediatrician told us she was going to be extremely disabled mentally and physically to the point that she would not know us,' Adela recalls. 'Her quality of life would be impaired significantly and most likely, she would never walk or talk.'

The decision by so many women to delay having children and the onward march of medical science has resulted in a dramatic growth in the number of children born with severe disabilities.

Statistics Canada found in 1999 that 3.1 million people – 12.5 percent of the population over the age of 12 – suffered from a 'long-term disability or handicap,' compared with 2.85 million or 11.6 per cent just two years earlier. In 1996, the National Longitudinal Survey of Children and Youth found that 436, 000 youngsters – 9.3 per cent of the population – were regarded as having special needs, from a learning disability to something as severe as a debilitating degenerative disease.

These are just estimates. Even the expert data collectors at Statscan [Statistics Canada] won't have a solid figure until they see the results from a major survey on the subject conducted as part of last year's national census.

But it's no secret that delivery room heroics now save thousands of disabled babies who once died shortly after birth. They also are creating a population of shell-shocked parents stunned to discover that, when it comes to rearing such children, they are largely on their own.

Source: *Globe and Mail*, 16 February 2002, pp. F4–5.

as well as what this reveals about the community of readers who regard disability as such.

Such an analysis requires attending to the concrete way that disability is textually enacted. To this end, I focus on specific components and the finer details of both the form and content of the newspaper text – titles and title shifts, words used and not used, the employment of the concept of disability – and I focus on the beliefs, values, and interpretive codes (Smith 1999: 157ff) that allow the text to make sense and that grant it legitimacy. I engage all of these detailed aspects of this single newspaper article in order to show how disability is enacted as a medical problem, and in order to uncover how the medicalization of disability actually works. In analysing what the text makes of disability, I will expose as well what it produces for and demands of 'us,' its disabled and non-disabled readers. I approach the practices, manifest in text, that tacitly achieve the medicalization of disability so as to show how these principled practices organize the ordinary ways readers have of being interested in disability and informed about it.

One way that a popular text comes to have both sensibility and legitimacy is by making embodiment appear as a medical problem and, therefore, as a problem best managed by a medical regime. Text is, then, site *for* and form *of* oriented social action. A single text suffices in this critical endeavour insofar as we can treat a text as an occasion, as Hannah Arendt suggests, to 'become humble again and listen closely to the popular language' (1994: 311ff). A single instance of sensible speech suffices since it is representative of our cultural logic, which surrounds bodies, mothers, and the birth of disability. Thus, I treat the analysis of a newspaper account as an opportunity to resist mystification. Let us begin to uncover and understand the medicalization of life.

Something Amiss

The first clue appeared on the ultrasound, a hint in the microscopic clenched fists' awkward inward curl and in the umbilical cord's missing artery that something was amiss.

The doctor called. It could be Down syndrome or some other
genetic fluke, the simple biological mistake of a spare chromosome that can render a child mentally or physically shortchanged.
Only amniocentesis – examining a sample of fluid from the womb
– could solve the mystery. (Philp 2002: F4)

This depiction of something amiss serves as the opening lines
of a newspaper article titled 'Of Human Bondage: How the System Martyrs Parents of Disabled Kids,' written by Margaret
Philp (*Globe and Mail*, 16 Feb. 2002: F4–5). The article, which
includes a relatively lengthy narration of the discovery of fetal
abnormality, as well as interview excerpts with parents of disabled children, statistics, and pictures of children, appeared over
two full pages. It was published in a nationally distributed Canadian newspaper, the *Globe and Mail*, within the special Saturday-
only 'Globe Focus' section.

Readers have been invited, and even seduced, into the genre of
medical mystery in an ordinary fashion: 'The first clue appeared
on the ultrasound.' By making a yet-to-be-defined bodily anomaly appear through some version of medical discursive practice,
such as granting agentive status to ultrasound machines, readers
are delivered a mystery. The mystery remains. Yet, what is amiss
is clearly delivered to pregnant women and readers alike in one
of the most familiar and ordinary of ways: the doctor will call,
and we are already expecting this.

This newspaper article can be regarded as ordinary and sensible, typical and reasonable, and thus this text provides for the
possibility of analysing it, for, in Judith Butler's words, the 'conditions of its emergence' (1997: 13). The text has come to make an
appearance in the midst of a variety of conditions, such as the
normative order of literate culture and the commodification of
knowledge as these intersect with a popular press industry that
includes trained and accomplished authors such as Philp. An
analysis could treat the text as symptomatic of these larger structures that help to organize the text's status in the world as an
intelligible object. Still, there is more. There is the matter of the

text itself as a context for inquiry. What conditions the meaning of this newspaper story of martyred parents and disabled children, a story whose given starting point is the discovery of bodily anomaly presumably located within a woman's body? How does that which conditions the sensibility of this text make women, bodies, and disability meaningful as medical matters?

The condition of the text's emergence is empowered by, and simultaneously empowers, the genre, or language game, of medicine.[7] The sensibility of the text reflects that which has conditioned its existence just as much as the text activates a form of medical language and seduces the reader into a taken for granted relation to this language use. In the context of the text resides the ongoing activity of not only making up the meaning of people and issues, but also constructing the appropriate relations between these people and those issues. I am speaking here of the issue of 'governmentality' or, as Foucault puts it, the conduct of conduct, which governs our governing of our selves (Martin et al. 1988: 16ff).[8] Operating at the confusing intersection between science and technology on the path of everyday life, medical discourse seems to offer all who attend to its directions a clear organized relation to embodiment. The text can thus be made to disclose how it serves as one way women are made into problems, just as disability's iconic status as abnormal lack is made to exist as if beyond question.

The newspaper article begins with the lead title, 'Of Human Bondage: How the System Martyrs Parents of Disabled Kids.' However, when the reader turns to page F4, where the two-page article is presented in its entirety, a different title appears. Such shifts in lead titles are a convention within the current newspaper industry. Thus, on page F4 readers find the title 'Victims of Love' appearing in large bold print, topping both the text and some of the various pictures of disabled children that fill the centre of the article. 'Victims of Love' is followed by other subtitles, such as 'Cares and Woes.' As the first title indicates, the text makes the explicit claim of being an informative exposé of the failure of the safety-net systems of state agencies to live up to collective expectations to respond to the needs of parents of disabled children.

The shift in title to 'Victims of Love' demonstrates the article's adherence to the formal conventions of the journalistic genre while, at the same time, the shift introduces some ambiguity into the reading situation. Are disabled children the victims, or are the parents? Either way, what makes up this victimage, of what is it comprised? The ambiguity of the meaning of 'victim' is intensified by the fact that the article opens by highlighting the problem of women's decisions to give birth even while they possess knowledge, or at least 'clues,' of fetal abnormality.

Since reading, like writing, occurs in time and space, title shifts such as 'systems,' 'love,' 'victimage,' and 'medical problems' are not discrete interpretive relations to disability; they are instead organized by the text and by the reader steeped in the normal conventions of reading.[9] Addressing how, for example, one interpretive category, such as medicine, wields authority over others means allowing the ambiguity that exists between the different renderings of the problem of embodiment to emerge.

Still, the author, Philp, presents an unambiguous liberal orientation to disability. For example, she accepts the conventional understanding of disability as an unquestionable abnormal matter representing only limit or lack. Later, Philp does inform her readers of the history of the rise of the independent living movement that sprung many disabled children and adults from institutions. She writes, eventually, of parents who care about their disabled children, and in so doing Philp implicitly shows that she too cares about what is and is not happening to these families. What is most interesting, however, is Philp's (lengthy) introduction, for it is here that the story of women and disability as medical problem is accomplished and, once established as true, remains present throughout the text. It remains as a set of instructions advising readers to regard disability as *essentially* a medical issue regardless of other responses. I turn now to a detailed analysis of the specific introductory narrative of the text, paying special attention to how the text introduces readers to the body as a problem, thus disclosing what interpretive instructions we follow when we medicalize our lives.

Victims of Love: The Constitution of Medical Issues

Establishing the Problem

The introductory tag lines, 'Of Human Bondage: How the System Martyrs Parents of Disabled Kids,' 'Victims of Love,' and 'Cares and Woes,' are followed by a short block of text that introduces not only disability but also the author: '... *Margaret Philp* finds that many Canadian families are on the verge of despair ...' (Philp 2002: F4, emphasis in text). Interestingly, her exposé of this despair begins with a depiction of an ultrasound test. Again:

> The first clue appeared on the ultrasound, a hint in the microscopic clenched fists' awkward inward curl and in the umbilical cord's missing artery that something was amiss.
> The doctor called.

Philp defers to the authoritative image of the ultrasound.[10] This image 'voices over' Philp's own voice and displaces her as author. Still, the beginning of the text seems almost personal in its poetic description of an abnormal happening. There is a writer, of course. But in the face of the startling clues of something amiss, it seems almost natural that the 'really wrong' will appear as if it is outside of the human acts of noticing and interpreting. The clue to something really wrong is made to appear *as if* it is not produced by human interpretation, but is instead produced by the stark and undeniable *authority*, which has the ability to *see* inside the body – the ultrasound image of medicine.

Critical media studies demonstrate that news is an 'end product of a complex process' (Hall et al. 1996: 424) involving many decisions, including how to define newsworthy problems and how to do so in readily recognizable ways. Making the author's voice disappear, while making it appear as if technology alone

delivers the problem, is a move in this play of establishing legitimacy. The displacement of the author's voice is a common
practice. Nonetheless, the practice accomplishes meaning. It
demonstrates a desire to offer the reader an up-close look at something going wrong, while simultaneously making it appear as if
this desire exists in the starkness of the *wrong* and not in the relation between writer and reader.

A departure from the normal configuration of fetal development as narrated by the ultrasound becomes a 'clue,' and
through this description the reader is delivered a sense of a problem, namely, imaged symptoms of a fetus that, in general, *is* a
problem since it *has* a problem. The problem is not that of a system that martyrs parents of disabled children, at least not so far.
In the introductory part of the text, nothing is attended to outside
of the fetus and the technology geared for reading it for 'microscopic clues' of abnormality; this is the domain of the ultrasound,
which is, for some, the most socialized and politicized of all the
diagnostic imaging procedures (Cook 1996: 76; Hartouni 1998:
208; Stabile 1998: 187–8). The reader is given a sense of a type of
problem discovered and documented only by the authority of a
medical practice. This represents the birth of disability as abnormality conceived of as a medical problem.

When disability is given birth to by medicine, medicine must
labour to separate women from their bodies. There is no mother
mentioned in Philp's depiction of the ultrasound image, and it is
difficult to remember that 'the division between woman and
fetus is historically unprecedented' (Stabile 1998: 172). In the face
of the authoritative image of something wrong, it is relatively
easy to forget that the image-maker, like the embryo and stories
given it, has a history (Sawicki 1999: 191–3). Moreover, medicine
must further enact a separation between bodies and any sense of
a wider social context. As Irving Zola reminds us, constituting a
medical trouble requires that medicine be enacted as that which
'locates the source of trouble as well as the place of treatment primarily in individuals and makes the etiology of the trouble asocial and impersonal' (1977: 62).

Ultrasound is used to provide the reader with a legitimated

sense that there can be the discovery of objective clues of abnormalcy. This legitimacy is predicated upon a collective understanding that it is sensible to not acknowledge our ordinary interpretive relations to medicine as a powerful separator of human bodies from that which conditions them (this conditioning includes texts that provide us with legitimized ways of regarding embodiment). Readers are provided with texts of some 'thing' objectively wrong and are not provided with images that reflect culturally specific ways to imagine wrongness. Without signs of medical decision-making and interpretation, it becomes difficult to remember that imaging something is a way of forming the decision to look. As Rod Michalko says, any look is 'essentially a social act. Looking and noticing is located within a social web of interests, purposes, hopes, fears, anxieties, and so on' (1998: 40). The ordinary phraseology for noticing something wrong – 'The first clue appeared on the ultrasound' – accomplishes the extraordinary work of displacing not only the author but the entire sociality that grounds contemporary ways of looking at bodies. Through separations, such as the one between women and their bodies, and through displacements, such as displacing an imager by the decontextualized image, the authority of the medical domain is achieved, and its coherent articulation of the whole of human embodiment is accomplished.

I have disclosed the ways that medical language operates. Its operation, ongoing and prevalent, enacts the set of instructions for the appropriate, typical, or legitimate way of orienting to something as a medical issue. For example, readers are being instructed to regard disability as fully encapsulated by a negative ontology: somehow it is appropriate to regard disability as nothing but lack and limit, as wrong, abnormal, incorrect ... It is something amiss.

Something Amiss

As the objective knower, ultrasound need not be depicted as social action, and any details of its contexted existence are made absent within, and by, the text. This technology is presented as an asocial objective mirroring of some-body, but this presentation is reliant upon a number of veiled social acts – separations, displacements, and absences. 'Ultrasound' is used in such a way as to establish the power of the god trick (Haraway 1991: 189), and through this trick the reader comes to an unquestioned sense of something amiss. Disability is thus defined as the anomalous, the missing; it is defined as lack and as abnormality, which is articulated, documented, and treated by the call and concern of medicine. Not only is there no clue as to how the system martyrs parents of disabled children, there is also no reference to a social context of any kind, not even that of a woman's body. Techniques and clues appear as if they happen outside of the social organization of hospital or clinic, and technology appears to produce its results without the need for the reader to imagine even a technician operating the body-imaging machine, let alone to imagine the presence of an actual woman's body. Ultrasound is the linguistic device that serves the function of abstracting the body-as-problem from social life.

Then, the doctor calls. This is an often used phrase, since positive medical test results are accompanied by the promise of, the expectation of, even the deed of, the doctor's call. But how does this phrase work and what work does this phrase do?

It does not matter who this doctor is or where the doctor is; nor does it matter when the doctor is calling. The doctor's name and gender are not given; nor is the reader given any sense of the doctor's training, specialty, or social location. An anonymous agent (Sawicki 1999: 194), the 'doctor' who 'calls,' is the only necessary identity marker. The only thing the reader needs to remember is that when medicine calls there is a good (medical) reason for it to do so, and this reason has been provided for by Philp's account of the ultrasound image with its authoritative discovery of abnormality. No question about it, something is amiss, something is wrong, since the doctor will call.

The abstract doctor who calls is a textual enactment of medicine that hides the wielding of its decisive authority in the cloak of expertise, objectifying and fragmenting the body in this process. The socially abstract and disembodied doctor normalizes the notion that some human problems are beyond a need to attend to their social organization and production, thus reproducing the belief that some practices of medicine are not grounded in decisive and, thereby, oriented human action. This sensibility allows the reader to experience 'The doctor called' as clear and obvious, while not experiencing the doctor's particularity as missing. This is not a strange way to speak of doctors. It makes sense. The disembodied, decontextualized doctor can call and can be called. While bodily uncertainty or pain may make this call most welcome, the call nonetheless is a masterful organizer of that uncertainty and that pain.

Seeing Abnormality as Disability

> The doctor called. It could be Down syndrome or some other genetic fluke, the simple biological mistake of a spare chromosome that can render a child mentally or physically shortchanged. Only amniocentesis – examining a sample of fluid from the womb – could solve the mystery.

These words represent the spirit of what the doctor said when the doctor called. The medical call of abnormality transforms the ultrasound 'image' into the doctor's 'actually seeing' of abnormality. The doctor calls in order to communicate (organize) what she or he has seen. Still, what is wrong is a mysterious problem to be unravelled by an amniocentesis test.[11]

Dealing with the problem involves two aspects. First, medicine wants to solve the mystery as to what type of disability it is dealing with; for example, Down syndrome or some other genetic fluke.[12] In the words of Nikolas Rose, 'Our modern medical experience is, first, constituted in certain *dividing practices* ...' (1994: 50). The amniocentesis test will allow for medicine to divide one type of problem from another, but for now the diagnosis of a *type* of disability remains a *mystery* and medicine is depicted as guessing at what 'it could be ...' Nonetheless, the consequences of disability are not mysterious; someone (and not medicine) will be, as Philp puts it, 'shortchanged.' Medicine is

depicted as already successfully actualizing a dividing practice –
the contours of the short-changed life are seen as separate and
distinct from the contours of normal fetal development, and the
woman is separated out so radically that she is yet to make an
appearance. It is now the self-proclaimed task of medicine to
'locate subjects in different relations to the decisions and actions
made about their problems' (Rose 1994: 52).

The second aspect of dealing with the problem involves articulating these consequences to whomever the doctor calls. Ultrasound in hand, the doctor calls the possessor of the womb that is
carrying a fetus that displays an apparent abnormality. The doctor gives a partial diagnosis by regarding the abnormality as
caused by something, for example, a faulty genetic configuration.
A caused abnormality, even at the microscopic level, grounds the
doctor's ability to also provide a prognosis – this fetus represents
something mentally or physically short-changed. At this point in
the text, not only has the fetus been interpretively transformed
into a child, but also a clue of abnormality has been transformed
into a living lack. This prognosis is related to medicine's 'social
vocation' to determine where embodied differences fit and where
they do not (Rose 1994: 52).

It is easy as a reader to not be startled by the text's radical
movement from a description of microscopic abnormality to the
depiction of a child's form of life, a disabled one, a short-changed
one, a devalued one. Moving from an image of abnormal body
parts to the imagining of an entire short-changed form of life and
its life-course is presented within Philp's text as a normal fact
and not as a decision based upon an interpretive relation to disability. Still, there is no mention of the system nor of any other
social context, and while the title 'Victims of Love' may still
haunt the text, it is not yet a manifest issue. There are, however,
the beginnings of a cost/benefit analysis regarding faulty genes.
The reader is given the not-so-mysterious articulation of disability: it is a 'simple biological mistake,' a troublesome thing; it
exists in and of itself; disability becomes that thing that renders
the lives of some people short-changed.

Nonetheless, the medical mystery continues. The mystery
resides in the yet undetermined prognosis – how short-changed

of a life does this fetus represent? According to the text, this mystery can be solved by an amniocentesis test. That a medical test can be used to foretell life chances, or forms of life, makes sense only insofar as both the writer and reader conform to a set of taken for granted beliefs provided to us through group life informed by a medical sensibility. Both writer and reader must accept the efficacy of such tests; both must believe in and expect a straightforward equation between type of disability and type of life; both must subscribe to the belief that disability is a fluke condition of a nameable type within which there are few variations. The primary shared belief required of readers, and one actualized by the text, is that a named problem condition is not merely a prediction of a form of life, but is also a reasonable depiction of a life conditioned by such problems.[13] Disability is made not only to appear as a problem condition found, diagnosed, and treated by medicine, but also as a way of being, the meaning of which is clarified by medicine – disability *is rendered* as a life which is abnormal and short-changed, of little to no value, but unrelated to human interpretation. The clarification of this meaning, too, becomes part of the doctor's call – s/he calls about the abnormal thing found.

It is, say Janet Price and Margrit Shildrick, 'the enduring power and authority of biomedicine to reproduce bodies as predictable collections of matter, fixed and held in place by empirical scientific analysis ...' (1999: 147). Within the realm of new reproductive technologies, 'fixing' (as in remedy) is often not a viable option and thus is not a sensible ground for medical authority.[14] However, 'fixing,' as in pinning down with precise specificity a type of problem, is something that medicine can do. The mass media news reports daily on one genetic 'breakthrough' after another, and such breakthroughs are operative only at the diagnostic level. This ever developing ability to pin down a specific problem provides proof of medicine's authoritative ability to name the condition, to claim the condition as some-thing wholly within the purview of medicine, and impart to medicine the power to slip from saying 'what' the problem *is* to describing what the problem *means*. Rosi Braidotti describes this expanding field of medical meaning-making as a 'practice that consists in deciphering the body, transforming the organism into a text to be read and interpreted by the medical gaze' (1997: 72, 73). Deciphering, transforming, and interpreting the problem-matter are practices oriented, according to Braidotti (ibid.), by an unexamined belief in the perfectibility of the living organism and the gradual and eventual abolition of anomalies.

The text governs our consciousness of embodiment (Titchkosky 2003b, 2002; Pratt and Valverde 2002; Foucault 1988: 16ff). Writer and reader can govern their relation to disability by the understanding that disability is an objectively given lack that is assembled *as if* it is completely unrelated to the symbolic realm of social meaning – unrelated to systems that offer poor supports, unrelated to medical techniques and knowledge, and unrelated to alternative interpretations that might be held by pregnant women or parents.

Governing Objectivity and Subjectivity

The yet unnamed but objectified problem reported by Philp, unencumbered by any mention of a woman's body, or an actual doctor, is made to exist on its own, and made to appear completely within the purview of medical technology, practices, and beliefs. But when the doctor calls, she or he calls a woman to whom this problem apparently belongs, and the meaning of disability expands well beyond the medical issues of diagnosis and prognosis:

> Adela Crossley searched her soul. Her first child, Jason, was a strapping boy who seldom fell ill. If her second child turned out to be cursed with a debilitating genetic defect, would she opt for an abortion?
>
> No, she decided, 'Francine was conceived in love.' Adela, 34, now says, 'and we loved her with all our hearts even before she was born. The fact she was born disabled, didn't make her any less of a child.' She refused the amnio, leaving the doctors to shake their heads as successive ultrasounds revealed ever more starkly the subtle deformities of a fetus with a severe chromosomal disorder.

Crossley is the bodily container (Purdy 1990) upon which the ultrasound was performed and who will be delivered the diagnosis, prognosis, and treatment issues that accompany a medical noticing of abnormal fetal development – she will be delivered the issues of deformity, disorder, defect, disability. Adela Crossley is whom the doctor, of unknown gender, name, experience, or place, has called. The disembodied doctor (objectivity) calls the embodied and socially located woman (subjectivity) who possesses the womb that carries a problem in order to recommend further examinations.

Whatever Crossley's lived actuality of this complex event might have been, it serves in the text to introduce the soul-searching problem of cultural interpretations of health and illness, disability and ability, anomaly and normality, as they emerge and take place in and on women. Here illness becomes a 'falling' and disability a curse that is located in a context described only as a mother's love. As much as it is a cliché and even as banal as this sounds, Crossley becomes the occasion to articulate complex and messy relations between disability (all that is bad and not strappingly normal) and women as the subjects who bear this objective wrong. 'The fact she was born disabled, didn't make her any less of a child.' Child and disability are separated, and somehow this separation, like the medical separation between fetus and woman, makes sense. Crossley is depicted as splitting disability and personhood, and, on the basis of this split, all sorts of other soul-searching considerations enter into the meaning of disability.[15] The neater medical distinction between normal and abnormal *conditions*, resulting in functional or short-changed lives, becomes messy and unclear upon the advent of an imagined personhood, whose meaning inevitably exceeds the sensibility offered by medical discourse.

Regarding the fetus as 'Francine' or regarding it as a 'severe chromosomal disorder' requires human acts of interpretation. The act of imagining the future child readily displays its human origins. Imagining the fetus as Francine displays the context of interpretive decisiveness by making reference to institutions such as motherhood, to orientations such as love, and to situations such as age, gender, and a family nexus. The act of imagining the fetus as a severe chromosomal disorder represses its own decisive character and requires a form of imagination able to abstract *how* it sees from *what* it sees. In the text, 'Crossley' functions as a set of interpretive relations that brings out the decisive character behind any act of noticing or treating disability. Once a fetus has been made to materialize, it is, of course, caught in the web of interpretive life. However, this inescapable fact is something we can attend to or not.

Orienting to the medical meaning of disability as if it is both 'natural' and 'objective' hides medicine's active interpretive relation to disability and makes Crossley appear all the more troublesome, indeed mistaken, in her thoroughly subjectivized stance. Indeed, Crossley's reasoning seems attached only to a surfeit of subjectivity – 'love.' She refuses to regard the ultrasound's sound version of the fetus as something that can be totally contained by the singular unity of a medical conception of disability as organic lack of function and thus as abnormal. In the process of intersecting with extra-medical institutions and contexts (such as motherhood), diagnosis, prognosis, and treatment of disability become more complex. But, like the doctors, readers are positioned so as to only shake their heads at Crossley's overly subjectivized stance. The juxtaposition of the singular patient, saturated with her own subjectivity, and the many doctors, abstracted from any form of subjectivity beyond their function, provides the reader with a sense of the woman's decision as strange – Crossley is knowingly giving birth to a disabled fetus. Moreover, she is humanizing that which medicine insists is best regarded as a departure from humanity, namely, deformed and disordered genes. That this appears unruly and even monstrous is steeped in an understanding of woman as dangerous; woman blurs and confounds the clear-cut categories of self and other, especially in matters of maternity. This brings to mind the work of Margrit Shildrick (2002: 30ff), who explicates the mother/other/monster cultural conceptions and shows how mothers 'as a highly discursive category, have often represented both the best hopes and the worst fears of societies faced with an intuitive sense of their own instability and vulnerabilities.' In such a context, disability 'is still positioned as the other that not only disturbs normative expectations, but destabilizes self-identity' (Shildrick 2005b: 757).

Victimage

The tacit meaning of 'Victims of Love' now begins to crystallize. Some fetuses are cursed by a faulty genetic make-up. Undoing this curse is difficult because the problem is in them at the microscopic level, manifesting in clenched fists, twisted arteries, and other deformities, deviations, and disorders. Currently, elimination of such fetuses is the only sure medical treatment. But there are times when the curse is not undone. Because of some people's failure to be mastered by the call of medicine (e.g., a mother victimized by her own [subjective] orientation toward pregnancy), the healthy management of an orderly and normal life is put at risk. A second level of victimization then emerges as the fetus is forced to live with its curse because of the mother's decisions. Under the medicalization of life, mistaken or risky bodies are made manifest as lives victimized by an impaired sensibility, a sensibility unable to fully subject itself to the ruling authority of the day. A third level of victimization lies in this: the birth of such a being is the birth of a short-changed life, in regard to which both parent and medicine will have to offer compensatory measures. If we do not heed the call of medicine and willingly submit to it as the best way to order our lives, we all pay for it in the end. (The price we pay in not accepting our subjectitude serves to remind all of us that a renewed acceptance of the medicalization of our lives is rational, necessary, normal, and good.)

The story of this victimage continues:

Francine Crossley was born with an enormous bump on the side of her head and a floppy rag doll of a body weighing little more than four pounds. In seconds, she was in the intensive-care ward, where three days later she was diagnosed with Trisomy-18, which medical texts describe as 'incompatible with life.' Most babies die before their first birthdays, the victims of heart failure or an infection their faulty immune systems are helpless to fight.

'The pediatrician told us she was going to be extremely disabled mentally and physically to the point that she would not know us,' Adela recalls. 'Her quality of life would be impaired significantly and most likely, she would never walk or talk.'

Adela Crossley, victimized by her own decision to not allow medicine to order her relation to her pregnancy, has become mother to a mistake. This mistake is fully enunciated by medical discourse – the infant 'was diagnosed with Trisomy-18, which medical texts describe as "incompatible with life."' This is a big mistake since Francine is so short-changed by her genes, and her mother's decision not to seek treatment, that her rare condition is described as incompatible with life. Francine's 'quality of life' is deemed to be impaired by her form of life. The life that is incompatible with life is the one that medicine must now treat and attempt to save. Francine is thus encapsulated by her condition. Symptoms: a huge bump on the side of her head, a rag doll body, and a low birth weight. Diagnosis: Trisomy 18. Treatment: intensive care. Prognosis: extreme mental and physical disability leading to the constitution of a child whose most notable features are that she will never recognize her parents, never walk, and never talk. Francine is defined via her departures from, even negations of, normalcy. This all can seem dramatic. However, Francine is defined via the most common, normal, and ordinary definition of disability – negative biological lack causing personal limits and a life of abnormalcy. She epitomizes the 'negative ontology' making disability matter (materialize) as not normal and as the life that cannot do. (I will flesh out this negative ontology in the following chapter.)

Philp presents the birth of Francine in such a way as to represent the generation of a mistake that is incompatible with many of our common-sense and taken for granted notions of motherhood, childhood, and family life. At the time Philp wrote her article, Francine was four years old. While Francine still lives and has been rescued from death before her first birthday, she certainly lives, as reported by Philp, outside any normal sense of familial relations. Adela Crossley, victimized by her own inability to deal normally with a simple biological mistake, imbues all of family life with all sorts of deviations from normalcy. For example, halfway through the newspaper article, and couched among stories of other families with disabled members, the reader is presented with the following:

> ... Adela turns to her son, now 12, and says: 'Jason, can you bring your sister down.' A friend has called to ask whether he can come out to the school playground, but not today, his mother says, he's needed at home. Jason dutifully slips away, returning a moment later with Francine in his arms. Now 4, she has survived repeated colds that have graduated to bronchitis and life-threatening bouts of pneumonia. She looks like an exquisite puppet, a delicate face with big green eyes, cascading brown hair and a body that flops helplessly when held upright.
>
> The pediatrician's prophecy has been borne out: Francine neither walks nor talks, lying on the living room floor of her parents' small house in Scarborough kicking her legs and squealing or shaking an infant toy in her grasp like a baby. A psychologist recently estimated her cognitive ability to be at the level of a six-month-old.

Presumably, if Jason had a normal life, family duties would not constrain his activity. But, according to the text, disability burdens the family. Jason cannot go out anytime he chooses; he must take care of the abnormalcy that is now part of his life. Insofar as disability is medically mastered as abnormalcy incarnate, we are provoked to imagine middle-class boys as 'normally' without family duties. This unquestioned imagined normalcy needs to be present if a community of readers is to align itself with the sensibility that a boy who does not go out to play with his friends is a sad calamity produced by disability. Symptom: a playful twelve–year-old boy acting dutifully. Diagnosis: a family that includes a disabled child who is the product of a mother victimized by her

own unruly individuality. Prognosis: 'Cares and Woes,' or normal group life severely victimized by the inclusion of the mistake
that is disability. Thus, according to Philp, '... everyone in the
family is paying a price.'

The social significance of disability is textually enacted as a
burdensome life, short-changed by its lack of normalcy. In the
face of a rare and severe impairment, pediatricians appear prophetic, and normal family life becomes pathetically abnormal.
While the medical prophecy of death has not been borne out, the
medical prophecy of disability as incompatible with life and as
that which causes all sorts of abnormalcy seems so true that it is
beyond question. Notice, too, that the realm where medicine is to
actualize its prophetic vision has been radically expanded. Philp
has moved medicine's search for the cause of abnormality outside the body and into the family nexus. This is how Jason
becomes burdened by Francine's needs and, simultaneously,
becomes another victim to the mother's disordered subjectivity.
As Irving Zola has reminded us, signs of the medicalization of
everyday life are accomplished 'through the expansion of what
in life is deemed relevant to the good practice of medicine [and]
[t]hrough the expansion of what in medicine is deemed relevant
to the good practice of life' (1977: 52, 59). The good practices of
life now include our collective ability to organize our consciousness of women and children in relation to medical definitions of
the situation, *while* not ever being requested to attend to this way
of ordering consciousness.

Excessive Female Subjectivity and Medical Heroics

I have analysed in sequential order the first part of the introduction which comes to a close with the visual aid of three diamond-
shaped ornaments (see page 80 above). These ornaments typically signify a shift within a newspaper text and provide the
reader with a sign that some space or distance lies between what
has come before and what is to follow. The reading of any text is
layered with meanings produced out of the interaction of what
comes before in a text and what comes after, and vice versa. The
meaning of the text is not to be found in its words alone, nor only

in the structured sequence of words. Instead, meaning resides in the flash that arises between and among words, where, as phenomenologist F.G. Asenjo suggests, words 'must be taken as ephemeral condensations of ambiguous malleable relations: they are the local incarnation of global meanings, meanings which vary in the process of writing, reading, re-writing, and re-reading' (1988: 24). One's experience of reading this writing can be consulted for the flashes of meaning that establish interpretive relations between women and disability.

While readers may imagine that these victims of love will now be discussed in relation to how the system fails to assist them with their 'Cares and Woes,' this is not what occurs. It does not occur because, it turns out, the introduction of medicine as it interacts with women and embodiment is not yet done. Thus, the social support system and its failures will not be introduced for yet another four paragraphs. Instead, we are informed that:

The decision by so many women to delay having children and the onward march of medical science has resulted in a dramatic growth in the number of children born with severe disabilities.

Statistics Canada found in 1999 that 3.1 million people – 12.5 percent of the population over the age of 12 – suffered from a 'long-term disability or handicap,' compared with 2.85 million or 11.6 per cent just two years earlier. In 1996, the National Longitudinal Survey of Children and Youth found that 436,000 youngsters – 9.3 per cent of the population – were regarded as having special needs, from a learning disability to something as severe as a debilitating degenerative disease.

These are just estimates. Even the expert data collectors at Statscan [Statistics Canada] won't have a solid figure until they see the results from a major survey on the subject conducted as part of last year's national census.

But it's no secret that delivery room heroics now save thousands of disabled babies who once died shortly after birth. They also are creating a population of shell-shocked parents stunned to discover that, when it comes to rearing such children, they are largely on their own.

Following the diamond-shaped ornaments, and six paragraphs into the account, readers discover that this is not really a story about Crossley and Francine. Mother and child are merely one case within a larger, troubling, and troubled, population. They are one of 3.1 million of Canada's entire population of approximately 32 million. The story of Adela Crossley's giving birth to a child with a rare form of impairment is transformed by the text into something not rare but typical. Crossley's story is made into a representation of the general population of parents with disabled children. The population of concern is women who have made decisions to delay having children and in their decisiveness are the producers of a highly problematic population. Women are thus depicted as victims of their own undisciplined desires. In the wake of this excessiveness, women become the producers of many more victims.

Philp now uses both statistics and medicalized discourse to deliver to the reader the sense that some women, far too many, are unwittingly giving birth to disabled children, and this is partly caused by medicine's rationalized efficacy and partly caused by women who fail to take medical advice due to their superfluous subjectivity. Thus, the story of interest becomes: 'The decision by so many women to delay ...' Women's decisions, already represented through details of Crossley's thoroughly subjective stance, are combined with the 'onward march of medical science,' already represented as authoritative, rational, and progressive. The product of this combination, especially if women fail to listen to the call of medicine, is a 'dramatic growth in the number of children born with severe disabilities.'

The article is making the claim that within the span of two years, the population of disabled people grew by a quarter million. Philp's particular use of statistics transforms systemic failure into natural shortcoming. Systemic failure, if it can be understood as caused, not by the system, but rather by the 'dramatic growth in the number of children born with severe disabilities,' is no longer a political issue, since what system could be expected to be prepared for such a dramatic growth? The dramatic rise in the disability rate, and not the failure of systems of support for parents, is what has become the *stunning* news.

A reasonably critical reader may come to notice how this empirical rendering of disability and women is, frankly, warped. It is inappropriate for Philp to use the statistical rendering of a general disability rate for an age group over the age of twelve as a way to provide proof for a 'dramatic increase in the number of children born with severe disabilities.' There is no reasonable correlation between those two sets of truth claims. There is something disturbing about moving so easily from disease to disability, from special needs to learning disabilities to severely debilitating conditions, all of which seem steeped in an unexamined assumption that the body-gone-wrong is clear and obvious to anyone regardless of definition and regardless of social context. Despite the fallacious statistical presentation of disability by Philp, much has been communicated about the imagined nature of the problem of disability as it is related to woman-as-problem. Through drawing upon the ruling relations of state-sponsored bureaucratic ordering of populations into discernible types (Smith 1990), disability becomes simply an objective departure from normalcy, clear and certain for all to see and for some people or agencies to count. The discursive regime that organizes the appearance of disability as objectively problematic remains untouched by questions.[16] The only question that Philp's article raises is that of the actual extent of the problem: 12.5, 11.6, 9.3 per cent, etc., are 'just estimates,' and thus we are encouraged to await the 'expert data collectors at Statscan' to tell us if the solid figure of disability as a major problem is even worse than we first imagined (estimated). If so, surely the surfeit of subjectivity that is woman will require a stronger form of governance.

The shift, indicated by the three diamonds and the move into the delineation of a population of women producing disability, represents the final medicalized account. The dramatic medicalized depiction of Crossley's decision to give birth to Francine, a particular child, does the work of preparing the reader to accept the truth claim that the birth of disability *in general* is just as dramatically disturbing as are the dramatically increasing, according to Philp, numbers of disabled youngsters. Disability transmogrified as matter gone wrong helps to produce, and is produced by, women regarded as those who make things matter wrongly. In the words of Merleau-Ponty, 'Every science secretes an ontology; every ontology anticipates a body of knowledge' (1964: 98). Our ways of knowing organize ways of being, and being a woman seems particularly subject to the necessity of knowing if we are going to manage Her excess.

The Crossroads of Knowing Women and Disability

Through this analysis of a newspaper text, I aimed to reveal at least two sciences and at least two ways of being in the world that these sciences presuppose and require. There is the way of knowing bodies, mothers, and anomalies that is produced by the discourse organized under the auspices of medicine. This way of knowing 'secretes' disability as a being (ontology), the characteristic feature of which is devalued difference produced by and producing abnormalcy. This way of constructing disability anticipates the knowledge that women who willingly and knowingly give birth to disability are not only derelict in their duty, but monstrously mistaken in their choices. This way of knowing is so certain in its understanding of disability that it can only shake its head, flabbergasted, at those who dare exercise women's right to choose in the face of disability. As authoritatively hegemonic as this way of knowing is, my analysis of the newspaper text both presupposes and demonstrates that there are alternatives ways of coming to know embodiment.

This alternative way of knowing (steeped in hermeneutics) begins from the assumption that there are, in fact, a plurality of ways of developing relations with bodies, mothers, and anomalies and that all ways, even medicine's, involve interpretive decisions and ontological commitments. A hermeneutic way of knowing, or science of understanding our interpretations of interpretations, requires the inquirer to begin from the assumption that we are all enmeshed in multiple and conflicting webs of interpretation. Despite conflict and messiness, this more reflective way of knowing attempts to understand all stories and all truths as engaged in and accomplished through the social action of interpretation and secretes an understanding of readers and writers as meaning-makers. As such, readers can read their readings and thereby provide for the reflexive space that arises upon establishing the possibility of alternative (plural) interpretations.

In the face of texts, we as readers exemplify the dynamic interchange among the text, the context of reading, and our effective histories as readers (Gadamer 1996, 1975). Moreover, that which conditions the text's existence as a sensible cultural object lies in-between all the words the text deploys in order to communicate its message and the possible orientations we can take to the flashes of meaning released though the text's organization. Texts are read by people located somewhere and with a variety of consequences, one of which is, as Dorothy Smith (1999: 214) shows, the risk of capture by the dominant discourses of the day. If every act of reading risks capture, then attending to the act of reading may be a way to resist such capture. (The next chapter explores this possibility.) Texts call out for us to be certain kinds of readers; they act upon our consciousness of the act of reading itself, organizing and governing what we may and may not come to know about ourselves as readers, as well as what we may and may not come to know about reading. This holds true for the medical mystery as much as it does for any other genre.

This chapter demonstrated that the medical mystery is this: what are the problems generated by the problem that is disability? The newspaper narrative contained an answer: disability is a problem that lurks everywhere. Not only does disability lurk in accidents of fate, in structures of everyday life, but it also lurks under, in, and around bodies, and, most poignantly, it lurks even in thoughts, desires, and decisions such as those surrounding an interest in bearing a child. Disability, we are told, is only the body gone wrong; it is nothing in itself but a haunted under-life. It is not an appropriate way of being in the world. The newspaper article participates in reproducing the established mystery of disability as beyond question; the mystery is then solved.

Disability as the devalued under-life of all the worthy and valued aspects of life comes with a further detrimental consequence. Disability, like all other forms of human life, is born of woman. Woman is responsible, yet again. Today, disability is born of

woman either because of her uncontrolled and unreasonable relation to the fetus or because of her 'natural ignorance.' Had she
known, had she considered the risk, had she had the test, had she
had a few more tests, disability would not be born. 'But it is not
simply that the feminine is presented only as a lack ... it is also the
site of an unruly excess that must be repressed' (Shildrick 2002: 5).
Perplexing still, woman is imagined as able to respond to (e.g.,
love) this devalued under-life, thereby putting into question
woman's own tie to a reasonable version of humanity. Woman's
lack is nonetheless clenched by her own surfeit of subjectivity,
and thus medicine's techno-sciences will recover a hold on her.

Perhaps the story of the birth of a life incompatible with life,
discovered and saved by medical technology, is a way to re-
achieve this hold on that which, left to its own devices, is nothing
but a surfeit of subjectivity – woman.

But still there is the alternative reading, one that posits and
assumes a different ontology. Disability here is that alternative
self-reflective space where we confront, not the 'true nature' of
embodiment, but the 'true character' of all that our culture can
make of embodiment as well as how we might live with and
through these bodies and their placement in culture. Disability,
as the despised under-figure of a 'natural and normal' body,
becomes the discursive space where we confront culture as it
makes our embodied possibilities out of the limits that it has constructed disability and women to be.

The Consequence of the Medicalization of Disability

Whatever else disability may be said to be, it is most certainly a
textual enactment worthy of sociological examination. This
chapter has shown that how we propose to make disability a
topic, to take it into account within the context of group life, a
community of readers, serves to enact disability as a particular
type of problem. To enact disability as a medical problem means
to assume the ideal of 'objectivity,' of scientific reasoning, and
this requires that the life of disability be transmogrified into an
object to which this reasoning can be applied. From a medical-

ized point of view, the significance of this object should not appear entangled in the reasoner's act of reasoning.

I have shown, however, that the meaning of disability is, in fact, enmeshed with medicalized definitions of it and is actualized through medical logic and its techno-science practices. Medicalization mystifies the life that disability is since it hides what I hope should now appear undeniable, namely, that disability only ever appears in relation to people, in relation to and through interpretation. Ironically, these practices of medical mystification also serve to make disability one of the primary sites where we could begin to uncover what our culture makes of us, of our embodied existence.

Of course, we will continue to seek medical help, but perhaps we do not need to be mystified by the types of relations this help generates and the types of meanings that it produces. Among all the other things that medicine gives us today, it also gives us a way of enacting disability as a straightforward and obvious departure from normalcy, and it gives us ways to ignore the fact that we all have something to do with the constitution of this sense of normalcy that is grounding our definition of disability through a series of negations. Disability is thus made to appear in the guise of a kind of not-being, a negative ontology, and this has consequences for all of us that certainly transcend medical help, since everyday life includes disability as a life and not just as a medical condition.

One key practice involved in the current enactment of disability and, thereby, normalcy is an ongoing denial, even rejection, of the notion that the appearance of any form of embodiment is tied to human interpretation. This is why I pursued a detailed analysis of a newspaper text as an instance of 'doing' disability, of making it appear and making it appear as a certain some-thing. I have tried to reveal what writers and readers, namely us, must actually do in order to notice, understand, and treat disability as a medical problem. A medical rendering of disability requires much interpretive work. But the one thing that a scientific rationality does not require is that its writers or readers pay attention to the decision and consequences of using only this form of rationality to make sense of disability. If a reader does pay attention to the decisive acts that ground his or her use of medicalized discourse, disability is no longer so easily totalized as a problematic thing, no longer so easily united under the singular assumption that it is nothing but the negation of the normal. Such critical attention means that it is no longer so easy to regard disability as a straightforward departure from normalcy, and it is no longer so easy to enact disability as that isolated thing which produces cares and woes for lone individuals or some 'special' group. By treating text as a form of productive social action, we can begin to see how group life, community, produces the social significance of disability as well as plenty of cares and woes for anyone who is disabled or who is interested in how the social significance of disability is enacted.

The most radical consequence of the unquestioned deployment of medical sense-making is that disability easily becomes meaningful as a type of problem a community would be better off not to have in its midst. That disability can and should be cured is a common-sense belief. This belief often appears as the only viable relation to disability and is powerfully supportive of the notion that it is rational to believe in the possibility of, and even desire for, the elimination of disability. With the help of medicine, or so the logic goes, we can achieve a greater state of perfectibility – meaning the absence or elimination of anomalous embodiment as well as an ever-expanding sense of what in human life ought to embrace and embody normalcy. The next chapter turns to an analysis of the ease with which the idea of disability as a life not worth living can both enter and organize the reading experience. This conception of disability as a worthless existence or a purely negative way of being in the world certainly supports and releases the growth of the eugenic orientation now widely reported in the news as 'discovery' and 'advancement' in genetic sciences. The next chapter assumes that the logic, the technology, and the talk that begin from the premise that disability is a way of being definable through negation are on the rise. I will make use of a media account that enacts disability as a life not compatible with life, or what Judith Butler calls non-viable life: 'Certain humans are recognized as less than human, and that form of qualified recognition does not lead to a viable life. Certain humans are not recognized as human at all, and that leads to yet another order of unlivable life' (2004: 2). The next chapter interrogates these forms of non-recognition as they appear in a popular text and explores as well how forms of non-recognition powerfully produce the meaning of our life with disability.

4 Reading and Recognition: Un-doing Disability's Deadly Status

Deformity of the body, troubles of the mind, loss of senses, have always worried social groups, just as sex, power, change, death and ancestors have. There is not a culture which has not worked out an explanation, a vision, in short, an *anthropology of infirmity*.

– Henri-Jacques Stiker, *A History of Disability*, 362–3

Worry and Explanation

Henri-Jacques Stiker suggests that every culture has worked out its explanations for worries about the body, mind, and senses. Every explanation offers a solution, a point of departure, a path of proceeding, in short, a way of living with the embodied experience that has been brought on by, or brought us to, worry. There is a kind of governance offered by those institutions and people who provide explanations, which demonstrates the tight tie between explanation and the dominant modalities of a culture.

Explanation also offers a solution to the problem of what to do with what worries us. There are a host of normative solutions available to address bodily experiences that exceed our normative expectations. If I can explain to myself that this worrying experience is due to what I did or what I didn't do; what my companions, community, industry, the courts did or didn't do; what my genes, synapses, chemical balances, organic apparatus can and cannot do; then I will be granted a solution to the problem of worry. I will obtain the 'appropriate' path of proceeding with or past my worry, and this path will become the dominant concern guiding me with my embodied experience. I can seek therapy or take medication, undergo treatment, support a research fund, etc., or go to court, launch a protest, or ... Whatever the case, I know that in the face of worry I ought to explain it and that I may even feel empowered when I do. (I have my own story of acquiring the explanation of dyslexia, as well as a sense of empowerment. See Titchkosky 2003a: 30–1.)

To wonder about the shape of worry seems to me to be a rare challenge. It is interesting that in our knowledge-based, technologically driven, capitalist times we are encouraged to linger as little as possible with the advent and form of worry. Ordinarily it is no one's concern that the experience of worrying about embodiment *might be more* than a call for solutions to symptoms of problems. The ordinary way to handle worry is to find an explanation and, whatever the explanation recommends, 'Just do it.' Living under the rubric of medicine and its tie to scientific explanations, Irving Zola suggests that an instrumentalism arises where there is an 'emphasis on doing – on doing something, almost anything, when confronted with a problem' (1977: 47). The dominant governing demand is to do something and get on with (dis)solving the worrisome bodily experience into the appropriately explanatory project – an anthropology of infirmity.

But even behind the powerful normative imperative *to just do something*, there is still that which governs what we worry about, how we worry, and what sorts of explanations we invoke. Again, worry is a form of social action informed by the meanings a culture enacts for and on embodied experience. So I will turn to a worry and linger a little there. I want to worry awhile about how we read and write disability as a questionable existence within our text-mediated everyday lives. As a way to do this, I turn to an examination of an experience that I had reading in which I unwittingly joined up with the idea that death and disability go together in some taken for granted fashion. I treat the death/disability connection, especially as it is narrated beyond the womb, as symptomatic of the medicalized assumption that

DISCOVERY

MEDICINE

Courtney Popken's disease may be unique, but finding a cure for her could strengthen us all

The only case in the world

BY BRAD EVENSON

Courtney Popken is stiff as a board. Whatever is wrong with the Chilliwack, B.C. child is unforgettably simple. She cannot bend. Cruel and untreatable, her illness causes almost every muscle fibre in her body to fire at once, 24 hours a day, an almighty clench that gripped her at two months of age and has never let go. She is five.

While rare diseases are usually named for the scientists who identify them – Huntington, Gaucher, or Parkinson – Courtney's affliction is nameless.

She is the world's only victim.

Doctors have given up trying to cure her. They now concentrate on keeping her comfortable until she dies, an act she has stubbornly refused to do, as if in joyful defiance of their predictions.

'As far as we can tell, there's never been anyone like her,' says Dr. Arthur Cogswell, a critical care specialist at B.C. Children's Hospital.

But in another context, there are many people like Courtney Popken. Rare diseases are astonishingly common. At least 5,000 have been identified, collectively affecting up to 2.5 million Canadians.

'And as we get better at keeping these kids alive, the number grows,' Dr. Cogswell says.

Most of us know of someone diagnosed with a disease that hits fewer than one in 100,000 people. A cousin, a neighbour's kid, a celebrity. Think of the legendary physicist Stephen Hawking, or football hero Walter Payton ...

Yet Canada, while justifiably proud of its vaccination and public health record, can boast little success with rare disease ...

Still, what country can afford to devote resources to exotic illnesses that harm only a handful of its citizens? Surprisingly, the answer is the United States, where health is more commonly associated with cost than compassion.

A 1983 law passed to help scientists reap profits from drugs for rare diseases is directly responsible for making the United States the global leader in biotechnology, helping create such corporate giants as Amgen and Genetech.

... It makes Courtney Popken a unique prism, a chance to gain precious insight into the greater human condition. Finding a cure for her could strengthen us all ...

Clara and her husband, Joop Popken, were overjoyed with the birth of Courtney ... She was perfect in every way. But several months after they brought Courtney home from the hospital ... 'We thought she had the flu,' ...

The following day, they took her to the emergency ward at a Chilliwack hospital in respiratory distress ...

Courtney never breathed on her own again.

While the doctors could not tell the Popkens what ailed their daughter, they believed she would not survive long. And so, when the hospital's ethical committee met in late 1993 to discuss her case, they recommended the Popkens 'extubate' their daughter.

In other words, let her die ...

Source: *National Post*, Saturday, 6 March 1999, p. B11.

1 disability is not recognized as an appropriate or viable way of
   being; and
2 disability is recognized as nothing but a limitation, even, a
   negation.

I assume, through a close reading *of how* I end up reading as if
death and disability are 'naturally' connected, that this chapter
can reveal the depth and breadth of the understanding that disability is dis-solved, imagined as a limit without possibilities,
and becomes something only to rid from daily existence. Moving
to the brink of some sort of equation of disability with death, I
use my analysis of this as a way to address the possibility that
embodiment confounds and exceeds attempts to contain it
within singular understandings. It is not my intention here to
conflate illness, injury, impairment, and disability. Instead, my
intention is to show *how* this conflation is done by the mainstream media, and done in such a way so as to produce the
meaning of embodiment, including the death/disability connection. That is, I want to worry about how disability is produced as
if only connected to limits, such as illness and death, and as if
such limits are not necessarily connected to possibilities, such as
life. Since there can be no conception of limit without a connection to possibility, it becomes interesting to worry about what is
made possible when disability is regarded as pure limit. I turn
now to a worrying experience I had while reading as a way to
begin to reflect on it.

Worrying about Reading

> While the doctors could not tell the Popkens what ailed their
> [infant] daughter, they believed she would not survive long. And
> so, when the hospital's ethical [*sic*] committee met in late 1993 to
> discuss her case, they recommended the Popkens 'extubate' their
> daughter. (Evenson 1999: B11)

I was feeling quite disappointed in myself. I don't know how I
missed it. Within a minute or so of reading the recommendation

to let the little girl, Courtney Popken, die since there was no cure, I picked up on what was going on. Still, I had missed it; I was simply swept along with the newspaper article's[17] aim to speak about the need to better fund research into rare diseases. The article made sure that I understood that rare diseases (less than one case in 100,000 people) are very common. Paradoxical as it is, I understood that the rare can be common; there is a lot of variety in the body; injury, disease, and illness, come in many different forms. As I read about this, I understood it well; after all, I was in the middle of writing my first book on disability, and reading disability studies and feminist theories on the body. I knew that not only was the rare common, but that it was common to think otherwise even as we become ill or impaired.

The newspaper article went on to present another rarity: it is uncommon to find anyone, especially medical researchers and drug companies, interested in rare disease research. Easily, I follow the text's point: drug companies and researchers do not get enough support from the Canadian government and thus do little research on rare diseases. It was difficult for me to believe that, with their huge profit margins, the drug companies need more support. But, whatever the cause, it seemed true enough that few are researching rare diseases, and such research seemed important too. Moreover, various real-life cases of people who had rare diseases with no medical solution, conceived of as something to worry about, were sprinkled throughout the article.

Courtney Popken was the feature case. The stiff little girl pictured in her stretcher-like wheelchair was discussed extensively: the early onset and symptoms; the likely genetic cause of her disease and nature of her impairments; the medical opinions and interventions; all were discussed and I followed the discussion easily:

> While the doctors could not tell the Popkens what ailed their [infant] daughter, they believed she would not survive long. And so, when the hospital's ethical [sic] committee met in late 1993 to discuss her case, they recommended the Popkens 'extubate' their daughter.
>
> In other words, let her die.

In 1983, a decade before Courtney was born, the U.S. Congress
passed a bit of unusual legislation ... The Orphan Drug Act gave a
special monopoly to companies that created a drug to treat a rare
disorder or condition ... Canada does not reward such research ...

I went with the flow, as meandering as it was, and moved from a
particular hospital committee's recommendation of death for
Courtney to the general need for special legislation to aid
researchers. Legislation, USA style – that was the point. I comprehended it. I read on.

The article returned to the feature case: all of Courtney's muscles have stiffened, so much so that her lungs would collapse
were it not for a ventilator pushing air into them and against her
muscles' deadly squeeze. (It is the tube of this ventilator that
would be removed if the extubate recommendation was followed.) Pictures of Courtney, now six years old, in her wheelchair on the street in ball hockey equipment and in her home at
her computer, are used to put a face on, or put our hearts into, the
matter of the need for more research into rare diseases. I supposed that both Courtney's life and her closeness to death were
used to show how worrying is the lack of support for rare-disease research. The explanation for such a worry is that drug companies are not rewarded for rare-disease research and, so, do not
conduct such research. The logic of the article suggests that since
rare diseases cannot be prevented or cured, extreme solutions
must be implemented.

As I read on, I arrived at an understanding of the strength and
breadth of the assumption that rare diseases that cause impairment can and should be eliminated: however briefly, it seemed
normal to regard Courtney's existence as questionable since her
stiff body represents that which ought to be eliminated. Elimination is the unquestionable solution to impairment. Twice more
the idea that Courtney should be *allowed* to die was presented in
the article. 'The doctors offered little encouragement. "She had
basically no control over her future and her bodily functions,
even her breathing," Dr. Cogswell said.' According to the news
article, it was the parents' religious beliefs and Courtney's eyes,
'brown and alert as a squirrel's,' that persuaded the Popkens in

1993 that their disabled daughter's brain was intact and she should not be allowed to die.

'Squirrel eyes' ... jarring: as signs of alertness and potential brainability, Courtney's eyes were serving as her horizon between life and death. Her eyes were serving as an argument for why she deserved to go on living. I wondered what sorts of children require such arguments? With that idea, I no longer felt at one with the text. I comprehended it, but this had come with a jolt, and disgust now enveloped my sense of the whole of the article, including my reading of it – and I began to worry.

Reaching the limits of sympathetic imagination, my concordance with the article now comes up against discord. I go on reading but only to experience myself as different from the text. Nothing flows. I read to see how far the article will go in attributing a fate worse than death to bodily impairment. I read to see how much it will ask of me: what other everyday assumptions will the article require me to invoke in order for it to make sense? Much later, in what has become an excruciatingly long article, I read: 'No one knows what direction Courtney's illness will take. Is it worth it?' My patience is tried. How do we so easily come to the question of worth in the face of disease, illness, injury, and impairment? How was it that I was not immediately struck by the fact that Courtney's existence had *been made* uncertain? On what grounds are some lives made measurable, questionable, and even extinguishable? *How does all this obtain its sensibility?*

Limits and Their Possibilities

Courtney's life served as evidence for the need for more research and better legislation regarding rare diseases, yet this same life barely managed to secure a sense of its own legitimacy. At the crossroads of being curious enough to read about different forms of embodiment and yet easily enough persuaded of disability's devalued character as nothing but a form of loss, lies the possibility of uncovering how our contemporary collective relations to the body actually get organized day-to-day. How do we explain disability as only loss and convince ourselves that the only appropriate response is to saturate this loss with a deadly status?

Phenomenologist Maurice Merleau-Ponty (1958: xviii, xii) reminds us that 'the world is not what I think, but what I live through,' and so all thoughts, whether they disappoint us, disgust us, or meet us as merely mundane, are 'grounded in' and 'destined for' the world. Treating the intersection of reading and text as a primary site for social inquiry, I am especially interested to interrogate the ways in which reading about impairment in mainstream media somehow sets readers up, or organizes consciousness, to perceive disability as a loss, and a worthless one at that. How in the world is disability *made sensible* as a kind of limit without possibility? As Kevin Paterson and Bill Hughes demonstrate, oppression lies not only in barriers, but also 'in corporeal and intercorporeal norms and conventions' (1999: 608). Reading the newspaper is certainly one such convention structured by a normative order, even as it helps to construct this order. Once we know something of how writing and reading achieves this limited representation of disability, what possibilities arise?

Disability studies, in general, and Jeffrey Cohen and Gail Weiss's discussion of the limits of the body, in particular, help to address these questions. Cohen and Weiss suggest that 'the body is ... a crossroads, a space of limit *as* possibility' (2003: 4). Any experience of limit refers to what our world already makes possible, while imaginatively engaging what is not yet possible. Hannah Arendt (1954) goes so far as to suggest that both constraint and creativity arise in the space between the 'no-longer and not-yet' (Titchkosky 2003a: 153ff, 228ff). Limit cannot be grasped without its other; so, limit refers to possibility, participates in it, and is a way of experiencing it. The tight connection between limit and possibility references the notion that limits are constituted as the middle space, between, as Cohen and Weiss put it, 'historically predetermined constructs and possible futures' (2003: 2). Yet, in everyday life we come across media representations of disability that depict disability *as if* it is only connected to limits, such as death, and represented *as if* such limits are not necessarily also possibilities, life. Facing disability oppression requires an analysis of the social significance of everyday ways of disconnecting limit from possibility.

Disability studies can be read as providing alternative representations of the ever-recurring problematic of the body *as both* limit and possibility. Vic Finkelstein (1998: 28, 29) is explicit about this when he says that 'human beings are, by nature, frail animals' and that which centres the constitution of our worldly reality is 'our ability to turn vulnerability into strength.' Still, a limit of this strength is that we easily forget human vulnerability has 'significantly shaped the development of all the machinery of modern social life,' and we accomplish such a forgetting by imagining that vulnerability belongs only to certain types of people. Finkelstein depicts bodily limit as always requiring response, and thus, from the body, proceeds the possibility of beginning something new. Other authors in disability studies – in fact, any person who has something to say about embodied existence, whether they acknowledge it or not – can be read as developing an implicit relation to the limit/possibility interconnection. The lived experience of disability, too, can be thought of as a way to begin to face the problematic of the intertwining of possibility and limit. As a dyslexic person, for example, it seems particularly ironic to me that all my efforts in learning to learn the appropriate things and learning to read and write 'normally,' may be the *limit* that has sponsored my strong sociological interest in text as a form of social action organizing consciousness.

Two interrelated questions arise, provoked by the understanding that limit is *already* an actualization of a relation between self and world. What possible relations to our being-in-the-world take shape as the experience of limit? And, how might the experience of limit, as distasteful as it often seems, be imbued with the possibility of knowing our world differently and consequently making a different world? I will now pursue these questions as they relate to reading and embodiment.

The Limits of Reading

Recall that in *Writing the Social,* Dorothy Smith (1999: 196) warns that to read is to risk capture. The notion of 'reading comprehension' seems to demand exactly this. Proficient reading, like proficiency in any task, entails a kind of perceptual involvement that no longer pays attention to the 'doing' of the task. Proficiency has been characterized by Herbert Dreyfus and Stuart Dreyfus as the 'moment of involved intuitive response [where] there can be no doubt, since doubt comes only with detached evaluation of performance' (1999: 108). I read the news article on Courtney Popken proficiently: it was clear that I went with the flow, following the article, intuitively grasping its various moves as somehow belonging reasonably together. Paterson and Hughes suggest that such '... "social competence" is informed and coded by non-impaired carnality' (1999: 607).

The 'easy read' usually provided by newspapers requires that we believe ourselves to exist within the confines of the text. Such confinement is, however, illusory; it is impossible since we always read as someone positioned somewhere. We read sitting in a chair, in our homes, through our histories and with our biographies. I can, however, act as if the text's intentions and aims are my only concern; that its focus is my focus. If we read otherwise, we get other things – we get reading difficulties slipping into our comprehension. When we begin to attend to how we are reading, we get the extra-textual ideas, we get the sense that something other than the words on the page are connecting one sentence to the next, or that something other than the text is allowing for the melding of one idea with another.

As I began to perceive my reading, I became disgusted, disgusted with myself for participating in linking together things I would otherwise never willingly link, such as children and their prescribed death. Recalling Dreyfus and Dreyfus, at the advent of doubt comes the limit of proficiency. At this limit, readers may begin to uncover the type of world that grounds the possibility of a text's existence and the reader's reading. The way Courtney Popken was both written and read points to a world coded as if non-impaired by marking only a few unique bodies as limited, serving only as a plea for others' life-work, and emptied of possibility. These unexamined notions of differential embodiment are exactly what make possible this text.

Ironically, very little in literate culture asks us to pay attention to our own literacy; rarely are we asked to 'read our reading.' We

are simply supposed to be readers who read. Those who experience learning difficulties may be the exceptions; we are asked to
read our readings, but typically only so as to ascertain our 'personal learning problems.' (Still, the perception of the possibility
of attending to reading in new ways can be developed in the process of addressing learning difficulties.) If it is true that through
activity we forge an identity, then through the activity of reading,
we forge our identities as readers. As a reader, I am enabled to
know much about whatever I read, but this possibility comes
with a limit. To know through reading, I need not attend to
myself as reader; I need not (should not?) concentrate on where
my identity is in my reading. Indeed, I need to dis-attend to the
sort of relation my reading actualizes. Being in the world as
expected, for example, being literate in literate culture, comes
with privilege, but it also comes with the risk that we will not
evaluate our capture by this culture and will not read our readings. Inasmuch as I embody the proficiency of the reader, I risk
not grasping how this identity governs my relation to others and
to myself.

The Possibilities of Reading

Still, it was through reading, first with the feel of proficiency and
its subsequent comprehension and then with the sensation of
disgust, that I came to discover my difference from the text.
While I was captured by the flow of the text, it was the very
places that the text took me that also left me behind. Eventually
what I read left me not wanting any unity with the text, even
though, paradoxically, it was my initial comprehensive unity
with the text that provided for the experience of my desired separation from it.

The meaning that arose between the text and my reading
exceeded the normal bounds of a normally proficient reading.
What Merleau-Ponty says of language, in general, applies well
here to reading, in particular that '... meaning appears only at the
intersection of and as it were in the interval between words'
(1974: 39). Meaning appears between the text and reader, even

though surely neither I nor the text expected this disquietude to arise. My reading began to be coded by something other than non-impaired carnality. This disruption, this doubt, this sense of uneasiness is not objectively given in the text, nor is it due to some sort of exceptional subjective intellectual prowess on my part. Despite the fact that the proficient practice of reading requires that we do not attend to its doing, reading is still an embodied activity that is part of the world. Reading is a way of being in, and destined for, the world, and so reading can be examined for the world it builds *and* relies on. Courtney is depicted as not having a secure place in life, and this can be overlooked, or read as a normal matter of fact, or read as disgusting. The diversity of possible readings underscores that disability *is* a realm of meaningful conflict. (Just as the medical and social models of disability are in conflict, so too is the life of disability in general.)

Reading is a practice whose meaning always exceeds its practical accomplishment. For example, it was not the practice of reading the news article that enabled me to join the recommendation of death for children. Instead, the initial joining-up was made possible by me joining my culture's very limited imagination regarding differential embodiment, which holds disease and impairment as interesting, but only as medical problems.[18] Nowhere does the text need to say:

Dear Reader,
Please make sure that you confine your interest in the life of Courtney to her being representative of a medical problem requiring only a medical solution and please don't imagine what it is like to grow up as a being that others easily imagine as better off dead.

Yet, how the reader can and cannot, should and should not, experience different forms of embodiment is what grounds the sensibility of the text. Somehow the *activity* of reading relies on and gives us a world where the reasonableness of recommending death for infants, as well as potential disgust, is made possible. The text, however, does not admit to its limited representation of disability as a life without possibility.

Of totalizing interpretive moves that try to reduce the meaning
of existence to a singular unity (e.g., totalitarianism), Hannah
Arendt advocates the need to *understand*, which is 'not to con-
done anything, but to reconcile ourselves to a world in which
such things are possible at all' (1994: 308). Put differently, the
'word is a gesture, and its meaning, a whole world' (Merleau-
Ponty 1958: 214), and this means that there is a need to understand the life of the word. Mainstream media's words on embodiment enact, that is, gesture the meaning of disability, a meaning
which allows the modern Western world to configure itself such
as it is. The task becomes explicating what in the world makes
possible this unified singular depiction of disability as a kind of
limit seemingly disconnected from all possibilities. Understanding this is a way to forge a critical relation *with and in* the world,
such as it is.

Headlining the Body

As a way to explicate the social accomplishment of disability-as-
limit-without-possibilities, I turn to an examination of news
headlines and tag lines regarding disability. I will consider how
headlines formulate a meaning of and for disability, and provide
ways of perceiving embodiment, worrying about it, and constituting body problems.

Headlines serve to frame a topic for an imagined reader. In
regard to news on disability, such framing must put a heading
on a body issue in such a way that makes it simultaneously sensible and yet potentially interesting for the reader. Headlines
announce how the reader might take interest in the yet-to-be-
read issue that the news article pursues. What makes headlines
particularly amenable to my current inquiry is that they explicitly participate in *governing* our ways of noticing, taking interest
in something, and explaining it (Rose 1999; Titchkosky 2003b,
2001a; Valverde 1998). Headlines do much to the reader's reading: they participate in the already existing ways our world
intends to give meaning to the body; they frame those ways pro-
vocatively, offering them to a reader as both substance and

guide; they imply intelligible sense and titillating interest; and in these ways headlines partake in and remake contemporary meanings of the body *as* news-worthy. Understood as representations of a common-sense grasp on the body and as reasonable ways to be interested in it, headlines are sites where inquiry can begin to uncover the background order that makes possible the appearance of bodies as news-worthy in the first place.

Whatever else our world may make of embodied existence, it makes possible the sensibility of the following headlines as well as their explanatory tag lines, gleaned from the mainstream media that is available in Canada:

Measuring Up: Should Genetic Testing Decide Who Is Born? When Linda and Gary Warner were expecting a baby, like most parents, they anticipated the perfect child. But their daughter Adele was not perfect. (CBC, *The National*, 11 March 2002)

Experts Say Failed Separation of Twins Was Ethically Justified. The attempt to separate two women joined at the head for 29 years was probably ethically justified despite its disastrous conclusion, several ethicists said Tuesday. (Canadian Press, 8 July 2003)

A Pill for Children Who Can't Read: Toronto Researchers Hunting for Clues. Experts foresee scenario akin to Ritalin. Some children can't read because of the genes. But one day they may be able to take a pill to solve the problem. (*Toronto Star*, 9 July 2003)

Quality of Society's Life Gauged by Care of Disabled, Says Pope, 'Rights Cannot Be Only the Prerogative of the Healthy.' The quality of life of a community is measured by the care given to the weakest, especially the disabled, says John Paul II. (Zenit News Agency [Vatican City], 8 January 2004)

No Way, No How: For Disabled and Old, Metro Station Stairs and Escalators Are Still Impassible Obstacles. Is It a Question of Money or Political Will? There's a metro station five minutes from Isabelle Ducharme's home and another stop next to her work. But the

Montreal woman can't use them because a 1988 car accident left her ... (*Montreal Gazette*, 27 May 2004)

Health Woes Ahead for Wheelchair-Bound People, Says Doctor. New provincial funding caps will mean more health problems for many wheelchair-bound ... says Patricia Forgeron, rehabilitation physician ... (*The Guardian* [Charlottetown], 3 June 2004)

When Alzheimer's Steals the Mind, How Aggressively to Treat the Body? (*New York Times*, 18 May 2004)

What do the Pope, parents, ethicists, and readers of these headlines share in common? This question may seem like the start to a bad joke. At first, it appears that the only existing commonality might be that of random bodily diversity as found in mainstream media available in the Canadian setting. This smattering of headlines does attest, however, to the ubiquitous character of the body understood as *problem*. These depictions of minds that do not work, injured bodies, or health woes represent people as having problems, problems that are located exclusively in their bodies, even in the case of Alzheimer's, where 'how aggressively to treat the body' becomes the problem. These people are depicted and thus explained as problems, not only for themselves but also for others: for parents, ethicists, researchers, communities, politicians, doctors, and people making decisions on treatment regimes. Apparently for all people, even the readers of these headlines, disability is a problem. The headlines highlight the diversity of people who conceive of the body in this singular fashion, and the headlines participate in *normalizing* this unified way of taking interest in the body as a medicalized problem. The sensibility of the 'problem-body' is achieved by the headlines, and this explanation governs the ordinary reading.

The body is depicted as potentially a problem in all phases of the life course, ranging from birth to death. Even though different experiences of the body can touch and remake any aspect of life at any time, the texts do not locate this diversity in the meaning of 'the body' itself. Instead, only particular bodies, those taken into account as already a problem, end up representing the differences and ambiguities that are the character of embodiment in general (Canguilhem 1991; Corker 1998a: 10, 40ff; Garland-Thomson 1997). The problem-body not only suggests the singular person (e.g., the Warners' child, Isabelle Ducharme), located in his or her personal troubles (e.g., not perfect, reading troubles, wheelchair use), but also a problem with a singular meaning, a meaning that in every case hints always of a negation, a negation that easily slides into the extreme – death. Directed at individuals with individualized body problems, the solution, any solution, including death, appears justifiable. As Lennard Davis (1997: 1) suggests, and as these headlines attest, disability is a *memento mori*. A reading coded for, and by, privileging non-impairment reigns. Representing impairment as nothing but limit means that the medical paradigm masters the meaning of disability as nothing but loss in need of annihilation. Disability becomes a kind of limit without possibility, but this is, of course, impossible since limit is always potentiated by possibility. How, then, is the impossible made to appear, enacted, at all?

In this meaning-making process, say Paterson and Hughes, disability is 'annihilated as subject, yet the disabled body-subject experiences this objectification at the very level of being that is denied by the process' (1999: 606). Making impairment represent nothing but limit oppresses the necessary possibilities that accompany any body experiencing limits. And there is more: differential embodiment is made present by making its tie to any sort of natality absent. Disability is not regarded as a productive gesture bringing something new or important into the world; it is not imagined as a way of perceiving that awakens new perceptions, such as attention to the social environment; it is not regarded as a chance to reflect on how decisiveness is tied up with the birth, life, and death of any-body. Instead of such potentially productive reflexive perception, there is a positioning of impairment so that even the Pope's words end up crowning disability with a negation, since disability serves as the exemplar of weakness against which a community will or will not demonstrate its strength. Headlines are not just provocative announcements for a yet-to-be-read text; they are themselves text delivering some preconceived notion of what will provoke readers to keep reading on. Headlines are a way of encountering the world steeped in a simultaneous form of perception of it. The headlines demonstrate that this world is one which encourages people to perceive disability as thoroughly encapsulated by negation, even though we must know that we all have bodies from which we not only perceive but, also, proceed. Detached from potential newness, impairment as pure limit belongs only to no-body.

The sense of such headlines rests on the assumption that readers understand that some embodied differences can be encapsulated by a negative ontology; for example, to be disabled *is* to be a negation of strength, and thus disability becomes weakness. A negative ontology is an illusion where some lives are made to appear as if contained only by limit. Impaired bodies are newsworthy insofar as they represent limit – are made to appear through lack; and what such bodies apparently lack is a strong connection to a taken for granted normalcy. Some bodies, noticed against an unexamined background of normalcy, are delineated by negation: some bodies are *not* perfect, *not* normally individualized, *not* reading, *not* moving normally, *not* walking, *not* in possession of a mind since it has been 'stolen,' as the headlines above remind us. This way of situating disability provokes Henri-Jacques Stiker to ask, 'To what ... am I referred by the existence of these multiple diminutions or insufficiencies: *mal-formation, disability, de-bility, im-potence*, etc? All these words, curiously negative (negating what?), evoke a fear' (1999: 3). (All the words for disability seem to negate the necessity of the non-impaired sensibility having to come to terms with the life that disability is.)

The headlines refer to a common-sense interest in defining disability through a negation of being – a negative ontology; they operate under the assumption that it is sensible to frame the body as lack, inability, as missing something – suggesting only that which cannot, ought not to, be. The orientation that holds disability as the ought-not-to-be is very powerful: it is what makes sensible the rapid move from a headline that begins with metro-station stairs as impassible obstacles to a tag line that depicts the body as the sole locus of a problem. Recall the story of Courtney. She is written about as futureless because she has no control over her breathing. Ironically, she is not written about as futureless because she faces a hospital ethics committee's decision to extubate her. Clearly, it ought not to be the case that little girls cannot control their breathing, and given that we can endow this form of embodiment with nothing but negation, it seems to follow that Courtney ought not to be. In very few words, headlines can transport readers into disability *as* a form of limit without possibility.

The words of the headlines are the gesture of a world view which holds the conception of disability as definable and graspable as a negation. Disability is first, foremost, and seemingly forever, 'not.' It is not strength, not ability, it is not *x*, *y*, or *z*. *As not*, disability is a difference that is not supposed to make a difference (Michalko 2002), and it is space where a 'different view amounts for nothing' (Goggin and Newell 2003: xiv). On the phenomenon of 'not,' Mark Taylor says: 'To think not is to linger with a negative, which, though it can never be negated is not merely negative ... Neither something nor nothing, the not falls *between* being and nonbeing' (1993: 1). If thought cannot think without thinking *not*, and if disability is typified in the negative, then we need to return, as Stiker suggests, to the question of what we refer to when we think *not* of disability, telling its story in the style of a negation. Different forms of embodiment can never only be negation, nor merely negative, since they are ways of perceiving and proceeding into a world, a world which nonetheless does grasp some bodies *as if* they were pure negation. Still, these headlines' typification of disability as 'not' requires the reader to join in the difficult, time-consuming, and energy-zapping activity of constituting a sense of being as a negation; this is an impossible task. Indeed so impossible is it that our culture must try to build up the deadly boundaries around disability everyday (Shildrick and Price 1996).

Perhaps the limits of *all* embodiment are feared and mystically assuaged by our contemporary enactment of disability. Perhaps this is the fear to which Stiker refers. But Courtney – like disability – lives. While impairment is regarded as a limit disconnected from possibilities, still possibilities, potentials, and newness arise in relation to societal attempts to confine disability to this negative ontology. Proof of this is our reading and writing disability differently in the here and now of this text.

Disability's meaning exceeds the confines of negation. Even within the headlines' powerful framing of body problems, the meaning of disability nonetheless goes beyond its negation, or, in Judith Butler's words, there is a trace, a 'unassimilable remainder' (2000: 24). Disability escapes the confines of its negative ontology even as the headlines and text produce it. Each headline and tag line, for example, does hint at the irrefutable fact that all human bodies are only locatable in the human-made world, in 'community'; for example, these bodies exist in relation to parents or ethicists, to subways and hospitals, to remedies and other social practices. No-body appears outside of interaction, social structures and practices, or outside of knowing all this. Acknowledging this, as Carol Thomas puts it, 'means starting out with a social relational conception of disability, and seeking to explain disablism in terms of its roots in the level of development of the productive forces' (1999: 143). (In literate cultures, reading about disability is one such productive force in need of examination.) The body does not appear outside the social world, within which it is made manifest. Just as the meaning of a text resides as much between its words and between reader and text, so too the meaning of a body resides between bodies, between those who live through them, in them, and those who bring them to mind. Each headline is thus marked by the reality that our bodies make available, and our bodies themselves are available through their situatedness, through the meaning of their place and time.

Yet, each headline makes it seem as if bodies exist in and of themselves. What the Pope, parents, ethicists, and anyone else are supposed to share is an ability to forget that bodies are a way of perceiving, proceeding into, and appearing in social space. Bodies are social entities always endowed with meaning. The body, in other words, is always a socially situated situation, and it is exactly our consciousness of this that the sensibility of disability as presented in the news asks us to *dis*miss and *dis*allow.

I have been hinting at the idea that the body, even while marked and organized by a world that understands disability as a form of negation, cannot be fully subject to this negation. The fact that the body is conditioned by its external circumstances still points to the idea that embodiment is more than conditionality. In the next section, I turn to a different negative ontology, one that is posited in the notion of 'throwing like a girl,' and to Iris Marion Young's work on this phenomenon. I use Young's explication of this negative expression of feminine comportment as a way to explore the possibility that devalued forms of embodiment (the feminine, disability, etc.) nonetheless represent possibilities necessary for remaking our relation to where we find ourselves situated. Through this exploration of devalued forms of embodiment, I will gesture toward a conception of disability that is tied to newness.

Some Possibilities of Reading Disability Differently

In *Throwing like a Girl*, Iris Marion Young aims to trace 'in a provisional way some of the basic modalities of feminine bodily comportment' (1990: 143). She says, 'If there are indeed typically "feminine" styles of body comportment and movement, this should generate for the existential phenomenologist a concern to specify such a differentiation of the modalities of the lived body' (Young 1990: 142). In order to address the feminine-styled body, Young is suggesting the following way of proceeding: notice some-body that is typically regarded negatively and attempt to discern the specific form of differences that gives rise to the typification. The typification Young considers is that of 'throwing like a girl,' that is, not throwing one's body more fully into what one is doing, limiting and distrusting the body's 'I can.' She is dealing with a perception of the body that attends to what this body is not or what it cannot do, a mode characterized 'by a failure to make full use of the body's spatial and lateral potentialities' (Young 1990: 145).

Young seeks to ascertain what in the limits of a Western woman's situation has led her to develop a body that 'throws like a girl.' In the face of this negative typification, Young recommends specifying the different modalities of the lived body, since she holds that we are 'defined by the historical, cultural, social, and economic limits of her situation' (1990: 142). Young suggests that situations give rise to differences; asked to watch their bodies, women not socialized to the full use of their bodies end up with a 'lack of confidence,' a 'double hesitation,' underestimating their 'level of achievement' and 'throwing like a girl' (1990: 146–7).

Young is interested in 'tracing' differences of lack once they have appeared. However, she has little to say about the situational horizon that allows her to notice the feminine *as* a troublesome lack in the first place. In the 'girly' catching of a ball, Young notices that 'women tend to wait for and then *react* to its approach rather than going forth to meet it' (1990: 146), and women pay attention to how this effort appears to others. What has made attention to the situated character of the body a locus of such negativity and not, for example, a locus for the beginning of a more social conception of embodiment as a situated phenomenon?

If it is true that 'every human existence is defined by its *situation* ...' (Young 1990: 42), then not only can we read the body as symptomatic of its situation (e.g., of capitalism, of patriarchy), but we can also read the body as responsive to, as oriented toward, and as acting on the situation. Let us return again to the throwing like a girl typification: what sort of situation are we in such that throwing like a girl can show up? What are we unlike when we are like a girl? How might throwing like a girl give us something other than the knowledge that 'women in sexist society are physically handicapped' (Young 1990: 153)?[19] Along with specifying the typical appearance of difference, I have demonstrated that inquiry can and should also address the specific background situation against which the typically different shows up at all (e.g., a non-impaired sensibility, a hetero-normative demand, or the hyper-individualism of capitalism). How, for example, does consciousness of body *as* a situated relation to the world show up only in the negative, only as 'throwing like a girl'?

I have proceeded in this chapter by discerning the specific typified form given to embodied differences such that texts can easily move readers to the idea that impairment is lack without a poignant way of being in the world. By turning to the typification of disability as a 'not,' I have attempted, for example, to discern the specific form given to embodied differences such that texts can move a reader so easily from the notion that disability is a form of not being to the idea that those with disabilities ought not be. I have not regarded the negative words on disability in the popular press as somehow a reflection of body-styles, but instead as a reflection of the historical, cultural, social, and economic limits organizing our collective perception(s) of bodies. I have tried to unpack the extreme objectivism of a medicalized gaze, which proceeds from a taken for granted sense that the impaired (or feminine) body *is missing* something. Also, I have attempted to not align myself with the extreme subjectivism of the liberal stance that insists that being disabled (or being a woman) is simply what the individual makes of it. Between objectivism and subjectivism, we thus have the opportunity to reconcile ourselves to the social fact that the body only ever appears to people in cultural situations and must be studied as such. For example, 'throwing like a girl' is not only a style of feminine bodily comportment; 'throwing like a girl' is a way of perceiving any-body at particular times and places and with particular consequences which are part of the achievement of that situation (e.g., 'Son, stop throwing like a girl!').

Perhaps the appearance of throwing like a girl can only show up when 'throwing like a guy' remains an unquestioned value and standard against which the gendered throw is formed and measured. Throwing hard, fast, without caution, or throwing to or for someone, are also types of throws that can show up; they appear against different (and also typically unexamined) registers of values and standards. Understanding this suggests that we examine our own relation to the typifications that have already made our lives appear in the ways that they ordinarily do. Judith Butler puts it this way:

> ... categories by which the world becomes available to us are continually remade by the encounter with the world that they facili-

tate. We do not remain the same, and neither do our cognitive categories, as we enter into a knowing encounter with the world. Both the knowing subject and the world are undone and redone by the act of knowledge. (2000: 20)

Typifications make the world available; they make disability or femininity appear, and even appear as a 'not.' Yet the appearance of disability, like feminine comportment, is situated in the potentiality of remaking what we know of our world, since embodied existence is always and forever an 'encounter.' It follows, then, that what has *already* been said and done to the body, such as putting it into newspaper texts as the problem of disability, can be analysed for the registers or taken for granted values against which disability is typically made to show up as lack and limit. This way of knowing seeks to reveal the encounter that has sustained dealings with the body, and yet this way of knowing risks undoing the typifications that have provided for the possibility of the encounter in the first place. In other words, reading and writing disability in this different way is to exemplify the belief that revealing the register upon which embodiment is made to appear 'is' a positive depiction insofar as it represents the promise of changing how our relations to embodiment figure and what they come to mean.

To understand the body as more than a mere symptom of a given situation, such as patriarchy or capitalism, is to begin to understand it as *a response*; the body is a way of being, even if this way is ordered, organized, and oppressed by its situation. The body (as thing, as object) is conditioned by its external circumstances; but it is more: it overflows its conceptual confines. There remains some difference between body and situation, so that in my body I meet more than the situations of patriarchy and capitalism. While reading the newspaper, I meet more than a body's newsworthy character, since I can also meet my embodied response to (acceptance, disgust) and acting on (critique) this news. The body, in all of its typifications, even oppressive ones such as 'girly or gimped,' is still an *acting-in-to-and-on-to* a world that has, of course, acted on the body and helped to constitute its types. This means that the body can be regarded as both symptomatic of *and* responsive to its essential situated-ness. The body means something, and in this meaning acts. As an oriented meaningful activity, the body can act upon that which has acted on it. From the typifications 'girly or gimped,' I can learn not only about the process of typification and its production of devalued difference, but also about the situations that allow these differences to show up and, in particular, show up today not only as objectively-given-natural-states-of-affairs, but *as* typifications, *as* something with which I work and live, and *as* that which might now invite reaction, response, or reflection.

Despite individual variations on these types, variations that are manifold and multifarious, there is a 'unity that can be described and made intelligible' (Young 1990: 142). This unity does not lie simply in the contours of the typical appearance of the typical type – its mode of being. It lies also in the type of world, the background situations, that, as Merleau-Ponty says, *release* the type: 'One phenomenon releases another ... by the meaning which it holds out ...' (1958: 50). Every type can be read as releasing a certain type of world *and* as responsive to it. No type need be read simply for shoring up the boundaries of the difference that it appears to be, since such an analysis may do more to contribute to the reproduction of a typification than to an analysis of its constitution. Negative typifications of disability, even those that depict disability as a limit without possibility, can be used to grasp the existential understanding that, as Stiker puts it, 'we are always other than what society made us and believes us to be' (1999: 51). The possibility that lies in exploring our limited and limiting representations of disability is to make our 'other than' more manifest. Reading and writing disability differently is to make manifest a commitment to retelling the stories of disability in such a way that resists the illusion that disability is a limit without possibility. Still, this is no easy task within a milieu that, with the rise of the new eugenics and its subsequent technology, necessitates a devaluation and dismissal of the life of disability for its own functioning. The meaning of embodiment is more than a mere product of discourse. Or, put differently, as much as discourse determines, it also makes possible, the retelling of disability stories that speaks back to that which has spoken.

Explaining Disability

Recall that this chapter began by discussing the fact that disability must first be enacted as a problem to worry about before any solution can be put forth. Different communities at different times accomplish this enactment of disability as a worrisome problem in different ways. This is why what counts as an impairment changes from one culture to the next, over time, and from one person to the next (e.g., see Holzer et al. 1999; Ingstad and Whyte 1995). As Henri-Jacques Stiker (1999: 362–3) reminds us, there is not a people who have not organized some relation to embodiment and how to worry about this. Thus, all peoples have worked out some way to explain bodily troubles. The working out of an explanation is an enactment of disability in that the explanation not only makes disability a problem, but makes it into a particular type of problem that requires the concerted and coordinated efforts of people (Smith 1999).

This working out of a way to understand disability happens in the context of group life. The working out of the meaning of things draws upon sensibilities that already circulate within a group's life. While meaning can be *reflectively* worked out by people, the meaning of disability is typically accomplished and performed on the grounds of pre-established and unexamined group values and assumptions regarding bodies, minds, and senses, and their interrelations. The daily appearance of disability in text is but one of the scenes where the presumption of disability's problematic character is enacted and where we are invited to be worried and to do something even if that something is nothing more than a sigh of pity. So, it is also in the scene of the text that people propose solutions to the problem of disability within the context of a group that enacts disability as a particular type of worry.

In Western(ized) cultures, the medical paradigm serves as the dominant way that disability is explained, enacted, and put into text. The sensibility of the text on Courtney Popken, for example, relies on the taken for granted authority of medical discourse. Taking a cue from Nikolas Rose's (1994: 49ff) work on modern modalities of control and governance, I conceptualize the medical paradigm as a particular way of making and coordinating human problems whereby our relations to problems are 'mastered by a form of truth regulated by rationalities proper to the codes of scientific reason.' The ideal of 'objectivity' in scientific reasoning requires an object to which this reasoning can be applied, an object, moreover, that does not appear entangled in the act of reasoning nor tied to the subjectivity of the reasoner. When embodied difference is mastered by medicine, it is demarcated and encoded as some 'thing' found wrong in individuals. Disability becomes some *thing*, which can be envisioned as *causing* a lack or a loss in and for individuals. Disability is structured as a problem in, and for, individuals. Moreover, what is not to appear is the medical paradigmatic stance that allows people to explain and 'see' disability as a caused entity and as a thing gone wrong.

The previous chapter attempted to reveal the actual workings of this medical mastery in the mainstream media. The current chapter has aimed to pursue the logical consequences of this mastery as it is currently being accomplished. I have been particularly interested in understanding the possible consequences that flow from our collective enactments of disability as an inessential figure in community life. Under the mastery of medicine, the appropriate path in the face of bodily worry, or in the face of a 'loss or abnormality of psychological, or anatomical structure or function,' as the World Health Organization (WHO, 1980; see also www.who.ch/icidh) puts it, is made manifest and is managed by medical speech and action.[20] Currently, it is medicine that wields the authority and takes the responsibility for telling people what disability is, where it is located, and how it affects individuals and populations; and, it is the medical domain that says how to prevent, manage, or live with disability. The dominant explanatory system of medicine starts from the presupposition that disability is *loss*. To worry appropriately about disability is to worry about a missing normalcy, an absent ability, a negative state of affairs. Under the rubric of medicine, disability is not a new way of being in the world. It is, instead, a departure from normalcy and a loss of a way of being in the world.

Through this disability-as-negation logic, we are existing more and more in a world that takes for granted the idea that we would be better off without disability since it is regarded as nothing in itself. It is only a sign of loss. Through medical explanations of bodily worries, embodied difference is observed, demarcated, and differentiated as a problem distinct from non-problems, as abnormal and distinct from 'normal' bodies, minds, and senses. Such discursive practice is thereby able to authoritatively render disability 'thinkable, describable, calculable, predictable' (Rose 1994: 62). Thoroughly explained as 'loss,' we now know what to do with disability – get rid of it or adapt – since who wants to live a life of loss?

At the socio-political level, one of the most interesting and perplexing features of the medical mastery of the meaning of embodiment is that disability too easily becomes regarded as a trouble distinct and separate not only from scientific reasoning but also from normal life. The demands for, and contours of, 'health' readily relieve us of the need to raise the possibility that there is no such thing as a normal or natural body against which disability obviously and objectively stands out (Bordo 1993; Foucault 1978; Michalko 2002). The problem of disability is explained as if it resides in embodiment alone, and the social processes of interpretation that help to constitute disability as such are typically excluded from collective consideration. Consequently, disability is enacted as a condition that pertains to an ascertainable number of individuals, usually imagined as very few and highly anomalous, and cultural and group life is enacted as the normal abode for those bodies, minds, and senses that count as normal, or near-normal. When disability is medicalized, culture and group life is made to appear as that which is unrelated to the making of disability as well as that which is unconnected to the constitution of interpretive relations to disability. Within a medicalized framework, disability becomes merely a thing, a problem, found in people, usually other people. Further consequences that flow from this way of making and knowing human problems are 'the valorization of health and of the sanitization of suffering, the powers ascribed to the medical personage in relation to the disquiets of the body, soul and social order, [and] the sense of ourselves as perfectible through the application of medical techniques' (Rose 1994: 50).

These consequences unintentionally create an abiding paradox which, in turn, creates a further unintended consequence, namely, the possibility of theorizing this paradox. The initial paradox lies in this: medical talk and conduct surrounding the thing make (disability) appear as if it has little, to nothing, to do with the actual constitution of group life. Despite appearances to the contrary, this talk and conduct are nonetheless accomplished among groups of people, as, among other things, normalized members' method for addressing worry. So, the medicalized talk and conduct that explain disability in an objectified fashion still provide for the opportunity to examine how group life, the grounds of our subjectivity, achieves itself, achieves its normal sense of normal worries. In so doing, such talk and conduct make disability appear, and yet appear *as if* it is unrelated to all people who explain and live with disability. It is this paradox that grounds the sensibility of Henri-Jacques Stiker's assertion that 'to speak at all pertinently of disabled people is to reveal a society's depths' (1999: 14). Addressing the topic of disability beyond the need to provide explanation is to reveal what a society makes of disability. If contemporary group life envisions disability as nothing but a loss with which we do not need to live, what might this say about 'society's depths'?

So non-viable is disability made to appear that its removal from group life is an idea that is often being proposed, or simply praised, by the mainstream media. For example, the discovery of genes (understood as the totalizing explanation of the problem of some impairments) is typically greeted positively. Gene discovery is positive, but not because it cures anything or makes life easier for anyone. It is one more factor that can be screened for in, and then (ideally?) eliminated from, a population. This project of eliminating disability, or at least desiring its elimination, is only partly guided by the politics of women's choice. Moreover, 'choice' is done in, and organized by, the social milieu within which it is accomplished and can be tied as much to oppression as to liberation (Kerr and Shakespeare 2002: 120–41). The research of Priscilla Alderson et al. demonstrates the practical ways that 'economic policies, such as whether society values and supports disabled lives or funds screening services intended to prevent such lives, are transformed into personal prenatal choices and private griefs for women to bear' (2004: 64). The advent of mass prenatal screening, and the growing normative demand to eliminate fetuses which bear signs of abnormality, are projects conditioned by the fact that disability is already understood not only as a problem but as problem a community would be better off without. *Still, how this explanation for the elimination of disability is actually enacted, accomplished, worked out, and worked into daily life remains a question.* Indeed, it remains an animating worry in my work.

There are many ways to reveal the depths of the understanding behind disability's current configuration as an unworthy participant and inessential way of being in the world. This configuration of disability could be documented, for example, by examining certain human acts (e.g., genetic testing, prenatal counselling practices, the development of policies that enforce fetal testing, etc.). These examples are all signs or symptoms of the veracity of the cultural understanding of disability as a life not worth living. Yet, genetic discourse is a difficult interlocutor. On one side, genetic discourse seems always to be tied up with all sorts of Enlightenment values: progress, industry, reason, and individual fortitude or gumption. On the other side, genetic discourse is not only complex, but is also highly malleable and shifty; thus, it seems empowered to change what we are to think of it. For example, in the span of a few short months, the multi-billion-dollar project of mapping the genome, the so-called new book of life, turned out to be of less use than people had imagined. The genetic map does not hold half the promise that the genomic industry predicted, and yet, our enchantment with genetic possibilities continues unabated. One further difficulty with genetic discourse lies in this: genetic discourse is just one realm, perhaps the most iconic, extraordinary, and powerful, but nonetheless just one realm that casts disability as limit without possibility.

Scientific industrial structures, as organized under late capitalism, may be, in part, the material reality organizing the manufacturing of the inclusion of disability as a site of institutionalized annihilation. It may well be that the grandiose project of designing ourselves has brought forth the normalization of a desire to make disability into non-viable life. However, it may also be something else that has caused disability to figure as a limit without possibility and as an unwanted problem. Whatever the cause, it is still in the mundane ordinary achievement of daily life, in our routine practices such as reading and writing, that disability is included as an excludable type, functioning as a scene of annihilation and understood as a life incompatible with life. First causes are illusionary, and while there are many explanations, they may not help us proceed toward an examination of how our participation in the ordinary doing of everyday life is tied to what and how disability has come to mean. Many millions of people, for example, have no contact with the genomic enterprise structure, with its people and processes, except through the practice of reading newspaper texts, pamphlets, or informative documents or exposés. Thus, I will leave behind the powerful and dramatic idea of the final solution: the total encapsulation of disability by the idea that it need only be recognized as a non-viable life that genetic discourse so often articulates while attempting to demonstrate its own necessity or profitability. I turn, instead, to ordinary everyday *solutions* to disability that still set up a diminishment of alterity.

PART TWO

Dis-solutions

IN THE FIRST PART OF THE BOOK I demonstrated, through an interrogation of texts informed by medical discourse, that 'disability' is typically regarded as a problem for the state, for communities, and for individuals. At all these levels, recommendations for addressing the problem are hinted at in the texts, and, in turn, the proposed *solutions* help to reconstitute disability-as-problem. The most radical of these, revealed in the previous chapters, is to understand disability as such a terribly negative condition, uncontrollably disruptive to individual and community welfare, that the prevention or elimination of 'worthless' forms of life comes to be understood as the only reasonable solution. Fortunately, we are always more than what is made of us.

There are stark and dramatic ways that everyday life enacts solutions to the problem of disability. Medical and technologically informed solutions often appear to achieve disability as worthless and non-vital. Still, while medicalized definitions of the *problem* of disability rule the day, medical solutions do not. Disability remains part of daily life. Nonetheless, solutions are sought since disability remains part of everyday life as, and typically only as, a problem. There are many different ways that solutions to the problem of disability are explicitly expressed within mainstream texts. Some prominent, and often overlapping, types of solutions include bureaucratic programmatic management, the development and use of assistive devices, as well as the suggestion that securing normal consumer rights can organize care and assistance in ways that dissolve the power of disability (already understood as a problem). In the chapters that follow, I explore two common neo-liberal solutions: first, bureaucratic language practices ordering inclusion; and, second, the common-sense demand to 'overcome' through a privileging of a transcendent human spirit. Such solutions still assume that disability is, at bottom, a medical problem. But these neo-liberal solutions are also geared to address the way in which disability is made to appear in everyday life; namely, only *in* individuals who appear disabled within settings, and where neither the setting nor the people appear as that which can be fully managed by medicalized discursive practices.

The logic behind genetic engineering assumes disability as a kind of contradictory living death that ought to be resolved through prevention and elimination. The consequences of being disabled are imagined, however, somewhat differently from within the confines of everyday life organized under the auspices of neo-liberal powers of bureaucracy, technology, and individualistic consumer culture. People with impairments are interpreted as individuals who face the problem of needing to secure their inclusion – seeking, organizing, and manifesting some form of inclusion is often deemed to be the solution to the problem of disability. This solution proposes that to be disabled means to be in possession of a problem condition that limits, disrupts, or even prevents the individual's normal participation in normal life, so that the problem needs to be diminished, perhaps even dissolved.

But an unquestioned adherence to the assumption that exclusion is the main problem faced by disabled people may be a dangerous one, especially if we are to maintain a critical focus on how the meaning of disability is being constituted through texts that aim to set forth ways to solve the problem of disability. A key task now is to interrogate those discursive practices that aim to provide for the *inclusion* of disabled people (as opposed to the elimination or prevention of disabled people). In Chapter 5, 'Governing Embodiment,' the focus is not on the efficacy of programmatic attempts to implement inclusionary practices. Instead, I focus on the government texts' claims to provide a 'blueprint' for the integration of disabled people, so as to reveal how the meaning of disability is enacted within and for communities of readers.

In chapter 6, I turn to what I experience as the most common and most ordinary way to solve the problem of disability, that is, to overcome it. I end with the common, mundane, and expected assumption that disabled people will try as best they can to overcome their disabilities. This ubiquitous expectation is expressed and celebrated daily in mass media texts, to which disabled people orient in a variety of ways, including conformity, rejection, and resistance. These orientations, too, find their way into the mass media. I treat overcoming as the prime discursive scene within which to ascertain what disabled and non-disabled people are making of disability, so as to reveal the cultural under-standings of embodiment that make possible the constant call to 'overcome!'

I address the bureaucratic management of inclusion for dis-abled people, as well as the common-sense assumption of the good of overcoming, in order to demonstrate that it is from rou-tine existence that we might learn about that which grounds the shape of possible lives and the future of possible worlds. These chapters demonstrate not only that the interrogation of routine life reveals the governance of embodiment under modern condi-tions, but also that critical reflection on the daily activity of inter-pretation represents a way to enact the meaning of disability differently. There is no final section of the book that posits a proper, more liberating, or more equitable way to textually enact disability. There is no such final section since the chapters them-selves have enacted a new way to read, write, and think disabil-ity. This new way actualizes the belief that disability has had much to teach us about contemporary Western forms of embod-ied existence. An ethics of alterity holds that, through reflective analysis, the notion that disability is only a problem in need of a solution can itself be dis-solved.

5 Governing Embodiment: Technologies of Constituting Citizens with Disabilities

The ethics of inclusion, which tries to bring otherness into a system while requiring it to manifest itself within the structure of the system, appropriates otherness, making it conform to the system. The ethics of alterity, in contrast, works not by inclusion but by openness – openness to otherness in a way that allows the other to deconstruct the system, to call into question the system's limits, particularly in its appropriation of others' otherness.

– Brian Pronger, *Body Fascism*, 17

Like the second chapter, this chapter, too, turns to Canadian government texts on disability. Instead of showing how government texts construct disability as a problem, this chapter pursues an examination of how these same texts sponsor solutions to the problem they have constructed. I interrogate the biomedically informed discursive practices of the Canadian government that aim to make the phenomenon of bodily, sensorial, or mental differences intelligible as conditions possessed by people who, with the correct programmatic support and the right attitude, can be integrated as participatory 'citizens with disabilities.' To this end, I make use of the *In Unison* documents produced by federal/provincial/territorial ministers responsible for social services in order to show how governing embodiment through bureaucratic discursive practices is one solution to the problem of disability. The two *In Unison* documents I consider here claim

ADVANCING THE INCLUSION OF PERSONS WITH DISABILITIES

Appendix 1: Chronology of Legislation and Initiatives

Canada has gradually developed a framework of legislation to protect those
rights of persons with disabilities that are within the Government of Canada's
jurisdiction. As well, a number of important initiatives have helped bring a
sharper focus to the Government's efforts to make progress on disability
issues. The following timeline summarizes key legislation and initiatives. For
more information, please see the Web-based technical report.

2002   Treasury Board Secretariat published a revised Duty to Accom-
              modate policy.

2001   In *Unison 2000* was released.

2000   Successive budgets announced improvements to tax measures
              in support of persons with disabilities between 1996 and 2000.

2000   The *Canadian Human Rights Act* (CHRA) Review Panel released
              its final report, *Promoting Equality: A New Vision*.

1999   The Minister of Justice announced a one-year comprehensive
              review of the CHRA.

1999   Social services ministers signed the *Framework to Improve the
              Social Union for Canadians*.

1999   The Government of Canada released *Future Directions*, which
              set forth the Government's disability agenda.

1998   The Government of Canada, in partnership with the provinces
              and territories, issued *In Unison*, described as a blueprint to pro-
              mote the full participation of persons with disabilities.

1998   Employability Assistance for People with Disabilities (EAPD), a
              joint federal-provincial initiative, was established to help working
              age adults with disabilities prepare for, obtain and maintain
              employment.

1998   The Auditor General's report recommended making the human
              rights system more effective.

1998	Bill S-5, *An Act to amend the Canada Evidence Act, the Criminal Code and the Canadian Human Rights Act as they affect persons with disabilities*, was enacted.
1997	Budget announced $30 million funding for Opportunities Fund to assist persons with disabilities to prepare for, find, and maintain employment.
1996	The Federal Task Force on Disability Issues (led by Andy Scott, MP) released its report, *Equal Citizenship for Canadians with Disabilities: The Will to Act*.
1995	The 1986 *Employment Equity Act* was revised.
1992	The House of Commons passed an omnibus bill that addressed access to the electoral system, access to information in multiple formats, acquiring citizenship, and testifying in criminal court, and added the words 'accessible' and 'persons with disabilities' to the policy section of the *National Transportation Act, 1987*. This was the first time Parliament had passed legislation explicitly dealing with disability issues.
1991	The National Strategy for the Integration of Persons with Disabilities was announced.
1990	The Treasury Board Real Property Accessibility Policy for the Government of Canada was released.
1988	Modifications to the *National Transportation Act* gave the National Transportation Agency new powers to make regulations and to resolve complaints regarding the removal of undue obstacles within Canada's federally regulated transportation network.
1986	The first *Employment Equity Act* was passed. The Act covered the federally regulated private sector and Crown corporations.
1982	The *Canadian Charter of Rights and Freedoms* came into effect as part of the *Constitution Act, 1982*, and prohibited discrimination based on disability.
1981	*Obstacles*, the report of the special Committee on the Disabled and Handicapped, was released.
1981	The House of Commons Committee on the Disabled and Handicapped was established out of respect for the United Nations International Year of Disabled Persons.
1977/1978	The Canadian Human Rights Commission was established.
1977	The *Canadian Human Rights Act* was passed.

Source: http://www.sdc.gc.ca/asp/gateway.asp?hr=/en/hip/odi/documents/
advancingInclusion/00_toc.shtml&hs=pyp [2003]

to represent the 'consistent vision' that grounds all sorts of future practices, such as producing more documents on disability; for example, *Advancing the Inclusion of Persons with Disabilities* (2004, 2005, 2006). I will reveal the socio-political consequences of this textual form of governing embodiment. The *In Unison* documents make the claim that they provide a 'blueprint' for the inclusion of disabled people into the citizenry of Canada, and these documents, used by government ministries and community groups, help establish and organize programs oriented to the integration of people with disabilities into Canadian society. The production of *In Unison* documents, written by a host of civil servants and other government officials, relies on statistics, survey data, community groups, and stakeholders, as well as disabled people. As I said in chapter 2, the *In Unison* documents have been distributed widely to readers who are part of the civil service, and given to many community groups and individuals who are seeking to do something about the problem of disability. It is important to remember that these documents both express and reproduce the ordinary and typical way that bureaucratic management of disability aims to solve the problem it, ironically, created.

The *In Unison* documents, and all such documents that have followed, make the claim that the concept of citizenship is central to addressing disability issues. Citizenship, in *In Unison*, means inclusion via participation in economic endeavours, community life, etc. This chapter will reveal that the government's discourse on disability and inclusion is a mechanism by which individuals and populations are constituted as a problem which *In Unison* seeks to solve, and is the mechanism through which collective relations to this problem of disability are governed. Finally, this chapter also shows how 'disability' has become a prime site for constitution of the neo-liberal version of the individual, whose participatory power is tied to an ability to conform to 'normal' society. It turns out that solving the problem of disability, through this bureaucratic governance of embodiment, requires the constitution of a new type of disabled person – the able-disabled individual.

I turn first to a discussion of the relation between the concepts of inclusion and exclusion, and how the work of Foucault, particularly his concept of 'governmentality,' plays into my analysis of these government texts.

Inclusion / Exclusion

Within the field of disability studies, much important work has been done on the extent and nature of disabled people's exclusion from industrial and post-industrial capitalist society. However, exclusion in any form contains an image or conception of disability that grounds the possibility of exclusion in the first place. *A culture only ever excludes those subjects it has incorporated within itself as exclude-able.* And yet, through our language and practices, disability continues to be included into Western cultures as just such an exclude-able type. For this reason, Henri-Jacques Stiker recommends that to speak at all meaningfully about the organization of disability requires the inquirer to take a radical stance, namely, 'to initiate an analysis of the social workings of disability by way of its integration' (1999: 15). With a focus on integration efforts, my question becomes: how do bureaucratic remedial policy and programs for the integration of 'citizens with disabilities' help to make disabled people into an exclude-able type?

The assumption that exclusion is the main problem facing disabled people may be a dangerous one, especially if we are to maintain a critical focus on how, and to what end, disability is constituted as it is within the contemporary minority world. One of the dangers of focusing on exclusion without taking into account the inclusionary practices that generate exclusion is that we might be tempted to ignore the constitutive powers of seemingly benign remedial programs, enacted through texts that claim to solve the problem of marginalized people. Textual renderings of remedial programs are never simply responses to an already existing problem. To know *how* disability is produced as a problem in need of remedy, to know how, for example, disability is given shape as an excluded population in need of programs requiring and thus empowering inclusion, is to come to know how and why disability matters. Recall Judith Butler, who suggests that 'to "matter" means, at once "to materialize" and "to mean"' (1993: 32). Disabled people are made to matter as excluded and marginalized, and this is what disability itself comes to mean. Today, for example, it is possible for governments to regard the matter of disability as a condition that in and of itself 'causes' a lack of participation, exclusion, and marginalization. The existence of remedial programs, and their professionals, is reliant upon disability mattering in this way (Albrecht 1992). It is professionally and bureaucratically generated narratives regarding the nature and consequences of disability that legitimize the existence, form, and content of such remedial programs (Mitchell and Snyder 1997: 1). And there is more: each and every programmatic attempt to institute inclusion is, at one and the same time, making disability materialize in particular ways, ways that perpetuate and support often unexamined conceptions of disability.

By focusing on the paradox of disabled people being included as an exclude-able type, I introduce a discontinuity into the systems of knowing disability by revealing the constitutive grounds of the paradox that makes disability matter as the problem-of-exclusion. Practices of inclusion involve ways of knowing who disabled people are and how to recognize the problem that is disability, as well as the development of appropriate programmatic responses. Given that exclusion is made possible on the basis of particular historical and social forms of including disabled people, the meaning of disability, which is made by and under-girds programmatic attempts at inclusion, is regarded here as an essential matter for critical inquiry. This is an inquiry that attempts to reveal that which governs our conceptions of, and potential relations with, disability. Such an inquiry is also political insofar as we can begin to understand that a consequence of employing unexamined conceptions of disability within a remedial program oriented by the goal of inclusion is that disabled people are reproduced as an exclude-able type.

My analysis of the *In Unison* documents' manufacturing of disability as a problem condition is methodologically informed by

Michel Foucault's notion of 'governmentality' (1988: 19) – the study of the conduct of conduct. As Foucault (1979, 1978, 1975) has demonstrated, discursive practices that surround a society's 'problem' people are more than a reaction to an already existing difficulty or problem condition.[21] These discursive practices are better understood as the technologies by which individuals and populations are constituted as a problem, and serve also as the means through which collective relations to this problem are governed. I do not treat *In Unison* as an implementation of programs that may or may not work to solve the issue of exclusion. Instead, I analyse these documents so as to show how they make disability matter as a problem of exclusion and integrate disability as exclude-able. The textual production of disability as a problem is based on coming to know disability through biomedically informed discursive practices. These biomedically based discourses reflect that which conducts the conduct of governments so as to generate policies and practices that make differential embodiment intelligible as, and thus matter as, 'individual citizens with disabilities.' My work activates an analysis of inclusion by uncovering the conception of disability that is conducting the Canadian government's conduct with disabled persons.

The government's formulation of a solution to the problem of disability continues to ground current practices of exclusion for disabled people by including, indeed, constituting, the abled-disabled individual (a new type of person) as *the* solution to the problem of possessing an embodied difference. Including disability as an asocial figure that is understood to be, in and of itself, a self-evident departure from normalcy, supports status quo relations to 'normal' bodies, minds, and senses, and 'normal' life as unquestionably real. The abled-disabled individual is a person who appears oriented to, and desirous of, this normalcy. Disability needs to be manufactured and included as an exclude-able type if current governing conceptions of the normal citizen, normal participant, and normal worker are to be maintained. Including disabled people as an exclude-able type allows the notion of disability to function as a discursive mechanism in service of normal society.

As a way to pursue this kind of inquiry, I interrogate the bureaucratically organized attempt to solve the problem of disability, as this is represented by documents, statements, programs, and practices of the federal/provincial/territorial ministers responsible for disability issues. Following Zygmunt Bauman (1990: 79–82; 2000: 3), this material can be characterized as bureaucratic not only because it is sponsored by the Canadian government, but also because it aims to implement a consistent, coherent, and rationalized recipe of rules and practices, which are deemed to apply equally to all individuals, regardless of differences, including the differences that are called disabilities. *In Unison 1998: A Canadian Approach to Disability Issues* is described as a 'Vision Paper,' and it claims to provide a 'blueprint for promoting the integration of persons with disabilities in Canada' (ibid., 5). The subsequent document, *In Unison 2000: Persons with Disabilities in Canada* (released in March of 2001), claims to be a 'report, which marks another step forward in the shared efforts of governments and the disability community' (ibid., vii). *In Unison 2000* (vii, ix) reports on the implementation of the 1998 *In Unison* 'vision,' and it claims that such reporting 'sets the stage for a new national consensus on disability issues that brings together all sectors' so as to reach the goal of 'full inclusion for all [disabled] Canadians.' These documents are surrounded by a history of many other documents and surveys, and are circulated and announced through a variety of other texts, such as pamphlets, websites, press releases, and interim reports, as well as through the creation of new policy and programs, together with training programs, which are implemented at the national, provincial, and community levels. While I keep all this material in mind, I more or less restrict my attention to the discursive reality of the two *In Unison* documents, in order to show how the government's solution is manufacturing disability *as* an organic and individual *condition* of abnormalcy, which, according to these documents, results in a lack of participatory citizenship and employment for 'persons with disabilities.' I turn to *In Unison*'s presentation of the problem of disability, and the 'fact text' first analysed in chapter 2 will be readdressed.

What's the Matter with People with Disabilities?

In a golden-coloured box, in bullet-point form, and set off from the rest of the introductory remarks, *In Unison 2000* reports:

- In 1991, 16 per cent of Canadians were considered to have a disability. That is 4.2 million people – 3.9 million living in the community, and 273,000 in institutions.
- Fifty-six per cent of people with disabilities were of working-age; nine per cent were children under 14, and 35 per cent were people over 65.
- In 1991, among working-aged women, 13 per cent were considered to have a disability.
- Slightly more than half of adults living with a disability were affected by a mild disability, one third were considered to have a moderate disability, and 14 per cent were affected by a severe disability.
- The 1991 Aboriginal Peoples Survey revealed that 31 per cent of Aboriginal adults reported some form of disability – almost twice the national average ... (5)

The federal, provincial, and territorial governments thus consider and reveal the contours of their target of concern. According to this government text, within the general population of Canada, 4.2 million people are disabled, and more than half of these people live with a mild disability. Recall that these figures are constituted from the 1991 post-census Health Activity Limitation Survey (HALS), which, through a 'lengthy series of questions,' determines levels of 'ability to perform various activities of daily living' as a means to identify and categorize people (*In Unison 2000*: 65). Using the World Health Organization's conception of disability, those people whose ability is impaired by a 'loss or abnormality of a psychological, or anatomical structure or function' and who are thereby restricted or unable to 'perform an activity in the manner or within the range considered normal for a human being' are counted as 'people with disabilities' (*In Unison 1998*: 33). HALS goes on to rank-order people into those who possess a 'mild, moderate or severe' disability, and it takes count of some types of impairments, namely, mobility, agility, mental, hearing, seeing, and speaking impairments (*In Unison 2000*: 69; see also Gadacz 1994: 27ff). Thus, disability is conceived of as a condition of organic abnormalcy attached to individuals, a condition that can vary according to severity, longevity, cause, and consequence (*In Unison 1998*: 11). Notice, however, that disability's meaning is transmogrified as biological matter gone wrong – disability's difference is thus principally constituted as negative effects caused by such abnormalcy, but it is also deemed amenable to bureaucratic ordering and management. It is this group of people that *In Unison*'s vision, policy, and practices aim to 'fully' include as 'citizens' (*In Unison 1998*: 8, 13, 15, 17–19; *In Unison 2000*: 4, 7). However, understanding disability as biological-matter-gone-wrong is a conception that does not readily fit with any conception of the 'citizenry.'[22]

Making disability matter in this way means that governments conduct themselves under the auspices of a dual consciousness of disability. This dual consciousness is reflected in the government's ability to conceive of human difference both as a thing (a biological condition imparting its negative effects) and as a group (a population distinct and distinguishable from the general population). The former makes possible the latter. Conceiving of disability as a condition and as a distinct population allows for activities such as surveys of conditions of embodied loss or abnormality, the generation of disability rates, and the implementation of programs geared at the group of individuals 'with' disabilities (e.g., 'special' assessment and training, 'innovative' work placements, funds to prepare for, obtain, and maintain employment, support for national disability organizations, or the disability income tax credit).[23] Such programs and practices go on to generate more information on the target population, further ratifying the documented reality (Smith 1990; Garfinkel 1967) of 'people with disabilities' as those people who are biologically driven to depart from realms of normalcy.

Moreover, *In Unison 2000* (17, 23–30, 39–47, 55–60, 70), in its accounts of best practices for inclusion, is interested in providing counts of the number of people who have benefited from such programmatic forms of inclusion. Of this North America–wide endeavour, Anita Silvers argues that interventions, guided by the 'tyranny of the normal,' aim to 'repair or restore or revise members of nondominant groups so that they qualify as citizens' (1998: 112–14). A consequence of this is that certain modes of functioning become reified as *normal* modes, and alternatives are belittled. Whether a return to an unquestioned normalcy is possible or not (or even whether such a normalcy exists), documents as to the number and nature of 'persons with disabilities' continue to proliferate – programs, policies, and especially government documents must show that they know both whom, and how many, they are helping to include.

Accounting for Conduct

Of this modern way of knowing people through such counting practices, Foucault says:

> Governments perceived that they were not dealing simply with subjects, or even with a 'people,' but with a 'population,' with its specific phenomena and its peculiar variables: birth and death rates, life expectancy, fertility, state of health, frequency of illnesses, patterns of diet and habitation. All these variables were situated at the point where the characteristic movements of life and the specific effects of institutions intersected ... (1978: 25)

Disabled people are counted from a variety of other population categories, such as 'age groups,' 'gender,' and 'Aboriginal Peoples.' Transforming disability into a countable population permits for a conception of disability as a potential aspect of any population insofar as disability is made to materialize as a variable (condition) that affects the population. Disability is a 'peculiar variable' of the general population, a 'rate' (16% or one in six Canadians), gleaned from the characteristic movements of life. Such documentation – the effects of institutions – builds up the reality of disability as a problematic, abnormal organic or biological matter. Disability is thus established as a kind of non-conformity, and Georges Canguilhem's suggestion that 'normal man is normative man, the being capable of establishing new, even organic norms' (1991: 139) rings true.

Even though it is characteristic of all of our lives to move within, toward, and between bodily, sensorial, and intellectual differences, these differences are taken to belong only to certain people, to the population category called 'people with disabilities.' Such population categories promote the 'idea that disability is a medical problem affecting a small proportion of the population,' and, as Colin Barnes goes on to remind us, this idea is 'no longer sustainable' (1998: 65). However, the idea of disability as rare, anomalous, and located only within individuals is sustained by shoring up an unexamined conception of normalcy from which disabled people *ipso facto* depart. That which is defined as essentially abnormal does not fit into the values of normative existence, but it does help to define that existence: 'A norm draws its meaning, function and value from the fact of the existence, outside itself, of what does not meet the requirements it serves' (Canguilhem 1991: 239). Appearing distinct from 'normal life,' and thereby serving as an example of what does not fit into this normative existence, disabled people, as well as disability facts, represent the meaning, function, and value of an otherwise unexplicated normalcy.

Even though disability can be conceived of as a relation between embodiment and the social and physical environment (Gadacz 1994: 5), *In Unison* reifies disability by conceiving of it as a distinct biological condition affecting certain individuals. For example, mobility impairment becomes 53 per cent of those counted with disabilities, and vision impairment becomes 9 per cent of those counted as people with disabilities (*In Unison 2000*: 69). A dual consciousness of disability as biological condition (thing) and as a distinct population governs the conduct of governments and makes possible the conscious grouping together of people with very different embodied experiences into one problematic group in need of a unified, consistent, and coherent set of programs and services. These procedures target *individuals* who are conceived of as excluded because of 'their' incapacity and 'their' lack of supports. As Zygmunt Bauman (2000: 30–8) argues in his *Liquid Modernity*, 'individuality' has become the key task and project of current times, and it requires people to believe and act as if all problems and all solutions can be located in the individual. Such a demand for individuality, Bauman claims, is opening up an ever-widening gap between an enforced 'individuality as fate and individuality as the practical and realistic capacity for self-assertion' (2000: 34). Disability is some people's individualized problem, one that those individuals should manage and, ideally, *overcome*. But disability is not enacted as something that is an essential matter of individuality, personhood, or the movements of life, which can thereby ground a practical and realistic capacity for self-assertion. Indeed, the belief in the 'strength of the individual' arises over and against disability, insofar as disability is a difference against which a self can actualize the task of individuality but should not be seen as a difference that influences, grounds, or organizes an individual's self-assertion.

Insofar as disability is conceived of as a difference that should, ideally, not make a difference (Michalko 2002: 93–103), many ways of knowing disability, beyond mechanisms for inclusion, become forms of useless knowledge. That is, these accounting procedures (Garfinkel 1967) make social conceptions of embodiment into a form of useless knowledge. It is useless, in relation to how the concept of disability is currently governed, to know that 'human beings are, by nature, frail animals' (Finkelstein 1998: 28), that we are all only temporarily able-bodied (Zola 1982: 246), or that disability 'is a social category whose membership is always open' (Gadacz 1994: ix). Even though government documents claim that 'injuries are a leading cause of disability in Canada' (Canada, *Future Directions* [2000]), it is useless to come to know how current economic relations produce disability, as well as economic and professional gains for mostly non-disabled people from disability (Albrecht 1992). However, governments do supply actual dollar figures for their 'Investing in Persons with Disabilities' (Canada, *Interim Report* [2001], 14). Still, it is useless, within the current governing of disability, to know what the movement of life 'looks like' to blind people, 'feels like' for wheelchair users, or 'sounds like' from the experience of hearing impairment. (After all, these sights, feelings, and sounds are not 'things' to be counted.) It is useless, moreover, to come to know how we are to reconcile ourselves to a technologized, bureaucratized, consumeristic culture that manufactures bodily difference and, yet, also invites us to orient to individual bodily anomaly as if it exists asocially, outside of human interpretation and action. Even the conceptions of 'levels' and 'severity' of disability, *as* they are created through relations between environment and body, are rendered useless knowledge since this knowledge cannot be readily employed in the production of notions of individualized abnormal biological conditions abstracted from social existence, that is, abstracted from the fact that our lives are lived in the midst of others and within a variety of contexts. Instead, within *In Unison,* characteristic movements of life and bodies are made into variables and rates affecting the functioning of a population and are counted (out) from among an ascertainable number of individuals (population). In contrast, social conceptions of disability do not so easily allow for the transformation of 'life' into 'variables,' and such a textually enacted transformation is essential if governments are to both 'know' and 'help' people with disabilities.

As a population, 'people with disabilities' can be documented, surveyed, treated, trained, supported, serviced ... or not, and all this occurs by ensuring that the characteristic movements of life, which *In Unison 1998* claims 'touches all of us' (4), are known only as a characteristic 'condition' of an ascertainable number of individuals. Disability comes to figure as a separate population with its peculiar variables. This population is documented through surveys concerning place of habitation, states of disability, levels of education, employment, and poverty. But, the alarming facts 'on' disability are overridden by the disturbing notion 'of' disability. For example,[24] *In Unison* informs its readers that a group of people in Canada face an unemployment rate double, and a labour non-participation rate quadruple, that experienced by other (normal) Canadians, and these differential gaps have been growing. When the variable of 'level of education' is added into the mix, the radical disparity reflected in the targeted group's employment rates does not fluctuate. Of those of the group that do have work (less than half), 50 per cent make less than $15,000 a year. However, understanding this group *as* individuals who suffer a loss or abnormalcy of a biological or anatomical structure or function, and *as* those who fail to accomplish things in a way considered normal for a human being, grants a peculiar sensibility to the data. *Disability is being conceptually included as a highly functional sense-making device for the exclusion of disabled people.* It becomes normal to conceive of, and thereby include, the matter of disability at the individual level separate and distinct from social considerations. How the physical and social environment is organized so as to accommodate only an imagined 'normal' citizen remains a devalued form of questioning.

The governing conception of disability, *In Unison*'s way of including disability, allows for the irony that disability discourse is used to reconstitute mythical 'normal' life, 'normal' body, or 'normal' movement as unquestionably real and to make real disabled people into an often justifiably excluded type. In a disability community group with which I worked and which was sponsored under the auspices of Human Resources Development Canada's implementation of the *In Unison* vision, people spoke of those whom they thought they were to help as the 'abled-disabled.' The 'abled-disabled' served as a term that made sense of the fact that measures of inclusion that would receive government funding were targeted at young people leaving school, or newly disabled and newly unemployed people. 'Abled-disabled' appeared to function as a gloss for those people who were deemed, by the members of the community group, to have the best chance to reflect, desire, or imitate 'normal people' or, at least, 'normal functioning.' They were the closest to 'ability' yet distanced from it by impairment, a distance which could be closed by programs and services directed at individuals with disabilities. Moreover, it appeared that some people believed that 'servicing the abled-disabled,' as they put it, would also attest to the community group's efficacy and thereby secure ongoing government funding. The *In Unison* text, as well as its concomitant funding rules and mechanisms, encouraged and required the set of beliefs that accompanied the deployment of the term 'abled-disabled.'

Having revealed the way in which the *In Unison* texts establish what is the matter with disabled people, I turn now to an examination of the 'abled-disabled,' which serves as a depiction of how the problem of disability ought to be solved according to the Canadian government.

The Abled-Disabled

The success stories and effective practices narrated in *In Unison 2000* can be understood as enacting the new social identity – the abled-disabled – a conception that implicitly provides a cause for the plight of disabled people in Canada, while supporting an unquestioned belief in a normal able citizen. *In Unison 2000* claims that in its presentation of 'statistics and stories, this report identifies barriers and areas where it may be possible to make continued progress toward full participation' (4). There are twenty-one pages dedicated to the description of 'effective practices,' reflecting provincial and community attempts to solve the problem of disability. There are four narratives of individuals with disabilities who, presumably, signify the way in which some people, supported by effective practices actualizing the *In Unison* vision, are continuing to 'progress toward full participation.' The first such story appears in bold print on page one, and begins in the following fashion:

Melissa Rezansoff's Story
There is not time for pity in Melissa Rezansoff's world. Melissa, who is a quadriplegic, is too busy improving herself and working for the betterment of others in her position as the Saskatchewan Regional Manager for the Neil Squire Foundation. (*In Unison 2000*, 1)

Enabled by her success in securing work, Melissa, 'who is quadriplegic,' is also disabled. The combination of an ability to secure work, and disability as her personal condition, is that which frames 'Melissa Rezansoff' as a story that can be told by, and that fits within, *In Unison*'s conception of disability. Given the aims and vision of *In Unison*, a story of disability needs to function as an illustration of what is meant by a citizen, progressing toward full participation, while displaying the possession of a well-managed disability that will not serve to exclude her.

While there may not be time for pity in Rezansoff's world, there is time given to telling a story that can provoke pity. Two full paragraphs locate disability as a personal condition caused by a host of other troubling personal conditions. The story of the genesis of Rezansoff's disability, and her subsequent ability to become a fully participating citizen of Canada, begins by narrating what caused her quadriplegia: Rezansoff grows up on the Kahakwisthaw First Nation Reserve; she is one of thirteen children; she attends residential school; moves around the country; begins to hang out with the wrong crowd; and has an argument with her boyfriend (ibid.). These personal details are the path the reader is provided so as to make sense of what happens next to seventeen-year-old Melissa: '... she went to the basement of her home, where her father kept his guns, locked the door, took a .22 caliber rifle and shot herself' (ibid.). However, 'instead of entering her head, the bullet went through her neck, nicking the vertebrae and wedging a bone fragment against her spinal cord, paralyzing her' (ibid.). This is a story of the genesis of disability that is very personal indeed – it is caused by a person's individual actions on herself. Disability is narrated as a condition caused by an individual's response to happenings and circumstances within that same individual's life.

However, recall the introduction, where there is no time for pity for the tragic condition of disability insofar as the disabled individual is 'busy improving herself and working for the betterment of others in her position.' Given that the story is introduced to the reader as a success story (and not, for example, an attempted suicide story), the intertwining of ability and disability is both striking and dramatic. The drama, I argue, is that of the constitution of the abled-disabled type. The telling of Rezansoff's story by *In Unison* continues, but its telling does not include the individualized details that accompany the depiction of her tragic response to her life. Instead, we read that 'During the long months of rehabilitation, Melissa "reinvented" herself' (ibid). This reinvention occurs when all the movements of Melissa's life come to an abrupt halt, symbolized by the named, but never described, condition 'quadriplegia,' and this reinvention is supported by the effective practices (programs and policies) she comes in contact with once she has become disabled and has left behind the characteristic movements of her life.

Reinventing herself does not include any discussion of her self-assertion as she negotiates a place as a disabled person, while she is regarded by others as the embodiment of abnormalcy. Nor is there any discussion of how Rezansoff must operate from within contexts that expect only a 'normal citizen' and are structured so as to exclude her. Instead, reinvention is spoken of in the most normal of ways: Melissa pursues an education, she sets a goal, and she gets a 'big break' when, as a program participant at her current place of employment, she secures a position as an administrative assistant. Today, the story concludes, Melissa works, and she 'draws from her many experiences and has transformed her job into a way of life' (*In Unison 2000*, 2). The final message of the story comes by telling the reader about how Melissa feels. She feels 'everyone has something of value to contribute, and therefore should be encouraged, not pitied' (ibid.). Melissa, like everyone else, or so the story goes, knows that her value is to be found in participating in the normal order of social life.

Here we have a story that begins with a depiction of a disordered life. It is a life consumed, not by unbearable social circumstances, nor by the desire to die, but instead by disability, which through individualized reinvention becomes orderly and successful. That is, Melissa becomes educated, lives on her own, and secures work. More importantly, the story about Rezansoff depicts the cause of disability (in this case, actions of the self), and it depicts the correct and proper way to conduct one's conduct in the face of disability. Nothing, for example, is said of her thoughts, feelings, or experiences of now being a wheelchair user. Nothing is said of the structural and attitudinal barriers she faces daily. However, much is said regarding what she is now able to do, and, it appears, she is much more successful at doing these normal things now than she was prior to becoming disabled. Melissa seeks her own betterment and the betterment of others; she seeks education, work, and independent living. Regardless of all the movements of life – reservation life, residential school, transience, and disability – Melissa's life is used to tell the story of how the individual can focus on individual betterment and realize that 'everyone has something of value to contribute.' This thing of value is depicted as an ability to fit into and embody that which is regarded as the normal order of life – education and work. Indeed, all the happenings in Melissa's life are now the stuff that she can draw upon as she makes 'her job into a way of life.'

The story of Melissa Rezansoff is the story of the abled-disabled individual who can work against all odds, especially disability, and especially a self-produced disability, and who can display to others the necessity of orienting normally to the normal order of daily life. She adds value to the taken for granted value of current society as essentially normal and thereby okay. Thus, the only barrier that needs to be hinted at in the story of an individual's pursuit of ably adapting to society such as it is, is an individualized one. Melissa can either subtract value (kill herself) or add value (act as ably and normally as is possible). The three other stories of disabled people follow the same narrative structure (*In Unison 2000*, 14, 15, 31): the person is introduced as a person with a disability; the condition of disability is named (progressive spinal-cord muscular atrophy, anxiety and depression, and developmental disability); and its consequence or requirements are detailed (the need for technology and the efforts to find disability-related supports; therapy, medication, and support from agencies and peers; sheltered workshops and ways to seek inclusion in mainstream life and work). Then, this individual with a disability is depicted as coming into contact with 'effective practices,' at which point nothing more need be said about disability, but much will be said about an individual able to fit into normal society, by securing work, volunteerism, and independent living. The disabled person is thus depicted as asserting their individualism over and against the condition of disability, and disability is once more emptied of any life. The stories conclude by articulating the person with a disability as an abled-disabled person. The abled-disabled are those people who can exclude attending to disability by attending fully to their ability to participate, as normally as is possible, and they ultimately and inevitably signify having a 'positive effect on others,' 'contributing fully to the community,' and 'maximizing their potential' (*In Unison 2000*, 2, 14, 15, 31). The abled-disabled demonstrate that 'even' disabled people are able to fit in and take up an appearance, which shows that their conduct is undoubtedly oriented to an unquestioned normalcy. Through this way of textually enacting disability, disability becomes the space upon which the value of the normal shines forth without ever having to be directly spoken of, and disabled people are held to be asserting their individual ability when they can be seen as oriented to serving this normal order.

Through the *In Unison* texts, both its stories and its statistics, we get the first hint of the paradoxical inclusion of disabled people that functions so as to exclude. As part of the general population, people with a certain 'problem condition' are separated out from the population *by* documenting them as people with disabilities. Programs and remedies for the inclusion of problem people are then implemented. Thus, from beginning to end, disability is included as a problem condition only to be excluded from any general conception of the movements of life. Disability is, then, reincluded as people who have problems functioning within the characteristic movements of life. Throughout, the reader is not prompted to think about 'normal life,' which encourages the reader to continue to imagine normal life normally. As Rod Michalko (1998) claims, one of the least normal things we can do is think about normalcy. One ordinary rendering of normalcy is as that which is unconnected to differential embodiment. A consequence of leaving normalcy unquestioned is that connections between the assumptions, values, and struc-

tures of normal life, and how disability is actually lived in Canada, are almost obliterated. For example, if it can be proven that
a piece of technology, such as a wheelchair, will aid in an individual disabled person's 'employability,' then this person can apply
to a fund which may provide such technology. Still, the structured actuality of the characteristic movements of life remains
untouched and unquestioned; for example, the building code of
most Canadian provinces still sustains a minimum doorway
width narrower than a typical, motorized wheelchair. Disability
is included as an exclude-able type and included as the figure
which allows 'normal' life and 'normal' bodies, and thus 'normal' societal structures and artifice, to remain unquestioned.

Through an analysis of *In Unison*'s use of stories and statistics,
I have demonstrated how the figure of the abled-disabled is textually enacted. I argue that, while the abled-disabled is proposed
as a solution to the problem of disability, it is also part of the constructed artifice protecting normalcy from critique, questioning,
and theorizing. As a way to continue to question normalcy, I
return to Foucault so as to further explicate the primary conception of disability governing the government's conduct with disabled people.

Bio-Politics

Regarding the constitution of problematic people as a distinct
population within more general populations, Foucault says that
this occurs through two interrelated poles of power:

> One of these poles – the first to be formed, it seems – centered on
> the body as a machine ... [and] was ensured by the procedures of
> power that characterized the *disciplines: an anatomo-politics of the
> human body.* The second, formed somewhat later, focused on the
> species body ... [bodies as]: propagation, births and mortality, the
> level of health, life expectancy and longevity, with all the conditions
> that can cause these to vary. Their supervision was effected through
> an entire series of interventions and *regulatory controls; a bio-politics
> of the population.* The disciplines of the body and the regulations of

the population constituted the two poles around which the organization of power over life was deployed. The setting up ... of this
great bipolar technology – anatomic and biological, individualizing and specifying, directed toward the performances of the body,
with attention to the processes of life – characterized a power
whose highest function was perhaps no longer to kill, but to invest
life through and through. (1978: 139, emphasis in the original)

The organization of the matter of disability can also be located
between these two poles. *In Unison* reinforces 'disability' as the
problem of functional difference located at the level of the organism. The Health Activity Limitation Survey (HALS, 1991; see
also chapter 2) generated data that is used in both *In Unison* documents. HALS asks: 'Can you read ordinary newsprint? Can you
hear normal conversations? Can you walk up a flight of stairs?
Can you cut your toenails?' HALS data is certainly based upon
an 'anatomo-politics of the human body.' (The next such survey,
the Participation and Limitation Activity Survey, or PALS,
occurred in 2001, and its data became available in 2003.) There
are other surveys and data employed throughout the *In Unison*
literature, all of which reflect a reliance on a conception of disability as biological matter gone wrong. This conception finds its
most extreme expression in the form (Canada 2000a) used to
certify a person for a 'Disability Tax Credit.' It asks: 'Can your
patient see? Can your patient walk? Can your patient speak? Can
your patient perceive, think, and remember?' etc. These questions, with some qualification, are to be answered with a check
mark in a 'yes' or 'no' box. The policy, programs, and practices of
the Canadian government make disability materialize through
an anatomical individualizing in which disability is, first and
foremost, lack of function located, not in social structure, but in
individual anomaly. This is how different embodiments come to
consciousness as mild, moderate, or severe lack of functionality.
Disability is seen as such lack, defined via negation and then
counted, giving rise to the conception of 'disability' as a rate
among the general population and as a subspecies within the
population that can be further counted and more specifically

rated – 'a bio-politics of the population.' All of this, suggests Foucault, has the effect to invest life through and through. But, with what has the life of disability been invested?

In order to consider this question, notice what the government has come to know about, and invest in, this distinct population. In contradistinction to the four stories of disabled people told by *In Unison*, the majority of people with disabilities live among the general population, the majority are adults (working age: 15–64), and the majority of these people have a 'mild disability,' which more likely than not was caused by their work environments or modern technologies. What, then, is the matter? While living in the community, somehow disabled people are not 'of' it (even if the disability was produced by community life). According to *In Unison 2000*, 'For many people with disabilities, paid or voluntary work – whether full or part-time – is key to independence and full participation in their communities' (32). However, the majority of this majority of people with disabilities do not work – i.e., are unemployed or are not participating in the labour market. 'Labor Force Participation' charts (*In Unison 2000*, 72–5) inform the reader that in 1990 44 per cent of men with disabilities and 57 per cent of women with disabilities did not work, and in 1995 these figures rose to 52 per cent and 62 per cent respectively. This represents a 34 to 42 per cent difference in work rates between people who are and who are not disabled, and this difference is even more radically disparate if one is an Aboriginal person. Other radical differences between disabled people and non-disabled people are traced out as they are made to appear through other work-related variables, such as levels of education or of income, amount of full-time work, or amount of time spent as unemployed, etc.

The processes of life that governments are primarily concerned with are those surrounding 'employment,' namely, a life 'able' to make a living. Disabled people are invested with significance as those who possess a faulty body, mind, or sense, which puts the ability to work at risk. 'People with disabilities' are understood as normally and potentially workers who are not working, normally and potentially participants within society who are not participating. Through the discourse on disability, 'normal people' are invested with an unquestioned ability to participate, to work – to be a normal citizen. Through the two poles of power, embodiment is organized as a life that functions (works) normally, or does not, and a citizen is constituted as one able to make an economic contribution. 'A normalizing society is the historical outcome of a technology of power centered on life' (Foucault 1978: 144). People with disabilities are those invested with abnormalcy. Attention to the performances of the body is, as Foucault suggests, intimately bound to considerations of ability to fulfil the 'processes of life.' The governing question becomes: how are we to invest a disabled life (which is regarded as inherently abnormal insofar as it removes one from the normal processes of life) with some touch of normal life, that is, a life that is able to make a living?

Investing in Normalcy

The government conducts itself in the face of the characteristic differences among human embodiment *as if* some of these differences are best understood as abnormal conditions of loss or lack of function affecting 4.2 million individual Canadians with varying degrees of severity. This leads to programs and practices which create a separate and knowable population whose individual members *are* 'people with a problem.' However, the problem condition affecting this population, even if defined as mild, cannot be used to justify nor remedy the further problems this population has with employment and general lack of civic participation. Governments have so thoroughly invested the meaning of disability with lack, limit, abnormality, pathology, and absence of normal functionality, that now 'people with disabilities' must be invested with some other meaning if they are to gain access to the normal processes of life. (Yet, it is important to remember, that the 'characteristic movements of life' do not include that which is imagined as the sporadic individualized anomaly called disability.)

The governing solution to this problem is to remind all people that this population of problem people are still people and as such are citizens. For example, addressing the implementation of the 1998 *In Unison* 'vision,' an interim report, *Future Directions*, says that the 'first' challenge of living with a disability is 'living with a disability and the individual barriers to full participation one must overcome' (Canada 2000b: 2). Still, a further investment is required:

> The second [challenge] is the attitudinal barriers that still exist among many people who do not understand that persons with disabilities can and do make a positive and meaningful contribution to our economy and our society. Too many people see the disability, and not the person. (Canada 2000b: 3)

The concept 'disability' is made distinct and different from the concept of 'personhood,' yet some sense of personhood can still be found in those who possess a disability. This personhood can be found if others possess the right attitude and can see past disability to the inner core of an essential self – the economic and social contributor. This requires that disabled and non-disabled people govern themselves in such a way that their conduct does not hint at a connection between being embodied and being a person; nor should their conduct hint at the connection between the organization of community life and how it produces embodied differences. Such an interpretive investment in the meaning of disability also requires that the current conception of citizen as an economic contributor remains unexamined.[25] It also means, ironically, that the millions of people in Canada who make a living through their professional dealings with disability remain unquestioned 'normal' figures of economic contribution and 'normal' citizens. All the while, disability remains devalued and is depicted as an expense.

The ongoing split between personhood and disability both supports and orients the 'vision' that the *In Unison* documents aim to actualize. In bold, double indented, or highlighted, and repeated throughout the literature, the government's 'vision' is articulated as follows:

> Persons with disabilities participate as full citizens in all aspects of
> Canadian society. The full participation of persons with disabilities
> requires the commitment of all segments of society. The realization
> of the vision will allow persons with disabilities to maximize their
> independence and enhance their well-being through access to
> required supports and the elimination of barriers that prevent their
> full participation. (*In Unison 1998*, 8, 13; *In Unison 2000*, 4, 6, 7)

This vision aims to focus everyone on 'seeing the person' behind
the disability. Disability should come to light as an abnormal condition attached to persons. Still, similar to other (normal) persons
in Canadian society, these people too are citizens and, with the
right vision, should be able to participate as citizens. The actualization of this vision is reliant upon the possibility that all seg-
ments of society focus their gaze on disability as simply a
condition attached to persons – to focus on disability as that
which, at best, ought not to make a difference (Michalko 2002: 93).
Following a presentation I did on the chronic institutionalized
marginalization experienced by disabled people, one Canadian
government official responded this way: 'I don't care what's
wrong with them, they are people too.' Seeing 'only the person'
will happen if all persons, including disabled persons, realize that
disability is nothing more nor less than an impediment to the
aims and interests of any normal person who wants to be a normal citizen. According to this vision, all citizens should want to
participate so as to maximize their independence and enhance
their well-being. What needs to be accessed and supported is the
sense in which people with disabilities can be invested with the
meaning of being 'just people.'

The requirement to continually invest in personhood as the
grounds for participation in society helps to make sense of the
fact that *the* most often mentioned 'barrier' requiring elimination
in the *In Unison* literature is not discriminatory building codes,
exclusionary transportation systems, ineffective application of
human rights laws, work- and technology-produced injuries, or
the failure to consider how ordinary life is, indeed, embodied
and as such continually and constantly intertwined with flux,

change, variation, and vulnerability (Finkelstein 1998). Instead, the barrier of concern throughout the *In Unison* literature is the 'attitude' which reflects the understanding that disability is something that makes a difference and is some form of human experience connected to the characteristic movements of life, yet excluded by normative society. To conceive of disability as part of the movement of life, and as something all persons are indeed interpretively engaged by, would cease to invest normalcy with its taken for granted status. To begin to understand disability as connected to, and revelatory of, the human condition would begin to disrupt the normal order of the physical environment, of knowledge production, and of interaction, even economic inter- action, and it would begin to show how, in the words of Irving Zola, 'a society has been created and perpetuated which has excluded so many of its members' (1982: 244). But no such possi- bility exists within *In Unison*, as there is either the wrong attitude that sees and stigmatizes disability or the right attitude that aims not to see disability at all. All the while, 'society' remains an unquestioned good or, at least, very normal.

Through maintaining a strict separation (barrier?) between 'person' and 'disability,' the government urges us all to govern our relation to disability so as to implement a common and uni- fied desire to participate in this normal citizenry with its con- comitant normal life. The aim of this sort of inclusion, claim David Mitchell and Sharon Snyder, is to '... return the incomplete body to the invisible status of a normative essence ...' (2000: 8). Still, the implications seem to reach well beyond individual incomplete bodies. *In Unison*'s form of inclusion represents the dominant societal 'take' on disability, namely, to employ any dif- ference experienced in the movement of life as a technique to return *all of us* to an unquestioned relation with status quo ren- derings of normative social existence. This marks the constitu- tion of a subjectivity, a citizenry, oriented to, and by, normalcy. In the words of Henri-Jacques Stiker,

> There is no better way to escape the fear of strangeness than by forgetting aberrancy through its dissolution into the social norm ...

figuring disability as an anomaly to be made to disappear through integration into social conformity is to represent society, empirically given, as a norm not to be transgressed, as a sort of universal capable of assuming, through annulment, all differences. (1999: 136–7)

At best, disability is made to matter as that discursive arena within which unquestioned and unexamined Enlightenment-based, normative notions of an essential and autonomous individuality of self are reproduced. While disability is imagined as having no place in the processes of life of the normal individual, the people to whom disability is attached should still be accorded a place within the citizenry. By conducting themselves as if there is no movement of life *in* disability, governments are able to make disabled people matter as those who need to 'get a life' (usually configured as employment), and sometimes even have a 'right to life,' *despite* the fact that something has forced such people outside of normal existence. Thus: 'See the person and not the disability.'

This, of course, raises the question as to what exactly is being integrated through the governing conception of disability that aims to make us see that 'persons with disabilities participate as full citizens in all aspects of Canadian society.' According to *In Unison*, what is integrated are citizens:

THE VISION OF FULL CITIZENSHIP

- Citizenship refers to the full inclusion of persons with disabilities. The intent of *In Unison* is to ensure that persons with disabilities have access to the systems and programs open to other Canadians ...
- *In Unison* translates this vison of full citizenship into objectives and policy directions within three interrelated building blocks: disability supports, employment and income. (*In Unison* 1998, 8)

Again, in 2000, printed within a golden coloured box:

Citizenship

The concept of citizenship is central to disability issues. Citizenship is the inclusion of persons with disabilities in all aspects of Canadian society – the ability of a person to be actively involved with their community. Full citizenship depends on equality, inclusion, rights and responsibilities, and empowerment and participation.

Different people choose to participate in various ways, so there is no single measure of whether or not a person is able to exercise full citizenship. Citizenship can be reflected in economic activity, involvement with community activities and organizations, political participation and in other ways.

A person is able to exercise full citizenship when they do not face barriers that significantly reduce their ability to participate fully in their community. Persons with disabilities and their advocates have argued that ensuring full citizenship is not just the right thing to do, but is also a matter of fundamental rights under Canada's Charter of Rights and Freedoms.

First Nations, Inuit, and Métis people have a somewhat different vision of citizenship due to their unique position in Canada, as Aboriginal people seek full citizenship both within their own Nations and in Canada. (*In Unison 2000*, 7)

The citizenry is that population for whom all the movements of life that could be disability are regarded as inessential except as variables that negatively affect the individual's ability to make a life as a citizen. Recall, too, that it is this same citizenry that has somehow decided not to educate or hire very many disabled people. Despite living within a citizenry that has manufactured the exclusion of so many, disabled people should want to become just like any other citizen. Citizens are persons who can conform to society 'such as it is' – they are people who participate, work, live in, and adapt to society, again, such as it is. Disability is deemed to be that thing which impairs participation, but participation, especially in the form of 'normal' economic contribution, is the measure of one's full citizenship. A citizen figures as a person who can participate, in economic and other ways, and as a person who imagines that disability 'really' has nothing to do with the citizenry, even though many people make a living from it and many other people make a life in it, and some do both.

Perhaps it is this unified and coherent demand to treat human difference as deeply the 'anti-value' (Canguilhem 1991: 239) of any notion of participation and citizenship that moves the authors of *In Unison* to forget (insofar as they are reminded by an *argument* put forth by disabled people and their advocates) that disability *is* included as a prohibitive ground of discrimination in the Charter of Rights and Freedoms. In fact, *In Unison 1998* insists that 'voluntary action to ensure inclusion' should 'reduce the need to invoke the Charter as an instrument of litigation. Ideally, it should be seen more as a beacon whose spirit guides all government actions' (18). Reduction of the need and desire to employ the law is being actualized on the basis of transforming the social and political matter of disability into a mere condition attached to individuals that is essentially inessential, except that it serves to depict the 'normal citizen' in negative relief. Using the law would require people to focus on the ways in which disability is made to matter as the grounds for discrimination and exclusion. Human rights law, for example, can make people focus on how citizens, disabled and non-disabled, develop interpretive relations to disability as they participate in social life and economic practices. Such critical activity is not, however, part of the programmatic relation that the *In Unison* documents aim to establish, for it would blur the collective's fixed gaze on all people as 'just people' who, as people, desire to participate in, and seek integration and conformity with, the citizenry.

This does, indeed, beg the question articulated by Henri-Jacques Stiker:

What kind of integration are we talking about? ... disability is elevated to an existence and a consistency that it never had ... The 'thing' has been designated, defined, framed ... People with 'it' make up a marked group, a social entity... if we examine the rights that have been accorded them, they are only those that all citizens have and that have never been the object of any formal declaration: the right to work, the right to education, the right to a guaranteed economic life, and so on ... Paradoxically, they are designated in order to be made disappear [*sic*], they are spoken in order to be silenced. (1999: 133–4)

Speaking of disability so as to silence it and making disability into that which is void of any value as a movement of life has real consequences for real people. Disabled people are granted the right to, or at least a touch of, potential normalcy insofar as disability is made to matter as a thing-like condition that is imagined as having nothing to do with being a person. Thus, 'the disabled person is integrated only when disability is erased' (Stiker 1999: 152). This, however, is a tricky manoeuvre since this 'thing' called disability, despite all attempts to designate, define, and frame it as only a thing, is nonetheless manifest *in* people's lives with each other in an historical context not of their own choosing. Even if disability could be totally 'thingified' (Crawford 1980), it is still part of human life.

Thus, disabled people are existentially positioned in a liminal[26] space. Disabled people are situated between:

1 the possession of an abnormal thing that leads to a departure from normalcy; and
2 the desire for inclusion in an abstract version of normal citizenry detached from bodily, sensorial, or mental differences.

Neither one nor two, neither the thing nor the desire, is inclusive of the other, yet both are included within a 'person with a disability.' One consequence of this liminal production and positioning of disability is that disability becomes a life that is invested through and through with cultural contradiction. To borrow from Susan Bordo (1993), disabled people are to function as the site where the psychopathology of a culture crystallizes. What is to crystallize are 'citizens with disabilities,' who are those types of selves able to adapt to and live with such cultural contradiction. These citizens with disabilities, if they become the abled-disabled, can now serve normative social order, for they stand as an image of an ability to participate 'against all odds,' which is the oddity of abnormal embodiment deemed to be far removed from any notion of personhood. The abled-disabled are those who can 'show that they are as good as anybody and that makes them better,' better able to exemplify the normative orders of ordinary life (Serlin 2002: 60). In fact, *In Unison*'s four stories of disabled people, its accounts of effective practices, and its inclusion of many pictures of 'citizens with disabilities' might best be understood as the new morality tale told to all of us: if people with disabilities can, then anyone can, conduct their conduct so as to actualize their participation in the normative order – all of us can crystallize our identity as the 'able-disabled.' After all, almost any difference from the demands of normative social order can be reified as a disability, and still we all can seek to overcome the challenge of difference and become able to function within society, such as it is.

A more radical and unintended consequence of this discourse on disability textually enacted through government documents is that disability discourse can become, if one is to take a critical standpoint, the prime location for the analysis of the production of just such a culture and its membership and citizenship requirements. This chapter is my attempt to take such a critical standpoint.

6 Overcoming: Abled-Disabled and Other Acts of Normative Violence

Recognition is at once the norm toward which we invariably strive ... and the ideal form that communication takes when it becomes a transformative process. Recognition is, however, also the name given to the process that constantly risks destruction and which, I would submit, could not be recognition without a defining or constitutive risk of destruction.

> – Judith Butler, 'Longing for Recognition,'
> in *Undoing Gender*, 133

In the last chapter, I considered how, through bureaucratic language and practices, the problem of disability is imagined to be solved by the constitution of the category 'abled-disabled.' It is, however, important to consider what happens to disability outside the more specialized or professionalized textual renderings of it. Thus, this final chapter turns to a more mundane and ordinary expression of solving disability, namely, the textual enactment of disability as something that can and should be *overcome*. In the daily life of reading, we might find it hard to discern whether we are more often confronted by text that recognizes disability through diagnosing a tragic problem or by text that recognizes disability through the unquestioned normative demand that it be overcome. I end my critical reflection on the textual enactment of embodiment by considering what I regard as likely the most common and most repetitive contemporary representation of how to solve the problem of disability – overcome it.

It is not only the professions of medicine, rehabilitation, and bureaucratic management and control that recommend overcoming as the ideal relation to disability. All of us are subject to and deploy the sensibility that disability ought to be *overcome*. Turning to this common and familiar way of positing a solution to the problem of disability is simultaneously a turning of attention to how we will spend our lives noticing disability. It is my aim that by attending to this relation to disability, we might better understand what texts on overcoming disability make of our collective relations to embodied existence.

Questioning Overcoming

Here are some ways that the mainstream media attends to disability:

> *Blind Student Earns M.D.* (CNN.com, 'Health: Associated Press,' 2 April 2005)

> *Given a Chance to Be Little Ballerinas, and Smiling Right Down to Their Toes* ... The eight little ballet students, who have cerebral palsy and other debilitating physical conditions, are assisted in class by teenage volunteers with strong healthy bodies and infinite patience. (Corey Kilgannon, *New York Times*, 5 May 2006)

> *Pedal Mettle: Competitive Cyclist Ryan Arbuckle Hasn't Let a Disability Get in the Way of Thriving in His Sport.* (Grania Litwin, *Times Colonist*, 5 July 2005)

> *Able Scientists Overcoming Disabilities.* (Von Rushkowski, *NextWave Science Magazine Canada*, 6 June 2003)

> *Deaf Parents Turn Disability into Advantage.* Taking care of a new baby creates a whole new world of challenges. But what about parents who are deaf? Global News met a Calgary couple who have no choice but to use sign language with their children. They say their children have actually benefited. (Global Calgary, 20 April 2005)

The Flesh Is Weak, the Spirit Willing. (Raymond De Souza, *National Post*, 17 July 2002)

Can't See ≠ Can't Do: Blind Student Tackles Life like Anyone.' Being visually impaired is not quite as difficult as it seems. I believe that the key to living a successful life is not only five senses, but determination as well. (Shermeen Khan, *Sunday Herald*, 7 February 1999)

Where in these texts about overcoming disability does recognition reside? Who or what is recognized? Someone has endured and overcome something, something that gets in the way, something that is a disadvantaging weakness. Some people, maybe even many people, read about this overcoming of disadvantage. What is recognized as we read about other people's strong and wilful endurance? In the face of such stories, do readers overcome anything, and are we ever overcome, perhaps, by our own joy or, even, disgust in the story? One thing is certain, given the ubiquitous repetition of the overcoming narrative, this form of recognition is not an individual act but is a participant in the normative order. If Butler is right and recognition involves the risk of destruction, what or who, then, is at risk in our recognition of disability as a story of endurance, will, and overcoming?

The overcoming story honours the sort of humanness that belongs to the enlightened liberalism of late capitalism, in which lone individuals pursue a competitive striving, making use of a transcendent intellect, or otherwise displaying the strength of the human spirit. This sort of 'strength' is generated from the basis of neo-liberalism's constant downward shifting of responsibility onto the individual (Robson 2005: 222). Still, sometimes I recognize the remarkable achievement of disabled people, and at other times, I scoff at the heroism heaped upon people who are made to re-present a rigorous performance of ordinary doings in everyday life as a kind of extraordinary personal challenge. There must be a problematic tension to which overcoming is a response, a tension that is kept alive when I read and am moved, sometimes disgusted, by the overcoming story. There must be some meeting of alterity between disability and non-disability in overcoming stories. There must be some way of recognizing disability that does not destroy alterity by making impairment nothing but that which points to the 'truly human,' even as this impairment is excluded from our conception of humanness. Can disability be more than a sign and thus be recognized as something other than an unexamined indicator of a unified symbol of humanness? Butler suggests that there is a 'constitutive risk of destruction' in the act of recognition. What risk might lie in recognizing disability as the site of an unquestioned desire for overcoming, and what risk might lie in recognizing disability as more than this?

By making use of the iconic, repetitive genre of the overcoming disability story, I now turn to an exploration of questions about what is at play in reading such stories. I will attempt to ascertain the sort of problem the overcoming narrative needs disability to be and interrogate what becomes of disability when it is overcome. My ultimate aim, though, is to explicate the possible relations between ability and disability as they represent contemporary notions of embodiment, that is, I want to reveal what is at stake in the relations of recognition established between ability and disability.

Why Study the Overcoming Story?

'Understanding the body as lacking and as in need of strategies to accumulate resources to protect itself against the dangers of lack is, of course, a strikingly familiar way of thinking about the body' (Pronger 2002: 157). Brian Pronger suggests that it is worthwhile to proceed from the assumption that it is the familiar and the everyday that are most in need of critical attention.[27] The task is to make the familiar strike us in new ways. Overcoming narratives are a familiar everyday strategy invoked to deal with the dangers of disability imagined as lack. Perhaps such stories are even a way to accumulate resources against such lack, since these stories suggest that in the face of disability there is always at least one promise – we can overcome.

The ubiquity of the act of narrating disability as a story of overcoming seems very clear. Such stories typically take shape by framing the noticing of impairment as a kind of hopeless hardship, as a barrier to the good life, or even as an assault on what is deemed vital. As Paul Hunt (1998 [1966]) puts it, disability is taken for granted as a *critical condition*. The overcoming story proceeds by depicting an individual feature or trait as an enabling universally human *force*, such as courageous perseverance, reasoned tenacity, positive attitude, or sheer will. The routine mass media appearance of overcoming as a 'human interest story' makes humanness interesting by working to exclude anything called disability from the nature of humanity. Disability becomes strictly an obstacle that, if overcome, seems destined to serve as a reminder of our common fate as human. Such stories almost always position readers as non-disabled, but, like any other human, non-disabled readers may encounter problems someday that will also need to be overcome. Overcoming inspires others to believe in the strength of the human spirit insofar as the human is recognized through the destruction of the idea that embodied differences are part of human existence. Disability is not regarded as an ordinary and common fate of all, but instead it is regarded as an exceptional circumstance and a unique problem against which 'special' people can show their spirit. Recall Colin Barnes's reminder that 'the idea that disability is a medical problem affecting a small proportion of the population is no longer sustainable' (1998: 65). Yet, it is precisely this non-sustainable notion that overcoming stories textually achieve and thus sustain. What ends up mattering is not so much correct knowledge about accurate disability rates, as it is the governing of ordinary taken for granted conceptions of disability. Overcoming narratives, then, are part of how our consciousness of disability is governed.

Overcoming stories are common, repetitive, and frequent. It would be difficult to find a daily newspaper at either the national or local level that did not daily print one such abled-disabled overcoming story. Indeed, some newspapers have a daily columnist dedicated to this genre; for example, 'Bright Spots' in the *Province* (Nova Scotia). So, it is important to acknowledge abled-disabled overcoming stories, not as personal quirks or private interests, but rather as repetitive structures in, and likely in service of, Western culture. I am interested, however, not in quantity but in the quality of these stories, that is, in re-collecting those features which define a story as a story of overcoming. Carrier Sandahl and Philip Auslander (2005: 3) suggest that the performance of disability is achieved through distinct scripts, such as the sweet innocent, the freak, the charity case, or the inspirational overcomer. I focus on overcoming because it seems to be, in part, a narrative form that is able to accommodate or incorporate other scripts of disability into its narrative structure. Consider also that charity and pity are typically interpretations taken by non-disabled people and bestowed upon disabled people. The narrative structure of the overcoming story, however, seems most amenable to questioning the straightforward divide between ability and disability. After all, non-disabled scientists or parents, non-disabled teachers and professionals, and even teenage volunteers with strong healthy bodies and infinite patience, as well as many others, are depicted in everyday texts as also overcoming disability, albeit that of others. The repetitive, inclusive, and thus common character of the overcoming story makes it particularly worthy of examination. Moreover, there is a potent social regulation that needs to be addressed here. From the point of view of common sense, it seems almost immediately certain that the best thing that could happen, if the problem of disability must appear, is that it be overcome.

Looking beyond Disability

As a way to continue to unpack what is involved in constituting a story as one of overcoming and reveal what such stories might do to or for its reader, I will make use of a *Maclean's* magazine article titled 'Look beyond the Leg Brace: You'll See a Whole Person Who Just Happens to Have a Disability' (Lindenburg 2004). There is nothing particularly unusual about this title; it makes sense. Such familiar sensibility has much to teach us about the sort of world that provides for both its sensibility and possibility. In 'Look beyond the Leg Brace ...' the author, Mark Lindenburg, writes about his cerebral palsy to an audience positioned as non-disabled or, at the very least, sighted, since the audience is invited to 'look beyond ...' Unique to this overcoming story is the fact that Lindenburg reflects on how others imagine overcoming, even while he goes on to tell his own overcoming narrative. Lindenburg has this to say:

> ... I can see my reality – as others perceive it – any week on TV. Pick a telethon, it doesn't matter which one. I'm the one standing wordlessly next to the presenter, or moving unsteadily on my crutches, or hunched over my walker, but still smiling. The host is a local celebrity who tells you about my courage, my zest for life despite such a hardship, and how, 'if you contribute to (insert name of organization here), we'll be able to give/send/buy Mark access to some much-needed services/activities/ mobility aids. Your donation helps so many people like Mark lead active/happy/healthy/ normal lives.' Cue close-up of smiling sufferer and/or supporting family members. Watch the screen fade to black and open your wallets. I'd be helpless if you didn't.

Wordlessly still smiling seems an apt metaphor for the aggression of attending to disability as a hardship suffered by some. The person other to disability – in this case, the celebrity host – speaks of the courageous overcoming individual and does so aggressively; that is, any joy, pleasure, or even mere utility of personal comportment can be transposed into a *sign* of maintaining a zest for life despite the hardship *of* disability. Nothing can or will be heard of the life *in* disability, for such a notion does not ordinarily connect us to active, happy, healthy, human life. We do not recognize disability as such a life. Yet, Mark is recognized.

Mark is known before we have any conversation with him; Mark is like any other 'person with a disability' who is worthy of recognition. Mark needs; but he is more than his needs, since he is working to overcome his neediness. Mark needs any number of things; he needs access, services, technology, etc. He needs things that others are imagined as already having, or simply not needing since they are not disabled. In the overcoming narrative structure, Mark is known as needy since Mark represents disabil-

ity. The good life is one that is able to overcome disability imagined as a non-social and lifeless obstacle. In so doing, Mark is
also known as an Overcomer since he represents something
other than disability, in this case, a zest for life.

A defining feature of the overcoming story is that the disabled
other is made into a kind of ablest opportunity. Putting pedal
to the metal, able-ist 'can do' values shine forth as if they are
merely normal and even natural. The *inter-dependence* that signifies and makes all reality is covered by the myth of the lone
individual acting over and against disability imagined as a non-
social condition. In the Lindenburg story, the transcendent
strength of humanness is granted to the non-disabled other,
who is enabled to give even in the face of the pitifully passive
impaired body. Ironically, the body depicted as passive and
impaired, from which no word will be uttered, is precisely the
sort of body needed in order to forcefully make the reader recognize a 'hardship,' and so send the overcoming story on its way.
Still, the hardship is overcome – through a gift, a smile, a crutch,
a phone call, a project, a zestful display of a desire to live – and in
one way or another, such stories represent the transcendent
human spirit. The hope that people are more than that which
conditions them is actualized in the overcoming story by making
disability into nothing but a negative condition, almost an inhu-
man condition. All people should, then, be more than that which
conditions their existence. An unrecognized irony is that disability must be emptied of life in order for it to become nothing other
than an occasion to display a zest for life. Again, this is what
Susan Bordo (1993) refers to as the cultural contradiction that
accompanies the psychopathology of our culture, which organizes embodiment through its own need to maintain its contra-
dictoriness.

Encouraged to 'look beyond the leg brace,' readers are
prompted to look at those who can endure different forms of
embodiment by ensuring that this difference is totally encapsulated by notions of hardship and suffering. Seeing the person who
'just happens to be disabled' is to imagine a form of humanness
that is literally disembodied. Bodies *just happen* to be attached to

humans, but bodies are not signifiers of humanity, at least not the disabled body found in the overcoming story. The non-disabled body of the celebrity host serves, then, as the unexamined background of normalcy against which the figure of the disabled body shows up. Disabled bodies are at best an opportunity to show what humans are supposedly made of – spirit, soul, strength, character, courage, zest, and, ultimately, mind of a can-do attitude that is essentially no different from any other 'normal' person. That which can play host to the act of overcoming the disabled body can be anyone or anything regarded as non-disabled: a strong spirit or a telethon event. The disabled body seems to host nothing, since it is only the opportunity to show how humans can respond to suffering, adversity, limit, and lack. In the face of body problems, the overcoming story recommends that we all become minded-beings.

Looking beyond, that is, seeing humans as those who just happen to have bodies, requires people to develop an ability to look at the body as essentially unessential. This way of seeing the body is abstract, distorted, and even generates a kind of optical illusion, since, as Vivian Sobchack reminds us, 'both empirically and philosophically our bodies are the essential *premises* of our being in the world' (2004: 182). Still, the progressive narrative of the overcoming story requires that the body not receive recognition as an essential premise and be treated instead as one stage, among many, from which the self can act. But there is more: the best version of overcoming is when the self performs so strongly that the stage is forgotten, if only for a moment.

The ability to recognize disability as essentially unessential can be achieved by an organization or a profession, a celebrity, or the numbers of people who give sympathy or charity. This form of recognition can be found in a nod, a cheque, or coin, and sometimes it is even displayed by the disabled person him- or herself. Look to the abled-self, the one dealing with disability, and you are looking at the strength of all that is human right in the eye. The gracious acceptance of the others' pocketful of pity through a wordless smile then qualifies the disabled-other to function as a participant in this version of ability, a version that

Overcoming Disabilities http://www.kidzworld.com/site/p5280.htm

No arms, no legs, **no problems**. Kidzworld looks at those who have overcome their disabilities and become **star athletes**.

Disabled Athletes – Wrestling Warrior

Trevon Jenifer was born without any legs because of a condition called **congenital amputation**. That didn't stop him from getting actively involved in sports. After spending ten years participating in **wheelchair basketball** and track, Trevon joined the **wrestling team** at his high school in **Huntingtown, Maryland**. While **disabled athletes** are usually eliminated from many team sports, Trevon has more than held his own on the school's **wrestling team**. Trevon has managed to overcome his disability by using his combination of **balance** and **upper-body strength** to his advantage. Opponents often have trouble wrestling with Trevon because he has **no legs** to grab on to, which gives him another advantage. Trevon has a wheelchair but he prefers to make his way around school by **walking on his hands**. In his junior year, Trevon has posted an 8–7 record and is an inspiration to other members of the school's **wrestling team**.

Disabled Athletes – Olympic Star

Rudy Garcia-Tolson was born with **Pterygium Syndrome**, which gave him a club foot, webbed fingers on both hands and a cleft lip and palate. At the age of five, Rudy decided to have his **legs amputated** and use **artificial limbs**, rather than remain confined to a wheelchair. Despite having no legs, Rudy plays football, runs track and has even completed several **triathlons**. This amazing 15 year-old athlete uses two prosthetic legs, so he can run, swim and play all the other sports he loves, including **rock climbing**. Rudy Garcia-Tolson also won two gold medals in swimming at the **2004 Paralympics** in **Athens, Greece**.

Rockclimbing

Disabled Athletes – Shark Surfer

In October 2003, **Bethany Hamilton** was surfing off the coast of **Hawaii** when she was attacked by a 14-foot tiger shark. Bethany managed to swim back to shore but not before the shark ripped off her left arm and ate a good chunk of her **surfboard** for lunch. Did a savage shark attack stop Bethany from **riding waves**? Not all all. Just four months later, Bethany Hamilton was back on her surf board and placed fifth in her age group at the **National Surfing Championships**. Bethany says she has to kick a lot harder to make up for the loss of her arm but she still **loves surfing** as much as ever.

Disabled Athletes – Paralympians

The **Summer** and **Winter Paralympics** have given athletes with disabilities a chance to shine on the **world stage**. From **swimmers** with no arms, to **skiers** with no legs, to **wheelchair sprinters** who burn around a track at record speeds – the Paralympics show that having a disability shouldn't stop someone from enjoying the **challenges, thrills and inspirations** of competitive sports.

Do you know of any athletes at your school or in your community who have **overcome a disability**. Send their stories to Kidzworld.

Related Stories:
- Weight Training Tips
- Wheelchair Sports
- Celebrity Workouts – How Stars Get In Shape
- More Sports and Fitness Stories

recognizes the body as essentially unessential. Suffering the body-as-obstacle, the disabled person becomes the symbol of overcoming *par excellence.* Overcoming stories make disability a scene where people are likely to find themselves in the play re-achieving able-ist values.

The Structure of the Overcoming Gaze

Through the overcoming story, a human difference is noticed but noticed as somehow not quite human. This stigmatized difference (Goffman 1963b), however, is not regarded as a mere marker; it is more than a disqualifying attribute. Indeed, the human difference (made not-human) is transposed into a demand: respond! This demand takes shape as 'Respond! Respond well; respond so well that we forget (look beyond) what you are responding to.' The well-structured overcoming story should enable the audience to believe that the Overcomer is responding to a body-object void of the subjective interpretive context through which the appearance of the body as such an obstacle is achieved.

The following excerpts from *Kidzworld* magazine illustrate the notion that Overcomers respond to the body as if it is an asocial object:

> No arms, no legs, **no problems**. *Kidzworld* looks at those who have overcome their disabilities and become star athletes ... Trevon Jenifer was born without any legs because of a condition called congenital amputation. That didn't stop him from getting actively involved in sports ... (http://www.kidzworld.com/site/p5280. htm [accessed August 2005])

To see 'no problems' while perceiving 'no arms' or 'no legs' does require some work. It requires the work of translating 'no arms' into something disconnected from the environments within which arms appear, environments that are set up as if there should always be arms, and always two, which function similarly to other people's two arms. Seeing 'no problem' requires the work of translating 'no arms' into the reasonable assumption that this lack belongs only and totally to individuals who, despite no arms, exude a spirit that makes no arms into no problem. In order for the overcoming story to function, 'no arms' cannot make anyone focus on the background order of everyday life that allows us to notice and worry about 'no arms' in the first place. Thus, under the organizational force of the overcoming story, no arms and no legs are recognized as conditions that could be a problem for an individual, but are not a problem since the individual is recognized as one who did not allow that which is regarded as a problem to stop them from active involvement in able-ist realms of normative values.

The *Kidzworld* article demonstrates that the overcoming story frames the object to be overcome as if the demand 'Respond. Respond well!' emanates from the spirit of mind situated in the impaired body, as if it has nothing to do with able-ist realms of normative values within which all people find themselves. Thus, *Kidzworld* can go on to say rather remarkable things that nonetheless might remain unattended to since all details are subsumed under the structure of the overcoming narrative:

> Rudy Garcia-Tolson was born with Pterygium Syndrome, which gave him a club foot, webbed fingers on both hands and a cleft lip and palate. At the age of five, Rudy decided to have his legs amputated and use artificial limbs, rather than remain confined to a wheelchair. Despite having no legs, Rudy plays football, runs track and has even competed in several triathlons. (Ibid.)

The remarkable notion that a five-year-old has decided to amputate his legs, as well as the absent medical and social context within which a five-year-old would 'make' such a decision, gain their sensibility and even ordinariness under the organizing force of the overcoming story. Thus, Rudy is depicted as overcoming his body's confinement to a wheelchair by deciding to amputate his legs and by using prosthetic devices. His decision, as well as the devices he uses, are taken up by the narrative as the artifice of the overcoming story makes it seem as if it is Rudy's five-year-old body that is calling out the demand, 'Respond.

Respond well!' The initial response that makes embodied differences essentially unessential once more disappears.

The conclusion of the *Kidzworld* article on overcoming illustrates how almost any disabled body can be pictured as a life-less obstacle:

> The Summer and Winter Paralympics have given athletes with disabilities a chance to shine on the world stage. From swimmers with no arms, to skiers with no legs, to wheelchair sprinters who burn around a track at record speeds – the Paralympics show that having a disability shouldn't stop someone from enjoying the challenges, thrills and inspirations of competitive sports. (Ibid.)

Within the space of a single page, the *Kidzworld* text has expressed wheelchair-as-confinement and wheelchair-as-liberation, in the latter of which athletes sportingly burn up the track. What makes it possible for us to read the *Kidzworld* article depiction of wheelchairs as not a blatant 'contradiction in terms'? It is the overcoming narrative itself with its demand 'Respond!' On one page and within one paragraph, the wheelchair can figure in a contradictory way as confinement as well as freedom since the overcoming narrative frames the body for the reader so that it seems only normal that all people submit to able-ist values as if they emanate from the 'natural' inclination of the self. The sensibility of textualizing wheelchairs in such opposing ways is structured by the taken for granted understanding that the self who overcomes is a self who decides how best to respond to their problem-body. The overcoming self is one that can focus the reader on the desire to get as close as possible to able-ist values. Rudy escapes the confinement of his wheelchair by deciding to have his legs amputated. Others can burn up the track in their wheelchair. Either way, we are learning to focus on wheelchairs insofar as they function as an exhibition of ability. Seeing the wheelchair as confinement in one instance, a liberator in the next, and looking beyond it at some other time are all related to the gaze that unfolds disability as the spectacle of the value of non-disability. This gaze does not need its subject to experience the different ways of perceiving wheelchairs as a contradiction or even as interesting.

The need to attend to different perceptions of wheelchairs only arises when disability is read differently; read not merely as an object of the world, but instead as that which can reveal the sort of world that makes such contradictory perceptions possible. Focusing on that which allows us to perceive disability as a representation of overcoming is the only possible way to perceive contradiction, conflicting perceptions, and, in this way, an experience of ambiguity arises. Reading how disability is depicted as overcoming, and used to make overcoming appear, is a different sort of reading than taking for granted the good of overcoming and reading only for the details of its actualization.

It may be disturbing to imagine how it is that a five-year-old boy's 'decision' to have his legs amputated can become, in a matter-of-fact way, uninteresting, except for indicating the need to not stop, go ahead, and participate in sports. It may also be disturbing that this overcoming story was written for children. Still, it is also fascinating. It fascinates me that recognizing Rudy as an Overcomer transforms the complexity of bodily decisions into spirit, in this case, the spirit of athleticism, tenacity, and competition. The narrative structure of overcoming makes Rudy and Trevon's impairments into pointers; their bodies point to a set of values (e.g., nothing about embodied differences should keep anyone from taking pleasure in realms of able-ist values). This form of recognition certainly implies the 'constitutive risk of destruction,' of which Butler writes. It not only destroys the complexity of the living scene of disability, but it also destroys, or at least tames and diminishes, the complexity of the forms of recognition that can be pursued by those who attend to disability. Perhaps there is some good to this: the story – 'little boys can decide to have their legs amputated for good reasons' – may be destroyed through readers' recognition of the unquestioned value of overcoming.

Whether directed at children or directed at adults, as is the Lindenburg story, the narrative structure of overcoming remains remarkably consistent. The body that is to signify such hardship, to signify the necessity for the rising up of the human spirit, and to signify the beginnings of the overcoming story, is the same body that is rapidly discarded as mere object, mere obstacle, not human. This way of recognizing a disabled person is constituted through the risk of destroying any social, complex, or subjective acknowledgment of disability. Nonetheless, disability structured through the overcoming narrative remains a dominant form of cultural engagement with embodied difference. In the midst of these cultural contradictions, a hardship must be suffered; those who suffer or deal with the hardship do so in a way that focuses others on almost anything but embodied difference as signifier of humanity. This is how disability can so easily become a story about how all children can and should participate in sports; that anyone can give; that a smile in the face of adversity is good, etc. Perception of disability, when structured by the gaze of the overcoming narrative, achieves the sense that human differences are outside the purview of humanity. Still, bodies may vary. There are, for example, fast and slow runners with two arms and two legs. But, bodily variation is not the type of difference that needs to be recognized *out* of human existence. Indeed, the normalcy of bodily variation, as well as a taken for granted sense of where variation ends and difference begins, are constituted through the overcoming story. In risking the destruction of the connection between disability and human existence, a taken for granted sense of a divide between mere variation and problematic difference is accomplished.

The general structure of the sort of gaze that is needed and produced by the overcoming story is, then, as follows. A human difference is noticed, but noticed as somehow not quite human. Pity, pleasure, and astonishment arise as a demand to respond, but also to forget that both self and others have already responded. Forgotten is the fact that we have already responded by perceiving a line between variation and difference, and have already deemed a difference disturbingly different enough so as to warrant its control by making it an occasion to celebrate the charms of normative values of able-ist sameness. The all-too-human is now recognized in overcoming as the signifier of the non-human. Embodied difference, the premise of our human existence, can now be perceived as if in opposition to human existence. *Overcoming that which grounds the possibility of human life is now the signifier of humanity.*

There is undoubtedly a pleasure that comes with overcoming stories. This pleasure lies in actualizing a sense that people are more than what conditions them. But this pleasure is too quickly done in. The pleasure of witnessing the sense in which we are more than (or other to) that which conditions us is present, but it is also quickly erased and made absent. The sense of the more-than-conditions is radically diminished since the overcoming story will not make anything other than what *it has been conditioned* to make of disability – disability remains a lifeless obstacle. The productive force of disability understood as a form of alterity, which makes possible the demand to overcome, is suppressed by the overcoming demand that seems always to serve sameness, ordinariness, or norms. But, it is more complicated than this.

Ability/Disability

What is complicated is that there are disabled persons who face the ever-present demand to overcome. In the Lindenburg example, there is Mark Lindenburg, undergoing this demand and offering his critique. There is the fact that disabled people can be aware of the societal demand to be the 'poster child' of able-ism, where the complexity of our embodied existence is transformed into a singular meaning. Overcoming, oriented to and by able-ism, allows for the possibility of making, for example, a child's medicalized embodied existence into a signifier of decisive individualism, whereby a boy chooses amputation 'because' he wants to play sports. The life of disability can be colonized for the sake of sustaining neo-liberal able-ist values, and this too can be recognized by disabled and non-disabled people. We recognize how others recognize us, and in that reciprocal experience a variety of things can rise up, only one of which is the conforming acquiescence of the silent smile. There are other possibilities, such as joy or mortification, pleasure, taking advantage, playing around, being offended, or writing a news article about the need to overcome the representation of disability as an occasion for charity, which is an overcoming of able-ist demands. Whatever the case, it now seems that Butler's words, which began this chapter, need to guide us a little more firmly if we are to address the connection between recognition and transformation, which is all the while tied to destruction. Recall Butler's words, 'Recognition is ... also the name given to the process that constantly risks destruction and which, I would submit, could not be recognition without a defining or constitutive risk of destruction' (2004: 133).

Recall also that Lindenburg writes: 'I can see my reality – as others perceive it – any week on TV.' He recognizes how others recognize him. In this back and forth of recognition, Lindenburg gives shape to what counts as 'overcoming.' His form of overcoming recognizes non-disability as a set of beliefs and values. He does not recognize non-disability as neutral, as no position, or as a mere biological condition. Lindenburg imagines that non-disability sees disability as a plea for pity and charity, and now Lindenburg has a few things to overcome. He will overcome the hardship of his impairment as it is mediated by what others make of his impaired body (e.g., a worthy cry for help). Then, he must also overcome his ready-made position as a voiceless smiling representative of disability. For at least part of his account, disability is as other to Lindenburg as it is to his audience that imagines him as pitiful. There is a tacit battle regarding what should be and what should not be overcome in any overcoming story, and this should remind us that the body never appears outside of the meanings made of it. We are not alone in our bodies.

There are conflicting interpretations not merely of disability, but of the ability/disability relation. For example, is Lindenburg overcoming disability when he indicates the need to highlight able-ist attitudes? His text does suggest that disability can be recognized as the need to transform 'the trouble with my body' into 'my body's trouble with you,' and this certainly destroys the sensible allocation of pity onto disabled persons alone. Lindenburg's text attests to the fact that the meaning of the story of overcoming has something to do with the complicated relation that lies between disability and non-disability.

Lindenburg's description of his need to overcome the telethon-type depiction of disability (his need to overcome overcoming) suggests that while the overcoming story is climactically structured through the demand 'Respond. Respond well!' what is actually being responded to is not quite so clear as I first implied. 'I can see my reality – as others perceive it – any week on TV' means that the self responds to how others imagine and represent him or her. I can see myself as you perceive me; and to this I feel compelled to respond. Let us not forget the 'TV.' In the time and space of everyday ways of noticing that which is taken as worthy of public attention, the disabled person confronts a version of their embodied existence as merely a plea for pity and charity. All this has now entered Lindenburg's formulation of overcoming. His story is one of needing to overcome what others have made of him in the context of being recognized as having a different issue to overcome, namely his body as obstacle. The relations between disability and non-disability, as well as the relations between the body as perceived and the body as the subject from which a person proceeds, are being ordered through the overcoming story.

Through the structure of the overcoming story, the complex and ambiguous relation between what counts as ability and what does not becomes a binary pair, a dichotomy, a split. The splitting up of disability and non-disability appears in the taken for granted sense that Mark is disabled, but the celebrity host is not; non-disabled people feel pity and give to disabled people, but disabled people do not; Mark regards disability as a management issue, but non-disabled people do not. The overcoming story quells the complexity surrounding embodiment even as the story relies on these complex relations for its own possibility. The textual enactment of disability is achieved through a set of relations to embodiment that are actively ignored in the text but which nevertheless make the narration possible. Thus, the complexity of embodied existence is textually enacted *and* ordered *and* ignored by the overcoming narrative.

Lindenburg goes on to emphatically state that he is not a 'cripple,' and he is not in need of pity. Being understood as a pitiable cripple is a form of recognition he wishes to destroy. Indeed, overcoming pity is a key endeavour not just for Mark but also for disability activism (e.g., 'Piss on Pity' slogans on placards, buttons, and T-shirts) and for disability studies scholarship (e.g., Shapiro's *No Pity*, and numerous other authors critiquing the 'pity model' of disability practice and policy). Those who dish out pity make a variety of assumptions about what disabled people need to overcome. Due to the normative demand of recognition, there are also people who must deal with this allocation of pity. Pity and charity can be understood as a scene requiring overcoming: thus, '... I am many things, but I am *not* a cripple' (ibid.). Mark's difference, which has been transformed by others into a moment for pity, is transformed by Lindenburg into a moment to emphatically state he is not as others perceive him.

Those texts that suggest that what needs to be overcome is other people's versions of overcoming destroy the taken for granted sense that there is, or ever was, a unified and singular reality of, or for, differences called disability. This shows disability to be an irreducible difference, never at one in its identity, a powerful productive force of alterity able to remake what has been made, rethink what has already been thought (Diprose 2002: 137). Lindenburg is not a cripple, and disability does not need to mean cripple. While it is very true, as interactionist sociology teaches us, that every word is not only a label of a reality but also a prescription for, and evaluation of, this reality, the performance of the word in the constitution of reality is also more complicated than it first appears. The word 'disability' is used by people to perform an untold number of forms of recognition. Our words for each other are used to symbolize, enact, and accomplish our ways of perceiving how we are not the same. Consider, for example, the disability activist slogan 'Label Jars, Not People!' or its more recent appearance, 'Label CD's, Not People.' It is, of course, impossible not to label people. Even expressions phrased through person-first language codes are labels; for example, a 'person with a disability' is a way to label some people and not others. Person-first language is typically used to emphasize personhood, as well as the conditionality of disability, and the idea that disability and persons ought to be separate. The political efficacy of stating, 'We are people too,' is questionable since it asserts, 'I am the type of person that you may not imagine as fully human' (Titchkosky 2001b). Thus, in the battle for recognition and human rights, people-first language codes may reconfirm the notion that there are some people in this world whose humanness is debate-able.

Still, the person-first slogan 'Label Jars, Not People!' is a text that performs a recognition. Suggesting that disabled people have been labelled as if they were jars (e.g., basil, jam, sugar, or blind, paralyzed, lame) recognizes that labels serve as tags influencing not just the disabled person but also the labelers' relation to the person or thing so labelled. The labels tell us of an 'inside,' even tell us what is inside, and finally tell us that we have a relation to inside/outside, to presence and absence, insofar as we are engaged in the act of 'labelling.' The use of the slogan will not and cannot make labels disappear. 'Label Jars, Not People!' does, however, make different relations to labels begin to appear. The slogan addresses the perceptions of others in an attempt to overcome these perceptions and forge an identity as person-other-than-the-label-Other. For example, addressing how others perceive him, Lindenburg achieves himself as not silent, not smiling, and not a cripple. As I demonstrated in other chapters, being 'not' is never only a negation. By destroying the sense that he is a cripple, Lindenburg is making an identity. The identity that Lindenburg identifies with and aims to achieve is expressed by his notion that in overcoming how others regard him as a cripple he can 'get down to the business of being me' (ibid.).

The business of this selfhood is enabled by Lindenburg's conception of disability as partly others' mistaken perception of him and partly a mere management issue. Mark says that 'I am a person who just happens to live with, and manage, my disability' (ibid.). As a management issue, disability means thinking ahead, planning, acquiring the correct technology to get the job of being himself, on the road, so to speak. Lindenburg's text suggests that just like any other embodied being, he is getting 'down to the business of being' an authentic self (Anderson 2006). Under modern conditions, the job of being a self, or finding a self, or improving our self can be seen to be accomplished through implementing an illusionary split between being (thought and action) and embodiment. The assertion is that one is a person first. Again, embodied differences, part of the essential premise of our being in the world (Sobchack 2004: 182), are made distant through the accomplishment of a sense of separation between self and disability. Like the non-disabled person, who regards disability as the other (in need of pity), Mark, too, regards disability as the other. Disability is other to his self, a self that is other to the pity providers only insofar as Mark is a self who knows that management, and not pity, is needed in the face of the condition called disability. But note: both sides face disability as a condition of otherness, and in recognition of these alternative views, we can read and write disability differently yet again.

Both the pity providers, who seek to overcome disability through a gift, and Lindenburg, who rejects this and seeks to overcome the idea that he needs pity, rely on a disembodied return to personhood. Look beyond the cripple, look beyond the leg brace, and you've got a person who prefers to say, 'I am a person who just happens to live with, and manage, my disability' (ibid.). Narrating the need to overcoming the others' demand to overcome recognizes disability as a management issue by destroying the others' sense that disability is a pity issue. Thus, Lindenburg writes in his article of his technological and accommodation needs; while responding immediately to a friend's request to travel, he speaks too of owning a car, working, and otherwise just getting 'down to the business of being me.' His 'me' is one that has overcome what others think of him, *as if* what others think of him is not forever and always part of the business of being a self.

Texturing the life of disability through the overcoming story is a display of selfhood that attempts a reasoned distance from embodiment. What Judith Butler says of gender seems particularly applicable to the understanding of disability: 'If gender is a kind of a doing ... it is a practice of improvisation within a scene of constraint. Moreover, one does not "do" one's gender alone. One is always "doing" with or for another, even if the other is only imaginary' (2004: 1). What grounds the possibility of the overcoming story is that disability is never done alone; yet a function of the overcoming story is to enunciate the sense that disability is done alone. It is within the constraints of the over-coming story that imagines disability as somehow an uninhabit-able void and as invalid that disabled and non-disabled versions of overcoming can arise. The ultimate gift of any kind of over-coming disability story is that embodiment is textually enacted as essentially unessential while, at the same time, serving as the hidden ground from which the independent self acts and against which this self can achieve its sense of strength. This is not just the 'gift' of false consciousness; this is the gift of common sense under modern conditions. Why do we need to recognize disabil-ity in this way?

Narrative Production of the Self-Same-Self

Under the sway of the demands of the overcoming narrative, both sides, namely, pity providers and pity resisters, enact a need to meet and transform disability into an unessential happen-stance. Many texts do this. From the disabled person's point of view, the view structured by the overcoming narrative, looking beyond the disability is also looking beyond, or disrupting, what disability means to non-disabled others. It is not a call for pity. It is a call to disrupt how others experience disability as a trouble that needs to be overcome. From the non-disabled point of view, looking beyond any symbolic manifestation of disability, such as braces, wheelchairs, white canes, hearing aids, or speech synthe-sizers, is looking to or at the person who can overcome this piti-ful condition. Despite all the essential variety in and of our bodies, the concluding scene of the overcoming story ends with the enactment of a sense of the self-same-self 'standing' over and against disability. In this imagined self, ironically, disability and non-disability find some unity or some common ground. This is the constant and consistent common-sense version of self made through overcoming stories, whether they are told from the point of view of disability or of non-disability. This self is narrated as one that recognizes the alterity inherent in embodiment but quells this potential transformative difference by treating it as mere objective otherness – difference becomes thing-like (static) rather than life-like (fluid).

While the provision of pity and the practices of technical management are radically different relations to disability, they do share in common the fact that they are relations that need, and make, disability thing-like. (What would happen if disability was recognized as part of, as tied to, as necessary for 'getting on with the job of being me'?) The complicated relations between disability's and non-disability's interpretations of what counts as overcoming and what is defined as a legitimate obstacle to be overcome also strike Lindenburg. He says:

> Talk about confusing. Focus on my abilities and tell me that the world is full of accessible, wonderful opportunity. Or focus on my disabilities and assure me that I'm quite incapable of supporting myself without outside intervention. Which version do I trust? (Ibid.)

Either version depends on ability being very clearly distinguished from disability. Lindenburg, like able-ist others, is subject to the desire to overcome. Lindenburg does not begin from the fear of some sort of difference, but he does begin from the clear and present sense that disability and non-disability are schismatically divided; in this there is no confusion. Regardless of the point of view from which the overcoming demand is issued, these views all depend not only on a schismatically clear difference between ability and non-ability, but also on a clear set of meanings for one side and for the other: ability is good and enabling; impairment is bad, poor, unwanted, and disabling. Again, like the able-ist other, Mark's confusion is based on the certainty that ability, just like disability, belongs to him individually. The text enacts the taken for granted split that seems so readily recognizable in our everyday lives and thus reproduces this form of recognition. Our collective and typically unquestioned trust in the notion that capacity and incapacity, ability and disability, are not only readily distinguishable but also located inside individuals leads to the necessary problem of needing to develop a relation to 'my own differences.' The question, born of confusion, 'Which version do I trust?' is made possible through a variety of unquestioned certainties. Both sides are presumed to reside in Lindenburg: 'Talk about confusing ... which version do I trust?' Beyond trust, indeed beyond question, is that there are two distinct versions, or a clear binary opposition between ability and disability.

Lindenburg, however, is not the same as either side since he is positioned as in need of having to develop a relation to the dichotomy. While all people are only temporarily able-bodied, only some people are forced, in the here and now, to develop a relation to the dichotomy of ability/disability. Decision, trust, and management seem to be signifiers of the relation that Mark Lindenburg has developed to the dichotomy. These are relations that he writes about as he narrates his need to overcome the non-disabled others' pity. The focus on the question regarding which 'side' to trust may distract us from the very provocative notion that the issue of trust raises, namely, that developing a relation to embodiment is tied up with 'focus.' Lindenburg's sense of confusion tacitly shows that capacity and incapacity do not reside in the body; rather, bodily capacity is constituted through 'focus.' Both sides share the capacity to focus on embodiment as either an issue of ability or as an issue of disability, but not as an intermingling, thus, as an ambiguity, of both. Lindenburg's confusion does not lie in the clear and ongoing split between ability and disability that the overcoming story relies on. Instead, the confusion of whether to focus on ability or disability lies in the fact that this either/or is 'in' him; he is both ability and not ability, depending on focus, a focus which always seems to be made to disappear for the sake of 'overcoming.'

The question of focus, however, arises from the taken for granted relation between disability and non-disability that assumes they are split, as if these two sides are not always in constitutive conversation with one another. I suggest that in developing an awareness of our possible interpretive relations to such dichotomies, we can represent the radical productive force of alterity. It is by fully being neither ability nor disability, yet remaining in some sort of interpretive relation to both, that we can begin to imagine, to read and to write, embodiment differently. The activity implied in the term 'overcoming' makes it a form of narrative which does not allow those who are its subjects to dwell on the dichotomies that make possible the overcoming story in the first place.

Under the narrative structure of the overcoming story, the disabled person is confronted with the demand 'Respond!' That demand necessarily over-writes, or transforms, the initial response shared by both those who utter the demand and those who do respond to it. The primary or first response is to focus on embodiment in such a way as to divide it up, parcelling off not only men from women, white from black, straight from gay, but also abled from not. Overcoming seems to manage the focus that sees ability and disability as clearly split by treating embodiment as if it were natural, normal, and, ultimately, not questionable. Overcoming narratives, then, make use of disability in such a way that a sense of an ordered and clearly compartmentalized reality is built up. Moreover, overcoming narratives help to (re)constitute common-sense versions of the self able to exist in the compartmentalized world, imaginatively splitting self and body. Still ...

Recognition and Destruction

Any overcoming text requires an act of recognition. To recognize how others imagine who you are, one must perform an act of, or undergo, identification. For example, when Lindenburg says, 'I can see my reality – as others perceive it – any week on TV,' he can see his reality in the perception of others insofar as he recognizes himself in others' perception. There is an act of recognition insofar as he identifies with the presentation of a 'TV self' as a presentation of his embodied self. While he is not a smiling silent cripple, he is someone who can recognize his self as one that can be recognized by others as a smiling silent cripple. The others' attitudes of pity that Mark overcomes become part of him; whatever is overcome is part of who we are. Somehow the telethon depiction of disability calls forth a form of recognition – some people identify with how others have identified them. But this identification takes shape in the form of a negation:

> I see that you are speaking about me. That is what you say I am. But I am not what you say I am. My 'me' is partly constituted through your mis-recognition. I am a self that must establish who I am in relation to the fact that I know that I am mis-recognized.

Now, it could be argued that non-disability's recognition of disability as a lack that needs to be overcome is merely the simple reproduction of stereotype – the reproduction of a general negative conception of disability. Here is one way this argument has been put forward:

> The mass media perpetuate stereotypes of disability through their portrayals of characters. But there is no evidence that the mass media have any major effect on manipulating the attitudes and opinions of its audience. Researchers state that it is difficult to discover what are the precise effects of the media on public opinion. It is possible that attitudes and opinions change dramatically as a result of what is seen or heard. There are indications of selective perception of what is viewed, namely that audiences tend to identify with that which reinforces their existing beliefs ... Some speculation is in order, however, on the effect of negative stereotyping on the disabled themselves, especially children with disabilities ... To see oneself labelled and cast always in the role of the villain, helpless dependent or victim is not an enviable fate. (Dahl 1993)

Whether or not the media influences people's opinions, or whether the media reproduces already existing beliefs, are questions that require not only operationalizing what will count as influence, but also developing empirical methods to measure this influence. Instead of researching the effects of the media, a different set of questions is raised by asking what grounds the appearance of Lindenburg's text or any other overcoming text. More is going on here than our being ruled by stereotypes, since there is an interpolation. Some people, and not others, identify as this 'not'; some people, and not others, feel called upon to deal with the influence of other peoples' negative stereotypes; some people, and not others, identify who they are through the constitutive risk of destroying what other people think they are. Not everyone finds themselves needing to say, 'I am not a smiling cripple.' Such a self is one that is forming their self-recognition by understanding that

> I am not a smiling cripple, yet I am that in the others' eyes. I am both not that and that. You have made me exactly what I don't want and will not be. I am, again, both. I am a self who relates to both and this relation is a constitutive tension of who I am as I aim to become other to who I am not.

What overcoming narratives seem to actively ignore is this complex ambiguity of existence. While overcoming narratives need this interpretive complexity, they can also make readers forget it. The overcoming story can now be read as showing that both disabled and non-disabled people can be united in a desire to achieve a form of forgetfulness that lends a false certainty to everyday existence.

What is forgotten is that even though disability is defined as lifeless obstacle, it is still given by and produces life. What needs to be brought to mind is the ubiquitous power of natality, of the making of something new, that is, the mystery of newness even when we think there is nothing but loss, lack, limit, death. People are more than put down or diminished by the collective imagination that inscribes disability everywhere in text as a lifeless obstacle since the relation between the 'I' and the 'Me' is steeped in a 'We' (Mead 1934). Taken for granted relations to collective life (a 'We') are built up through how individuals ('I') must interpretively engage how others imagine them ('Me'):

> They say of him you are a cripple, his 'me' is crippled. He says to himself and to others, 'I am not a cripple.' They say, 'Look at how the cripple overcomes and displays a zest for life, courageously smiling.' He says, 'Look at how I overcome able-ist attitudes by showing that what I do, I do to get on with the business of being me, and not to prove that I overcome.'

In the midst of the conflict, disability is still essentialized as an empty life. Disability as a lifeless obstacle remains what 'we' believe; both parties make sense to each other since both rely on the self-same ground, which is the supposed re-achieved end-point of the overcoming story. But even while we think this, or know disability in this way, something new can and does emerge. What is new, for example, is the ambiguous alterity of recognizing that we are always in an interpretive relation to dis-ability and ability, which not only grounds overcoming stories, but also my text and your reading of it.

The overcoming story enters into life and calls out to readers. Our sense of who we are enters into the contexts of interpretive realities, which are always laden with the possibility of focusing differently on that which makes us attend to things, such as dis-ability, in remarkably similar fashions. Stories of overcoming dis-ability enter the life of readers as a demand, a disappointment, a chastisement, as worry, as a model, as a time for analysis, etc. There are different ways that overcoming can be experienced by its readers, and this attests to the social fact that the meaning of the narrative is not solely contained within the text. Various lives are made and remade even in the face of the same representation of disability. This life-filled possibility remains so long as the potential to read our readings (self-reflexivity) is not controlled to death.

Regarding matters of life and death, Hélène Cixous has this to say:

> ... my mother the proof, my mother who circulates within me, my mother who was in me as I was in her ... The most surprising is not

that I, I will die, it is that I was born, that I am not you, and that I
am me. I would like very much to know that me. (1998: 86–7)

Given what has mothered disability under neo-liberal late capitalism, it should not be surprising that everyday disabled people
undergo deadly forms of discrimination. The death blows of stereotype, or pity provision, or of the textual enactment of disability as the ubiquitous demand to 'overcome' are, in one sense, also
not surprising. We have done so little to appreciate alterity that it
is not surprising that alterity is more likely to be oppressed and
marginalized than nurtured. To appreciate or to live imaginatively with alterity is to begin to entertain the sensibility that who
I am, all my identifications, my common-sense renderings of a
sensible life, are constituted in contradistinction to that which is
deemed other, not me, alter. 'I am not you' holds a promise, or
potentially so. I can be other to that which creates me and not
necessarily be a destroyed other. Cixous's 'me' is not the presupposed independent self of modern neo-liberalism. Her sort of me
is regarded as it is embedded in a relation to others, to not being
you where that you circulates within me. The play of absence
and presence, of limit and possibility, does not cease in our dismissal of alterity. Even when the demand 'Overcome!' rises up as
the orienting power over embodied differences, the recognition
of difference represents the promise not only that one can be
mortally wounded, but also that one can live in and as alterity.

Quelling the experience of alterity, a rather common fate, is
tied up with the achievement of much of one's daily competence
as a member of society. This competence is connected to the
reproduction of the hegemonic orders surrounding social differences, including those differences called disability. Appreciating
alterity demands an awakening of the sense that 'I would like
very much to know that me,' since I am not you. Who is it that
struggles to maintain a sense of competence for not imagining
disability as strictly a matter to be overcome?

With Cixous, we can learn that death is not surprising; my
competent appearance as a normal member is predicated on my
ability to kill off alternative responses to what is typically
regarded as essentially a devalued difference. Still, something is

borne along with, or something new emerges, as we attend to interpretation, and this something is beyond intentions and expectations; it is the something that Cixous says she would like to get to know. A rather crass example of this can be witnessed in the icon of pity provision – Jerry Lewis and his 'kids.' Lewis's telethon infantilizes disabled people while obtaining millions of dollars in donations for people he describes as unable to have a life without the aid of his telethon. But, even here, something new is born. 'Lewis' is himself a multi-million-dollar company, an industry; and Cixous suggests that he would be better off awakening his desire to get to know his self as a producer and seller of pity. The commodification of pity has entered people's lives, and sometimes something other than death of the self, or the death of disability as a life, occurs. Surprisingly, people do not necessarily acquiesce; more imaginative relations to disability arise. Surprisingly, even though millions of dollars, glamour, glitz, and media support surround Lewis, something other than his version or control of the meaning of disability is born – there is protest, commentary, comedy, and other alternative articulations, which have given rise to new ways to imagine disability. Or, consider again Mark Lindenburg's text. He narrates how he is not as others imagine him. Between his assertions of what he is not (e.g., a cripple) and what he is (e.g., a manager of a condition of happenstance), there is much that we might like to get to know. Reading our reading of disability situated between cripple and management could awaken a sense of the need to address that me that knows that

> ... what I understand never quite tallies with my living experience; in short, I am never quite at one with myself. Such is the lot of a being who is born, that is, who once and for all has been given to [her/]himself as something to be understood. (Merleau-Ponty 1958: 404)

The constant modern demand to overcome disability might be the prime location to begin to develop an ability to not reduce disability to the 'other of the same,' and to begin to open ourselves to the 'radical difference, a difference otherwise, in which both terms are valued' (Shildrick 2005a: 8). This chapter, indeed this book as a whole, can be read as my attempt to find ways to value disability as the discursive space where the interrelation of ability and disability can be thought anew. I hope only to read how we commonly regard disability otherwise than the same.

Afterword

... who would attempt to know the body of the other, opens a relation to the other but also holds the potential for effacing the other's alterity, and so for finishing the other off.
                            – Rosalyn Diprose, 'A "Genethics" That Makes Sense,' 243

I end this book by highlighting how disability has not been finished off. Whether you identify as disabled or not, I have assumed that text can be an encounter with disability. Everyday textual expressions of disability can be oriented to as encounters allowing readers an opportunity to open relations between ourselves and alterity. Encountering disability is a chance to ascertain, and thus evaluate, that which gives rise to the appearance of embodied differences in the first place. Through a critical engagement with textual expressions of disability, meaningful encounters between self and alter can happen, since 'the body is already caught in the fabric of the perceived world and ... this openness of the body to its world is such that what is seen and felt is at the same time a being seen and a being felt' (Diprose 2005: 242). That which we see and feel about disability as represented in text has much to reveal about our taken for granted world. Insofar as disability is caught in the fabric of the perceived world, it is an occasion to examine the interchange of world and perception played out through disability experience, in whatever ways you or I come to that experience. Coming to this sort of disability experience is irregularly occasioned by the act of identifying as disabled.

The sight and feel of disability, its documented and narrated form, that is, the sense that can be made of disability, is the sense of our world. Being in the world, disability can teach us about that world. Even as disability is constantly put into the form of a devalued binary partner to valued notions such as ability, normality, or, even, naturalness, disability can be perceived as something much different from the merely not-abled, not-normal, or not-natural. If this were not the case, then the sensibility of my text, and what we come to see as we read our readings of other disability texts, would not be possible.

I have tried to direct attention to relations with bodily differences by opening up the ways that disability is put into text in everyday life within the minority world mass media. Such texts circulate through daily existence in common and ordinary ways. In attempting to uncover the sense of the body that provides for typical ways of textually representing disability, a form of alterity is released. By noticing the ordinary ways of reading and writing disability, a relation to alterity is established. This is a relation to alterity that is not absolutely committed to the reproduction of the ordinary and normal ways of reading and writing disability. Noticing our ways of noticing will not as readily efface disability, since such noticing represents an alternative form of perceiving alterity. This is not the sort of alternative found in rule books, or set principles, or in evaluative measures of 'new and improved' ways to better put disability into text and avoid offence as much as one may avoid encounter. Instead, the alternative represented by this book is the sort that aims to be alter to its alters and produce something other than the perceived world of the same. In this way, this book exemplifies a relation to alterity that does not efface it.

To know that the body is made manifest through our word-filled relations to embodiment actualized through our reading and writing of the body, is to know that any manifestation of language is an embodied activity that might open us to something other than what appears on the page. Reading and writing are socially oriented activities of embodied actors situated in the same world they are busy making. Attending not only to the sense in which texts give us versions of embodiment, but also to the ways in which we apperceive these versions, can teach us much about the ordering of relations to the bodies of ourselves and others through the medium of everyday texts. It is my hope that this book actualizes the recommendation that disability can be read otherwise by revealing how disability is normally put into text and ordinarily read.

While perhaps not in tune with common-sense expectations, I think that it makes good sense that this book does not end by positing a programmatic approach to reading and writing disability differently. This book *is* reading and writing disability differently, since it attends to the production and governance of our relations to disability as currently put into text and read by people in the here and now of everyday life. I have read and written the body otherwise by opening the text to the differences the text both imagines and produces. In this way, the possibility of imagining disability differently is developed since this writing has attempted to grapple with the alterity that others must have grappled with in order to narrate the problems and solutions of disability in the way that they have.

I am finishing off this book by suggesting that disability cannot be finished off. Its ambiguity of meaning has been opened and relied on, so as to approach even the most totally clear-cut textual representations of disability as containing the potential to be otherwise. Overall, *Reading and Writing Disability Differently* aims to allow us to feel and see limited forms of embodiment as potentially opening us up to the sort of world and the sort of selves that require disability to appear in these ways. This play between limit and possibility can potentially teach us to read and write existence toward the otherwise.

Notes

1 See Anna Mollow's work (2004), informed by critical race and gender theory, which questions the limits and possibilities of identity politics in disability studies. See also Nirmala Erevelles (2000) on the same issue, especially as it relates to the importance of considering the material reality of finding ourselves located in the midst of others.

2 Maurice Merleau-Ponty, Peter Berger and Thomas Luckman, Maurice Natanson, Dorothy Smith, Rod Michalko, Judith Butler, bell hooks, Rosalyn Diprose, and Hannah Arendt are some of the phenomenologically oriented social theorists who highlight the achieved character of existence and profoundly influence my approach to the study of disability in everyday life.

3 See, for example, Lemert 1997: 173; Hall 1996: 2; Rose 1999; Foucault 1978. Stuart Hall (ibid.) reminds us that 'identification turns out to be one of the least well-understood concepts – almost as tricky, but preferable to "identity" itself.'

4 Carol Stabile, in 'Shooting the Mother,' argues that the separation, or 'disarticulation,' of 'women' from 'pregnancy' is part of a larger, right-wing sponsored 'cultural logic of removing the laborer from the site of (re)production' (1998: 186). As a consequence, pregnancy becomes the terrain of the medical profession where 'any number of mappings and various technological surveillance systems' operate. Through such operations, a belief in a free-floating individualized fetus, both ahistorical and decontextualized, is established.

5 Snyder and Mitchell (2006: 5ff) refer to this form of oriented critical attention as a 'cultural model of disability,' in contrast to the UK 'social model of disability.' The social model of disability holds that

disablement is the result of society's failure to respond adequately to impairment (biology) (Oliver 1996, 1990). Rod Michalko's *The Difference That Disability Makes* (2002: 41ff) works to uncover the different versions of suffering in various models or conceptions of disability studies. My 'Disability Studies: The Old and the New?' (Titchkosky 2000) formulates the sort of conversations and questions granted by disability studies' perspectives. Beyond rejecting or accepting the social model of disability there is the need to recognize what other sorts of relations can be and have been established to the social model of disability, since it is one of the more dominant formulations of disability arising from the life and politics of disabled people.

6 It is important to note that social class and wealth are very cogent, yet unrecognized, variables in the filter questions' version of disability. After all, a wealthy person could pay someone to do the things they have difficulty doing, thereby making these things not difficult to do. Is such a person still disabled? Or, if you are wealthy and pay for the doing of the activities of daily living, are you not, perhaps, impaired by your wealth? Of course, such plays on the logic of a definition have no part in the actual taken for granted conception of disability, which, so long as it remains taken for granted, allows the questions to do the filtering they are designed to do.

7 On genre, see Bakhtin 1986 and Smith's development in 'Telling the Truth after Postmodernism' (1999: 96–130). On language game, see Wittgenstein 1980, 1958. For a self-reflective discussion of language *as* the problematic of our relation both to agency and to our being an effect of subjection, see Butler 1997: 1–30 and Bonner 2001.

8 On governmentality, see also Pratt and Valverde 2002, Rose 1999, and Ruhl 2002. For an analysis of some of the ways that embodiment is governed, as this is reflected in disability discourse, see Corker 1998, Corker and French 1999, Corker and Shakespeare 2002, Davis 2002, Goggin and Newell 2003, Stiker 1999, Titchkosky 2003b, and Tremain 2005, 2002.

9 As Elizabeth Grosz says, texts are constitutive of 'both their milieu and the means by which they become comprehensible and tamed… histories – stories and reconstructions of the past – are in fact illuminations of a present that would not be possible without this past' (2003: 13–14). See also Davis 2002, R. Garland-Thomson 1997, Mitchell and Snyder 2000, 1997, Michalko 1998, and Titchkosky

2005c, 2003a, 2003b, 2001b for a demonstration of the theoretical and political importance of developing an analysis of the multiple ways in which disability is made manifest, and manifestly meaningful, through text.

10 Ultrasound is today regarded as the authoritative text/image of many different aspects of pregnancy. See, for example, Carol Stabile and Valerie Hartouni's articles in *The Visible Woman: Imaging Technologies, Gender, and Science* (1998). Ultrasound is a technology that uses pulsating sound waves to produce an image of tissue. In relation to pregnant women who have access to such health care procedures, ultrasound imaging has become routine. A '...scanner moves over the abdomen of the woman, sound waves penetrate the uterus; these waves bounce back to a monitor that produces the image, which can be captured immediately by the Polaroid camera attached to the machine' (Cook 1996: 74). For an in-depth analysis of how the ultrasound image is subject to a wide range of historical and cultural interpretations, see Lisa M. Mitchell, *Baby's First Picture* (2001).

11 Amniocentesis testing is an invasive procedure that involves collecting a sample of amniotic fluid by inserting a needle through the pregnant woman's abdomen. Medicine conducts amniocentesis tests only in the light of a medical version of risk, such as the age of the woman, history of disability, illness, and, of course, an abnormal ultrasound image. While medicine conducts this test in the face of such risk, the test itself is risky, as one out of every two hundred tests results in spontaneous abortion (Berube 1996: 40–94).

12 That the problem of disability is located at the level of the gene is an important issue that is just beginning to receive theoretic attention. It is also an issue that, as I trace its renderings through the media, shifts in extraordinary, sophisticated, and dramatic ways, while always returning to the same unquestioned assumption of the good of making some forms of life, if not some people, prone to elimination. For documentation and critique of the mass media's enthusiastic endorsement of genetic technologies, see, for example, Albert 2001, Diprose 2005, Fitzgerald 1998, Fortun 2002, Melzer and Zimmern 2002, Rapp and Ginsburg 2002.

13 A belief in the efficacy of medical tests on women's bodies and fetuses to reveal not only problems but forms of life is, as Ruth Hubbard (1997: 197ff) suggests, empirically questionable and even fallacious. Moreover, such tests are completely unable to foretell

what *others will make of embodied human differences*. See Rapp 2000: 129ff and Rapp and Ginsburg 2002 for how disability imagery is actually lived in women's lives in a variety of ways.

14 For example, prenatal surgery, opening the pregnant woman's uterus (hysteronomy), partially removing and operating on the fetus, and then putting the fetus back into the womb, is a newly emerging field within medicine accompanied by a high risk of death for the fetus. According to Monica Casper, 'Approximately half of the fetuses that undergo treatment die, while those who live are unlikely ever to be fully healthy and *always* require postnatal treatment of some kind' (1988: 28, emphasis her own).

15 See Corker and Shakespeare 2002, Corker 2001, 1998b, Michalko 2002, Overboe 1999, and Titchkosky 2001b, on theorizing the meaning of the split between personhood and disability as well as on the splitting of impairment and disability.

16 The question of competing definitions and the real political and social consequences of the power of the definitional process to delineate problem people is typically not imagined within texts that start from the assumption of disability as a problem. As demonstrated in chapter 2, the disability population shrank in Canada between 1991 and 2001, or, at least, the new way of counting disability shrank the population by about 600,000.

17 The full-page article, by Brad Evenson, was published in the *National Post*'s 'Discovery' section and is titled 'The Only Case in the World: Courtney Popken's Disease May Be Unique, but Finding a Cure for Her Could Strengthen Us All' (6 March 1999: B11). All references are to this article unless otherwise indicated.

18 See Oliver 1990: 4–11 and Zola 1977 for expanded critiques on the medicalization of the body, individuals, and culture.

19 It is interesting that almost any form of alterity, so long as it is devalued, can be represented as a disability: my work here suggests that this is so since disability serves as the ultimate form of negation. Still, disability is reasserted as negative ontology even within theoretical work that claims to examine forms of embodied existence that are fashioned negatively.

20 For a discussion on how the WHO's 'insertion' of a social component into its definitions and measurements of disability has done little to change the on-going practice of producing data on disability as biologically based abnormality, see Snyder and Mitchell 2006: 5–9 and Titchkosky 2006b.

21 See Nikolas Rose's *Governing the Soul* (1999) for a more extensive
formulation of the concept of 'governmentality.' Arthur Frank's
(1998a, b, c) work explicates how, and to what ends, Foucault's
work can be used in the sociology of illness, especially as this pertains to the agentive orientation of the ill subject. Many feminist
theorists, especially those working in the area of medicine and/or
reproductive technology, have used Foucault's work in order to
show how the healthy or unhealthy subject is constituted via a variety of discursive practices, all of which come to govern interpretive
relations to women's bodies. See, for example, Balsamo 1996, Braidotti 1997, Rapp 1993, Haraway 1991, Shildrick et al. 1998, and Treichler et al. 1998. Others in the field of disability studies (e.g.,
Corker 1998b, 2001, Corker and Shakespeare 2002, Mitchell and
Snyder 2000, Tremain 2002) have begun the work of bringing 'disability' and 'impairment' into the realm of discursive analysis,
using Foucault's work as a way to do so. I am grateful to Tremain's
work on Foucault.

22 For an analysis of how far removed this particular conception of
disability is, not only from citizenship but also from personhood,
see Michalko's (2002: 103ff) work on the Latimer case. See also
Enns 1999, Davis 1995, and Silvers 1998.

23 A more extensive account of 'Investing in Persons with Disabilities'
can be found in *Government of Canada Response to a Common Vision:
Interim Report* (Canada 2001) and throughout *In Unison 2000*, which
provides descriptions of 'best practices' initiated at the local level.

24 The following examples are gleaned from *In Unison 2000* data (34–
6, 49, 72–7), as well as from *Future Directions* (Canada 2000b), which
is an interim report on *In Unison 1998*. For more on these facts and
figures, see *A Portrait of Persons with Disabilities* (Statistics Canada
1995).

25 For a detailed examination of the economic ordering of disability
policy and its normative basis see Bickenbach 1993b: 93–134 or
McColl and Jongbloed 2006.

26 For a reformulation of Turner's (1985) use of the concept of 'liminality' – limbo – see Murphy (1987), who employs liminality so as
to draw out the radically precarious position of disabled people in
North America. See, also, my 2003 work, where I demonstrate that
the liminal positioning of disabled people gives rise not only to
marginality, but also to the possibility that disability is a radical
space for critical inquiry of culture.

27 I intended and attempted to end this book with a consideration of the human genome, reproductive technologies, and the new eugenic movement that assumes the good of eliminating disability even as it uses the threat of disability to secure investment and government interest. However, the extraordinary claims, processes, and hopes that surround the bio-technology industry rapidly transmuted after the mapping of the human genome, bringing a whole new set of concepts and complexities. Also, it seems to me, despite complex 'advances' in the bio-technology industry, it remains beholden to the rather simplistic repetitive unquestioned assumption that disability can and ought be eliminated. So, I turn to the fact that disability is in our midst, the extraordinary elimination projects have not (yet?) won. In keeping with the spirit of my own methods of proceeding, I have decided that it is best to deal with the ordinary daily practices by which disability is addressed and through which disability's meaning is accomplished. Thus, 'overcoming' became the topic of this final chapter.

References

Abberley, Paul. 1998. 'The Spectre at the Feast: Disabled People and Social Theory.' In *The Disability Reader: Social Science Perspectives*. Ed. Tom Shakespeare. London: Cassell Academic. 79–93.

Albert, Bill. 2001. 'Genetics: Promising Cure or Delivering Elimination?' *Consumer Policy Review* 11(5): 166–71.

Albrecht, Gary. 1992. *The Disability Business: Political Economy of Rehabilitation in America*. Beverly Hills, CA: Sage Publications.

Alderson, Priscilla, Clare Williams, and Bobbie Farsides. 2004. 'Practitioners' Views about Equity within Prenatal Services.' *Sociology* 38(1): 61–80.

Anderson, Katherine. 2006. '"To Thine Own Self Be True": Self-Expression and the Ethos of Authenticity.' PhD diss., York University.

Arendt, Hannah. 1994. *Arendt: Essays in Understanding: 1930–1954*. New York: Harcourt Brace and Company.

– 1971. *The Life of the Mind*. San Diego: Harcourt Brace Jovanovich.

– 1954. *Between Past and Future: Eight Exercises in Political Thought*. New York: Penguin Books.

Asenjo, F.G. 1988. *In-Between: An Essay on Categories*. Lanham, MD: Center for Advanced Research in Phenomenology, Inc. and University Press of America, Inc.

Bakhtin, Mikhail Mikhailovich. 1986. *Speech Genres and Other Late Essays*. Trans. Vern W. McGee. Austin: University of Texas Press.

Balsamo, Anne. 1999. 'Forms of Technological Embodiment: Reading the Body in Contemporary Culture.' In *Feminist Theory and the Body: A Reader*. Ed. Margrit Shildrick and Janet Price. New York: Routledge. 278–89.

– 1996. *Technologies of the Gendered Body: Reading Cyborg Women*. Durham, NC: Duke University Press.

Barnes, Colin. 1998. 'The Social Model of Disability: A Sociological Phenomenon Ignored by Sociologists?' In *The Disability Reader: Social Science Perspectives*. Ed. Tom Shakespeare. London: Cassell Academic. 65–78.

Barnes, Colin, Geof Mercer, and Tom Shakespeare. 1999. *Exploring Disability: A Sociological Introduction*. Cambridge: Polity Press.

Barnes, Colin, and Mike Oliver. 1995. 'Disability Rights: Rhetoric and Reality in the UK.' *Disability & Society* 10(1): 111–16.

Barnes, Colin, Mike Oliver, and Len Barton, eds. 2002. *Disability Studies Today*. Cambridge: Polity Press.

Bauman, Zygmunt. 2002. *Society under Siege*. Malden, MA: Blackwell Publishing, Ltd.

– 2000. *Liquid Modernity*. Malden, MA: Blackwell Publishing, Ltd.

– 1990. *Thinking Sociologically*. Oxford: Blackwell.

Beck-Gernsheim, Elizabeth, Judith Butler, and Lidia Puigvert. 2001. *Women and Social Transformation*. New York: Peter Lang.

Benhabib, Seyla, Judith Butler, Drucilla Cornell, and Nancy Fraser. 1995. *Feminist Contentions: A Philosophical Exchange*. New York: Routledge.

Berube, Michael. 2000. 'Biotech before Birth.' Review of *Testing Women, Testing the Fetus: The Social Impact of Amniocentesis in America*, by Rayna Rapp. *Tikkun* 15(3): 73–5.

– 1996. *Life As We Know It: A Father, a Family, and an Exceptional Child*. New York: Vintage Books.

Bhabha, Homi K. 1994. *The Location of Culture*. New York: Routledge.

Bickenbach, Jerome. 1993a. 'AIDS as Disability.' In *Perspectives on Disability*. Ed. Mark Nagler, 2nd ed. Palo Alto, CA: Health Markets Research. 495–506.

– 1993b. *Physical Disability and Social Policy*. Toronto: University of Toronto Press.

Blum, Alan. 1993. 'Travesty.' *Symbolic Interaction* 15: 83–101.

Bonner, Kieran. 2001. 'Reflexivity and Interpretive Sociology: The Case of Analysis and the Problem of Nihilism.' *Human Studies* 24: 267–92.

Bordo, Susan. 1993. *Unbearable Weight: Feminism, Western Culture, and the Body*. Berkeley: University of California Press.

Braidotti, Rosi. 1999. 'Signs of Wonder and Traces of Doubt: On Teratology and Embodied Differences.' In *Feminist Theory and the Body: A Reader*. Ed. Margrit Shildrick and Janet Price. New York: Routledge. 290–301.

– 1997. 'Mothers, Monsters, and Machines.' In *Writing on the Body: Female Embodiment and Feminist Theory*. Ed. Katie Conboy, Nadia

Medina, and Sarah Stanbury. New York: Columbia University Press. 59–79.

Butler, Judith. 2005. *Giving an Account of Oneself*. New York: Fordham University Press.

– 2004. *Undoing Gender*. New York: Routledge.

– 2000. 'Restaging the Universal: Hegemony and the Limits of Formalism.' In *Contingency, Hegemony, Universality: Contemporary Dialogues on the Left*, by Judith Butler, Ernesto Laclau, and Slavoj Zizek. London: Verso. 11–43.

– 1998. 'Foreword.' In *The Erotic Bird: Phenomenology in Literature*, by Maurice Natanson. Princeton: Princeton University Press. ix–xvi.

– 1997. *The Psychic Life of Power*. Stanford: Stanford University Press.

– 1993. *Bodies That Matter: On the Discursive Limits of 'Sex.'* New York: Routledge.

Canada. 2005. *Advancing the Inclusion of Persons with Disabilities: Executive Summary*. Ottawa: Human Resources and Social Development Canada.

– 2004. *Advancing the Inclusion of Persons with Disabilities: Executive Summary*. Ottawa: Social Development Canada.

– 2003a. *Defining Disability: A Complex Issue*. Office for Disability Issues, HRDC. Ottawa: Human Resources Development Canada. (RH37–4/3–2003–E).

– 2003b. *Update: Advancing the Inclusion of Persons with Disabilities: A Government of Canada Report*. Ottawa: Human Resources Development Canada.

– 2002a. *Advancing the Inclusion of Persons with Disabilities: A Government of Canada Report, December 2002*. Ottawa: Human Resources Development Canada. (RH37–4/1–2002E)

– 2002b. *Technical Report: Advancing the Inclusion of Persons with Disabilities: A Government of Canada Report*. Ottawa: Human Resources Development Canada.

– 2001. *Government of Canada Response to a Common Vision: Interim Report: The Fourth Report of the Standing Committee on Human Resources Development and the Status of Persons with Disabilities*. Hull: Her Majesty the Queen in Right of Canada. (RH34–16/2001–1).

– 2000a. *Disability Tax Credit Certificate: T2201 E*. Canada Customs and Revenue Agency.

– 2000b. *Future Directions to Address Disability Issues for the Government of Canada: Working Together for Full Citizenship*. Hull: Her Majesty the Queen in Right of Canada.

– 2000c. *In Unison 2000: Persons with Disabilities in Canada*. A Visionary Paper of Federal/Provincial/Territorial Ministers Responsible for Social Services. Ottawa: Supply and Service Canada. http://social-union.gc.ca/InUnison2000.

– 1998. *In Unison 1998: A Canadian Approach to Disability Issues*. A Visionary Paper of Federal/Provincial/Territorial Ministers Responsible for Social Services. Hull: Human Resources Development Canada.

– 1996. *Equal Citizenship for Canadians with Disabilities: The Will to Act. Final Report to Federal Task Force on Disability Issues*. Ottawa: Supply and Services Canada.

– 1981. *House of Commons Special Parliamentary Committee on the Disabled and the Handicapped: 'Obstacles.'* Ottawa: Information Canada.

Canadian Broadcasting Corporation. 2002. 'Measuring Up: Should Genetic Testing Decide Who Is Born?' 11 March.

Canguilhem, Georges. 1991 [1966]. *The Normal and the Pathological*. Trans. Carolyn Fawcett and Robert Cohen. New York: Zone Books.

Carey, Elaine. 2003. 'A Pill for Children Who Can't Read: Toronto Researchers Hunting for Clues; Experts Foresee Scenario akin to Ritalin.' *Toronto Star*, 9 July. (Accessed 9 July 2005.)

Carniol, Naomi. 2004. 'No Way, No How: For Disabled and Old, Metro Station Stairs and Escalators Are Still Impassable Obstacles.' *Montreal Gazette*, 27 May.

Casper, Monica. 1998. 'Working in and around Human Fetuses.' In *Differences in Medicine: Unraveling Practices, Techniques, and Bodies*. Ed. Marc Berg and Annemarie Mol. Durham, NC: Duke University Press. 28–52.

Cicourel, Aaron. 1970. 'The Acquisition of Social Structure: Toward a Developmental Sociology of Language and Meaning.' In *Understanding Everyday Life: Toward the Reconstruction of Sociological Knowledge*. Ed. Jack D. Douglas. Chicago: Aldine Publishing Co. 136–68.

Cixous, Hélène. 1998. *Stigmata: Escaping Texts*. New York: Routledge.

Clough, Peter. 2002. *Narratives and Fictions in Educational Research*. Buckingham: Open University Press.

CNN.com. 2005. 'Blind Student Earns M.D.' *Health CNN*. 2 April. www.cnn.com/2005/HEALTH/o4/o2/seeing.no.limits.ap/index.html. (Accessed 4 April 2005.)

Cohen, Jeffrey Jerome, and Gail Weiss, eds. 2003. *Thinking the Limits of the Body*. New York: State University of New York Press.

Cook, Kay. 1996. 'Medical Identity: My DNA/Myself.' In *Getting a Life:*

Everyday Uses of Autobiography. Ed. Sidonie Smith and Julia Watson. Minneapolis: University of Minnesota Press. 63–85.

Corker, Mairian. 2001. 'Sensing Disability.' *Hypatia* 16(4): 34–52.

– 2000. 'Disability Politics, Language Planning and Inclusive Social Policy.' *Disability & Society* 15(3): 445–61.

– 1999. 'New Disability Discourse, the Principle of Optimization and Social Change.' In *Disability Discourse*. Ed. Mairian Corker and Sally French. Buckingham: Open University Press. 192–209.

– 1998a. *Deaf and Disabled or Deafness Disabled?* Buckingham: Open University Press.

– 1998b. 'Disability Discourse in a Postmodern World.' In *The Disability Reader: Social Science Perspectives*. Ed. Tom Shakespeare. London: Cassell Academic. 221–33.

Corker, Mairian, and Sally French, eds. 1999. *Disability Discourse*. Buckingham: Open University Press.

Corker, Mairian, and Tom Shakespeare. 2002. 'Mapping the Terrain.' In *Disability/Postmodernity: Embodying Disability Theory.* Ed. Mairian Corker and Tom Shakespeare. London: Continuum. 1–17.

Dahl, Marilyn. 1993. 'The Role of the Media in Promoting Images of Disability – Disability as Metaphor: The Evil Crip.' *Canadian Journal of Communications*. 18(1). http://www.cjc-online.ca/viewarticle.php?id=141&layout=html. (Accessed 27 June 2006.)

Davis, Lennard J. 2002. *Bending Over Backwards: Disability, Dismodernism and Other Difficult Positions*. New York: New York University Press.

– 1997. 'Introduction: The Need for Disability Studies.' In *The Disability Studies Reader*. Ed. Lennard Davis. New York: Routledge. 1–8.

– 1995. *Enforcing Normalcy: Disability, Deafness and the Body.* London: Verso Press.

Desouza, Mike. 2004. 'Tiny Call Centre to Handle Aid to Disabled: Move Will Save Quebec $500,000 a Year.' *Montreal Gazette*, 5 May: A12.

De Souza, Raymond. 2002. 'The Flesh Is Weak, the Spirit Willing.' *National Post*, 17 July.

Diprose, Rosalyn. 2005. 'A "Genethics" That Makes Sense: Take Two.' In *Ethics of the Body: Postconventional Challenges*. Ed. Margrit Shilrick and Roxanne Mykitiuk. Cambridge: MIT Press. 237–58.

– 2002. *Corporeal Generosity: On Giving with Nietzsche, Merleau-Ponty, and Levinas.* New York: State University of New York Press.

Dowd, Maureen. 2005. 'United States of Shame: Stuff Happens.' *New*

York Times: Opinions. www.nytimes.com/2005/09/03/opinion/
03dowd.html. (Accessed 3 Sept. 2005.)

Dreyfus, Herbert, and Stuart Dreyfus. 1999. 'The Challenge of Mer-
leau-Ponty's Phenomenology of Embodiment for Cognitive Science.'
In *Perspective on Embodiment: The Intersections of Nature and Culture.*
Ed. G. Weiss and H.F. Haber. New York, Routledge. 103–20.

Enns, Ruth. 1999. *A Voice Unheard: The Latimer Case and People with Disabilities.* Halifax: Fernwood Publishing.

Erevelles, Nirmala. 2000. 'Educating Unruly Bodies: Critical Pedagogy,
Disability Studies, and the Politics of Schooling.' *Educational Theory*
50(1): 25–47.

Ettorre, Elizabeth. 1998. 'Re-Shaping the Space between Bodies and
Culture.' *Sociology of Health and Illness* 20(4): 458–555.

Evenson, Brad. 1999. 'The Only Case in the World: Courtney Popken's
Disease May Be Unique, but Finding a Cure for Her Could
Strengthen Us All.' *National Post,* 6 March: B11.

'Experts Say Failed Separation of Twins Was Ethically Justified.' 2003.
Globe and Mail, 8 July: F7.

Fenstermaker, Sarah, and Candace West. 2002. *Doing Gender, Doing
Difference: Inequality, Power, and Institutional Change.* New York:
Routledge.

Finkelstein, Vic. 1998. 'Emancipating Disability Studies.' In *The Disability Reader.* Ed. Tom Shakespeare. London: Cassell Academic.
28–49.

Fish, Stanley. 1980. *Is There a Text in This Class? The Authority of Interpretive Communities.* Cambridge: Harvard University Press.

Fitzgerald, Jenniver. 1998. 'Geneticizing Disability: the Human
Genome Project and the Commodification of the Self.' *Issues in Law
and Medicine* 14(2): 147–63.

Fortun, Mike. 2002. 'Open Reading Frames: The Genome and the
Media.' *Gene Watch* 15(2). gene-watch.org/magazine/vol114–
6media.html. (Accessed 19 June 2002.)

Foucault, Michel. 1988. 'Technologies of the Self.' In *Technologies of the
Self: A Seminar with Michel Foucault.* Ed. Luther H. Martin, Huck Gut-
man, and Patrick H. Hutton. Amherst: University of Massachusetts
Press. 16–49.

– 1980. *Power/Knowledge: Selected Interviews and Other Writings 1972–
1977.* New York: Pantheon Books.

– 1979. *Discipline and Punish: The Birth of the Prison.* Trans. Alan Sheri-
dan. New York: Vintage Books.

– 1978. *The History of Sexuality: Volume I: An Introduction*. New York: Vintage Books.

– 1975. *The Birth of the Clinic: An Archaeology of Medical Perception*. New York: Vintage Books.

Frank. Arthur. 1998a. 'Bodies, Sex and Death.' *Theory, Culture and Society* 15(3–4): 417–25.

– 1998b. 'Foucault or Not Foucault? Commonwealth and American Perspectives on Health in the Neo-Liberal State.' *Health* 2(2): 233–43.

– 1998c. 'Stories of Illness as Care of the Self: A Foucauldian Dialogue.' *Health* 2(3): 329–48.

Gadacz, Rene. 1994. *Re-Thinking Dis-Ability: New Structures, New Relationships*. Edmonton: University of Alberta Press.

Gadamer, Hans-George. 1996. *The Enigma of Health: The Art of Healing in a Scientific Age*. Trans. Jason Gaiger and Nick Walker. Stanford: Stanford University Press.

– 1975. *Truth and Method*. New York: CrossRoad.

Garfinkel, Harold. 1967. *Studies in Ethnomethodology*. Englewood Cliffs, NJ: Prentice-Hall.

Garland-Thomson, Rosemarie. 1997. *Extraordinary Bodies: Figuring Physical Disability in American Culture and Literature*. New York: Columbia University Press.

Gatens, Moira. 1997. 'Corporeal Representation in/and the Body Politic.' In *Writing on the Body: Female Embodiment and Feminist Theory*. Ed. Katie Conboy, Nadia Medina, and Sara Stanbury. New York: Columbia University Press. 80–9.

Global Calgary. 2005. 'Deaf Parents Turn Disability into Advantage.' 20 April. http://www.canada.com/compentents/

Goffman, Erving. 1963a. *Behaviour in Public Places: Notes on the Social Organization of Gatherings*. New York: The Free Press.

– 1963b. *Stigma: Notes on the Management of Spoiled Identity*. Englewood Cliffs, NJ: Prentice-Hall.

Goggin, Gerrard, and Christopher Newell. 2003. *Digital Disability: The Social Construction of Disability in New Media*. Lanham, MD: Rowman and Littlefield Publishers, Inc.

Golding, Peter, and Philip Elliott. 1996. 'News Values and News Production.' In *Media Studies: A Reader*. Ed. Paul Marris and Sue Thornham. Edinburgh: Edinburgh University Press. 403–15.

Greenwood, Davydd, and Morten Levin. 2003. 'Reconstructing the Relationships between Universities and Society through Action Research.' In *The Landscape of Qualitative Research: Theories and Issues*.

Ed. Norman K. Denzin and Yvonna S. Lincoln. Thousand Oaks, CA: Sage Publications. 131–66.

Grosz, Elizabeth. 2003. 'Histories of the Present and Future: Feminism, Power, Bodies.' In *Thinking the Limits of the Body*. Ed. Jeffrey Jerome Cohen and Gail Weiss. New York: State University of New York Press. 25–38.

– 1996. 'Intolerable Ambiguity: Freaks as/at the Limits.' In *Freakery: Cultural Spectacles of the Extraordinary Body*. Ed. Rosemarie Garland-Thomson. New York: New York University Press. 55–68.

Hall, Stuart. 1996. 'Introduction: Who Needs "Identity" Anyway?' In *The Questions of Cultural Identity*. Ed. Stuart Hall and Paul du Gay. London: Sage Publications. 1–17.

Hall, Stuart, Chas Chritcher, Tony Jefferson, John Clarke, and Brian Roberts. 1996. 'The Social Production of News.' In *Media Studies: A Reader*. Ed. Paul Marris and Sue Thornham. Edinburgh: Edinburgh University Press. 424–9.

Haraway, Donna. 1991. *Simians, Cyborgs, and Women: The Reinvention of Nature*. New York: Routledge.

– 1990. 'A Manifesto for Cyborgs: Science, Technology, and Socialist Feminism in the 1980's.' In *Feminism/Postmodernism*. Ed. Linda J. Nicholson. New York: Routledge. 190–233.

Hartouni, Valerie. 1998. 'Fetal Exposures: Abortion Politics and the Optics of Allusion.' In *The Visible Woman: Imaging Technologies, Gender, and Science*. Ed. Paula Treichler, Lisa Cartwright, and Constance Penley. New York: New York University Press. 198–216.

'Health Woes Ahead for Wheelchair-Bound People, Says Doctor.' *Guardian*, 3 June.

Holzer, Brigitte, Arthur Vreede, and Babriele Weigt, eds. 1999. *Disability in Different Cultures: Reflection on Local Concepts*. Bielefeld: Transcript Verlag.

Hubbard, Ruth. 1997. 'Abortion and Disability.' In *The Disability Studies Reader*. Ed. Lennard Davis. New York: Routledge. 187–200.

Hughes, Bill, and Kevin Paterson. 1997. 'The Social Model of Disability and the Disappearing Body: Towards a Sociology of Impairment.' *Disability & Society* 12(3): 325–40.

Hunt, Paul. 1998 [1966]. 'A Critical Condition.' In *The Disability Studies Reader: Social Science Perspectives*. Ed. Tom Shakespeare. London: Cassell Academic. 7–19.

Ingstad, Benedicte, and Susan Reynolds Whyte, eds. 1995. *Disability and Culture*. Berkeley: University of California Press.

Iser, Wolfgang. 2000. *The Range of Interpretation*. New York: Columbia University Press.

Kerr, Anne, and Tom Shakespeare. 2002. *Genetic Politics: From Eugenics to Genome*. Cheltenham, UK: New Clarion Press.

Khan, Shermeen. 1999. 'Can't See ≠ Can't Do: Blind Student Tackles Life like Anyone.' *Sunday Herald*, 7 Feb.

Kilgannon, Corey. 2006. 'Given a Chance to Be Little Ballerinas, and Smiling Right Down to Their Toes.' *New York Times*, 5 May. www.nytimes.com/2006/05/05/nyregion/o5ballet.html. (Accessed 5 May 2006.)

Klaszus, Jeremy. 2005. 'Seeing Past the Disability.' *Calgary Herald*, 30 March.

Kolata, Gina. 2004. 'When Alzheimer's Steals the Mind, How Aggressively to Treat the Body?' *New York Times*. www.nytimes.com/2004/05/18/health/18DEME.html. (Accessed 18 May 2004.)

Konrad, Monica. 2003. 'From Secrets of Life to the Life of Secrets: Tracing Genetic Knowledge as Genealogical Ethics in Biomedical Britain.' *Royal Anthropological Institute* 9(2): 339–58.

Lemert, Charles. 1997. *Social Things: An Introduction to the Sociological Life*. Lanham, MD: Rowman and Littlefield Publishers, Inc.

Lindenburg, Mark. 2004. 'Look beyond the Leg Brace: You'll See a Whole Person Who Just Happens to Have a Disability.' *Maclean's*, 22 Nov. http://www.macleans.ca/switchboard/overtoyou/article.jsp?content=20041122_93422_93422 (Accessed 2 Aug. 2005.)

Linton, Simi. 2006. *My Body Politic: A Memoir*. Ann Arbor: University of Michigan Press.

– 1998. *Claiming Disability: Knowledge and Identity*. New York: New York University Press.

Linton, Simi, Susan Mello, and John O'Neill. 1995. 'Disability Studies: Expanding the Parameters of Diversity.' *Radical Teacher* 47: 4–10.

Litwin, Grania. 2005. 'Pedal Mettle: Competitive Cyclist Ryan Arbuckle Hasn't Let a Disability Get in the Way of Thriving in His Sport.' *Times Colonist*, 5 July.

Lock, Margaret. 1993. 'The Politics of Mid-Life and Menopause: Ideologies for the Second Sex in North America and Japan.' In *Knowledge, Power and Practice: The Anthropology of Medicine and Everyday Life*. Ed. Shirley Lindenbaum and Margaret Lock. Berkeley: University of California Press.

Martin, Luther H., Huck Gutman, and Patrick H. Hutton. 1988. *Tech-*

nologies of the Self: A Seminar with Michel Foucault. Amherst: University of Massachusetts Press.

Matthews, Beverly, and Lori G. Beaman. 2006. *Gender in Canada: A Multi-Dimensional Approach.* Toronto: Pearson.

McColl, Mary Ann, and Lyn Jongbloed, eds. 2006. *Disability and Social Policy in Canada.* 2nd ed. Toronto: Captus Press.

McRuer, Robert. 2002. 'Compulsory Able-Bodiedness and Queer/Disabled Existence.' In *Disability Studies: Enabling the Humanities.* Ed. Sharon L. Snyder, Brenda Jo Brueggemann, and Rosemarie Garland-Thomson. New York: Modern Language Association of America.

McRuer, Robert, and Abby Wilkerson. 2003. 'Desiring Disability: Queer Theory Meets Disability Studies.' *GLQ: A Journal of Lesbian and Gay Studies* 9(1–2): 1–24.

Mead, George Herbert. 1934. *Mind, Self and Society from the Standpoint of a Social Behaviorist.* Ed. Charles W. Morris. Chicago: University of Chicago Press.

Melzer, David, and Ron Zimmern. 2002. 'Genetics and Medicalization.' *British Medical Journal* 324(7342): 863–4.

Merleau-Ponty, Maurice. 1974. *Phenomenology, Language and Sociology.* London: Heinemann Educational Books, Ltd.

– 1964. *The Primacy Of Perception: And Other Essays on Phenomenological Psychology, the Philosophy of Art, History and Politics.* Evanston, IL: Northwestern University Press.

– 1958 [1945]. *Phenomenology of Perception.* Trans. Colin Smith. London: Routledge and Kegan Paul.

Michalko, Rod. 2002. *The Difference That Disability Makes.* Philadelphia: Temple University Press.

– 2001. 'Blindness Enters the Classroom.' *Disability & Society* 16(3): 349–59.

– 1998. *The Mystery of the Eye and the Shadow of Blindness.* Toronto: University of Toronto Press.

Mitchell, David T., and Sharon L. Snyder. 2000. *Narrative Prosthesis.* Ann Arbor: University of Michigan Press.

– 1997. 'Disability Studies and the Double Bind of Representation.' In *The Body and Physical Difference: Discourses of Disability.* Ed. David Mitchell and Sharon Snyder. Ann Arbor: University of Michigan Press. 1–31.

Mitchell, Lisa M. 2001. *Baby's First Picture.* Toronto: University of Toronto Press.

Mol, Annemarie, and John Law. 2004. 'Embodied Action, Enacted Bodies: The Example of Hypoglycaemia.' *Body & Society* 10(2–3): 43–62.

Mollow, Anna. 2004. 'Identity Politics and Disability Studies: A Critique of Recent Theory.' *Michigan Quarterly Review* 43(2): 269–96.

Murphy, Robert. 1987. *The Body Silent.* New York: W.W. Norton.

Natanson, Maurice. 1998. *The Erotic Bird: Phenomenology in Literature.* Princeton: Princeton University Press.

– 1970. *The Journeying Self: A Study in Philosophy and Social Role.* Reading, MA: Addison-Wesley Co.

– 1963. 'A Study of Philosophy and the Social Sciences.' In *Philosophy of the Social Sciences.* Ed. Maurice Natanson. New York: Random House: 271–85.

Office for Disability Issues (ODI). 2002. *Office for Disability Issues: Strategic Plan 2002–2007.* Ottawa: Human Resources Development Canada.

Oliver, Michael. 1996. *Understanding Disability: From Theory to Practice.* New York: St Martin's Press.

– 1990. *The Politics of Disablement.* London: The MacMillan Press Ltd.

Overboe, James. 1999. '"Difference in Itself": Validating Disabled People's Lived Experience.' *Body & Society* 5(4): 17–29.

'Overcoming Disabilities.' 2005. *Kidzworld.* www.kidzworld.com/site/p5280.htm. (Accessed 8 May 2005.)

Parens, Erik, ed. 1998. *Enhancing Human Traits: Ethical and Social Implications.* Washington, DC: Georgetown University Press.

Parker, Andrew, and Eve Kosofsky Sedgwick. 1995. *Performativity and Performance.* London: Routledge.

Paterson, Kevin, and Bill Hughes. 1999. 'Disability Studies and Phenomenology: The Carnal Politics of Everyday Life.' *Disability & Society* 14(5): 597–610.

Patterson, Annette, and Martha Satz. 2002. 'Genetic Counselling and the Disabled: Feminism Examines the Stance of Those Who Stand at the Gate.' *Hypatia* 17(3): 118–44.

Peters, Susan. 1999. 'Transforming Disability Identity through Critical Literacy and the Cultural Politics of Language.' In *Disability Discourse.* Ed. Mairian Corker and Sally French. Buckingham: Open University Press. 103–15.

Philp, Margaret. 2002. 'Of Human Bondage: How the System Martyrs Parents of Disabled Kids.' *Globe and Mail,* 16 Feb.: F4–5.

Pratt, Anna, and Mariana Valverde. 2002. 'From Deserving Victims to "Masters of Confusion": Redefining Refugees in the 1990s.' *Canadian Journal of Sociology* 27(2): 135–61.

Price, Janet, and Margrit Shildrick, eds. 1999. *Feminist Theory and the Body: A Reader*. New York: Routledge.

Pronger, Brian. 2002. *Body Fascism: Salvation in the Technology of Physical Fitness*. Toronto: University of Toronto Press.

Purdy, L.M. 1990. 'Are Pregnant Woman Fetal Containers?' *Bioethics* 4(4): 273–91.

Radley, Alan. 2002. 'Portrayals of Suffering: On Looking Away, Looking At, and the Comprehension of Illness Experience.' *Body & Society* 8(3): 1–24.

Rapp, Rayna. 2000. *Testing Women, Testing the Fetus: The Social Impact of Amniocentesis in America*. New York: Routledge.

– 1993. 'Accounting for Amniocentesis.' In *Knowledge and Practice: The Anthropology of Medicine and Everyday Life*. Ed. Shirley Lindenbaum and Margaret Lock. Berkeley: University of California Press. 55–78.

Rapp, Rayna, and Faye Ginsburg. 2002. 'Standing at the Crossroads of Genetic Testing: New Eugenics, Disability Consciousness, and Women's Work.' *Genewatch* 15(1). http://www.gene-watch.org/genewatch/articles/15-lcrossroads.html. (Accessed 4 Sept. 2006.)

– 2001. 'Enabling Disability: Rewriting Kinship, Re-imagining Citizenship.' *Public Culture: Society for Transnational Cultural Studies* 13(3): 553–6.

Rinaldi, Jacqueline. 1996. 'Rhetoric and Healing: Revising Narratives about Disability.' *College English* 58(7): 820–34.

Robson, Christa. 2005. '"Canada's Most Notorious Bad Mother": The Newspaper Coverage of the Jordan Heikamp Inquest.' *Canadian Review of Sociology and Anthropology* 42(2): 217–32.

Rose, Nikolas. 1999 [1989]. *Governing the Soul: The Shaping of the Private Self*. New York: Free Association Press.

– 1994. 'Medicine, History and the Present.' In *Reassessing Foucault: Power, Medicine and the Body: Studies in the Social History of Medicine*. Ed. Colin Jones and Roy Porter. London: Routledge. 48–72.

Rosenau, Nancy. 2001. 'Do Espoused Values of Diversity Include All Differences? The Representation of Disability in Popular Counselor Education Textbooks.' Paper presented at the Society for Disability Studies 14th Annual Conference on Democracy, Diversity and Disability, Winnipeg Convention Centre, Winnipeg, 20–3 June.

Ruhl, Lealle. 2002. 'Dilemmas of the Will: Uncertainty, Reproduction, and the Rhetoric of Control.' *Signs: Journal of Women in Culture and Society* 27(3): 641–63.

Rushkowski, Von. 2003. 'Able Scientists Overcoming Disabilities.' *Next-Wave Science Magazine Canada*, 6 June.

Sandahl, Carrier, and Philip Auslander, eds. 2005. *Bodies in Commotion: Disability and Performance*. Ann Arbor: University of Michigan Press.

Sawicki, Jana. 1999. 'Disciplining Mothers: Feminism and the New Reproductive Technologies.' In *Feminist Theory and the Body: A Reader*. Ed. Janet Price and Margrit Shildrick. Routledge: New York. 190–202.

Scott, Joan. 1998. 'Deconstructing Equality-versus-Difference; or, The Uses of Postcolonial Structuralist Theory for Feminism.' *Feminist Studies* 14(1): 32–50.

– 1995. 'Multiculturalism and the Politics of Identity.' In *The Identity in Question*. Ed. John Rajchman. New York: Routledge. 3–12.

Scott, Sue, and David Morgan, eds. 1993. *Body Matters: Essays on the Sociology of the Body*. Washington, DC: The Falmer Press.

Serlin, David. 2002. 'Engineering Masculinity: Veterans and Prosthetics after World War Two.' In *Artificial Parts, Practical Lives: Modern Histories of Prosthetics*. Ed. Katherine Ott, David Serline, and Stephen Mihn. New York: New York University Press. 45–74.

Shildrick, Margrit. 2005a. 'Beyond the Body of Bioethics: Challenging the Conventions.' In *Ethics of the Body: Postconventional Challenges*. Ed. Margrit Shildrick and Roxanne Mykitiuk. Cambridge: MIT Press. 1–29.

– 2005b. 'The Disabled Body, Genealogy and Undecidability.' *Cultural Studies* 19(6): 755–70.

– 2002. *Embodying the Monster: Encounters with the Vulnerable Self*. London: Sage Publications.

Shildrick, Margrit, and Janet Price. 1996. 'Breaking the Boundaries of the Broken Body.' *Body & Society* 2(4): 93–113.

– eds. 1998. *Vital Signs: Feminist Reconfigurations of the Bio/logical Body*. Edinburgh: Edinburgh University Press.

Silvers, Anita. 1998. 'A Fatal Attraction to Normalizing: Treating Disabilities as Deviations from "Species-Typical" Functioning.' In *Enhancing Human Traits: Ethical and Social Implications*. Ed. Erik Parens. Washington DC: Georgetown University Press. 95–123.

Smith, Dorothy E. 2005. *Institutional Ethnography: A Sociology for People*. Lanham, MD: Rowman & Littlefield Publishers, Inc.

– 1999. *Writing the Social: Critique, Theory, and Investigations*. Toronto: University of Toronto Press.

- 1990. *The Conceptual Practices of Power: A Feminist Sociology of Knowledge*. Toronto: University of Toronto Press.

Snyder, Sharon L., and David T. Mitchell. 2006. *Cultural Locations of Disability*. Chicago: University of Chicago Press.

Sobchack, Vivian. 2004. *Carnal Thoughts: Embodiment and Moving Image Culture*. Berkeley: University of California Press.

Sprague, Joey, and Jeanne Hayes. 2000. 'Self-Determination and Empowerment: Feminist Analysis of Talk about Disability.' *American Journal of Community Psychology* 28(5): 671–95.

Squier, Susan M. 1995. 'Reproducing the Posthuman Body: Ectogenetic Fetus, Surrogate Mother, Pregnant Man.' In *Posthuman Bodies*. Ed. Judith Halberstam and Ira Livingston. Indianapolis: Indiana University Press. 113–32.

Stabile, Carol. 1998. 'Shooting the Mother: Fetal Photography and the Politics of Disappearance.' In *The Visible Woman: Imaging Technologies, Gender, and Science*. Ed. Paula Treichler, Lisa Cartwright, and Constance Penley. New York: New York University Press. 187–8.

Stabile, Carol, and Valerie Hartouni. 1998. 'Introduction: Paradoxes of Visibility.' In *The Visible Woman: Imaging Technologies, Gender, and Science*. Ed. Paula Treichler, Lisa Cartwright, and Constance Penley. New York: New York University Press. 1–20.

Stacey, Jean Edwards. 2004. 'Beating the Odds: Youth with Learning Disabilities Receive Awards.' *The Telegram*, 25 June: A4.

Statistics Canada. 2002. *A New Approach to Disability Data: Changes between the 1991 Health and Activity Limitation Survey (HALS) and the 2001 Participation and Activity Limitation Survey (PALS)*. 89-578-X1E2002001. Ottawa: Housing, Family and Social Statistics Division.

- 2001. *Participation and Activity Limitation Survey: A Profile of Disability in Canada, 2001 – Tables December 2002*. Ottawa: Minister of Industry.

- 1995. *A Portrait of Persons with Disabilities: Target Groups Project*. Ottawa: Minister of Industry, Science and Technology.

- 1991. *Health and Activity Limitation Survey*. http://www.statcan.ca/english/Pgdb/People/Health/health12a.htm and http://www.hrdc-drhc.gc.ca/sommon/news/ 9821b3.html

Stiker, Henri-Jacques. 1999. *A History of Disability*. Trans. William Sayers. Foreword by David T. Mitchell. Ann Arbor: University of Michigan Press.

Stocker, Susan S. 2001. 'Problem of Embodiment and Problematic Embodiment.' *Hypatia* 16(3): 30–55.

Taborsky, Edwina. 1997. *The Textual Society.* Toronto: University of Toronto Press.

Taussig, Michael. 1993. *Mimesis and Alterity: A Particular History of the Senses.* New York: Routledge.

Taylor, Kerry, and Rozanne Mykitiuk. 2001. 'Genetics, Normalcy and Disability.' *ISUMA* 2(3): 65–71.

Taylor, Mark C. 1993. *Nots.* Chicago: University of Chicago Press.

Thomas, Carol. 1999. *Female Forms: Experiencing and Understanding Disability.* Buckingham: Open University Press.

Thomas, W.I. 1971 [1923]. 'On the Definition of the Situation.' In *Sociology: The Classic Statements.* Ed. Marcello Truzzi. New York: Random House. 274–7.

– 1931. *The Unadjusted Girl.* Boston: Little Brown and Company.

Thomas, W.I., and D. Thomas. 1928. *The Child in America.* New York: Knopf.

Titchkosky, Tanya. 2006a. 'Pausing at the Intersections of Difference.' In *Gender in Canada: A Multi-Dimensional Approach.* Ed. Beverly Matthews and Lori G. Beaman. Toronto: Pearson.

– 2006b. 'Policy, Disability, Reciprocity?' In *Disability and Social Policy in Canada.* Ed. Mary Ann McColl and Lyn Jongbloed. 2nd ed. Toronto: Captus Press. 58–86.

– 2005a. 'Acting Blind: A Revelation of Culture's Eye.' In *Bodies in Commotion: Disability and Performance.* Ed. Philip Auslander and Carrie Sandahl. Ann Arbor: University of Michigan Press. 346–63.

– 2005b. 'Clenched Subjectivity: Disability, Women and Medical Discourse.' *Disability Studies Quarterly* 25(3). Special issue on disability studies and technology. Ed. Gerard Goggin and Christopher Newell. www.dsq-sds.org. (Accessed 4 Sept. 2006.)

– 2005c. 'Disability in the News: A Reconsideration of Reading.' *Disability & Society* 20(6): 653–66.

– 2003a. *Disability, Self, and Society.* Toronto: University of Toronto Press.

– 2003b. 'Governing Embodiment: Technologies of Constituting Citizens with Disabilities.' *Canadian Journal of Sociology* 28(40): 517–42.

– 2002. 'Cultural Maps: Which Way to Disability?' In *Disability/Postmodernity: Embodying Disability Theory.* Ed. Mairian Corker and Tom Shakespeare. London: Continuum. 145–60.

– 2001a. 'Coming Out Disabled: The Politics of Understanding.' *Disability Studies Quarterly* 21(4): 131–39. www.cds.hawaii.edu or http://www.dsq-sds.org/_articles_pdf/2001/Fall/dsq_2001_Fall_15.pdf

- 2001b. 'Disability: A Rose by Any Other Name? – "People-First" Language in Canadian Society.' *Canadian Review of Sociology and Anthropology* 38(2): 125–40.
- 2000. 'Disability Studies: The Old and the New?' *Canadian Journal of Sociology and Anthropology* 25(2): 197–224.
- 1998. 'Women, Anorexia and Change.' *Dharma: The Changing Faces of Femininity* 23(4): 479–500.

Treichler, Paula A., Lisa Cartwright, and Constance Penley, eds. 1998. *The Visible Woman: Imaging Technologies, Gender, and Science*. New York: New York University Press.

Tremain, Shelly, ed. 2005. *Foucault and the Government of Disability*. Ann Arbor: University of Michigan Press.

- 2002. 'On the Subject of Impairment.' In *Disability/Postmodernity: Embodying Disability Theory*. Ed. Mairian Corker and Tom Shakespeare. London: Continuum. 32–47.

Tsang, Peral. 2004. 'Glad Hatters Bring Campaign to a Close.' *Calgary Herald*, 20 June: D7.

Turner, Victor. 1985. *On the Edge of the Bush: Anthropology as Experience*. Tucson: University of Arizona Press.

Valverde, Mariana. 1998. 'Governing out of Habit: From "Habitual Inebriates" to "Addictive Personalities."' *Studies in Law, Politics and Society* 18: 217–42.

Vanast, Walter J. 2003. 'The Best Gift Ever: She Was a Patient with a Mysterious Condition That Left Her without Vision.' *The Globe and Mail*, F7.

van Manen, Max. 1990. *Researching Lived Experience: Human Science for an Action Sensitive Pedagogy*. London, ON: Althouse Press.

Warner, Sam. 2001. 'Disrupting Identity through Visible Therapy: A Feminist Post-Structuralist Approach to Working with Women Who Have Experienced Child Sexual Abuse.' *Feminist Review* 68: 15–139.

Weber. Max. 1947. *The Theory of Social and Economic Organization*. Trans. Talcott Parsons. New York: The Free Press.

Weiss, Gail. 2003. 'The Body as a Narrative Horizon.' In *Thinking the Limits of the Body*. Ed. Jeffrey Jerome Cohen and Gail Weiss. New York: State University of New York Press. 25–38.

Weiss, Gail, and Honi Fern Haber, eds. 1999. *Perspective on Embodiment: The Intersections of Nature and Culture*. New York: Routledge.

Weitz, Rose. 2003. *The Politics of Women's Bodies: Sexuality, Appearance, and Behavior*. New York: Oxford University Press.

West, Cornel. 1995. 'A Matter of Life and Death.' In *The Identity in Question*. Ed. John Rajchman. New York: Routledge. 15–32.

– 1990. 'The New Cultural Politics of Difference.' In *Out There: Marginalization and Contemporary Cultures*. Ed. Russell Ferguson, Martha Gever, Thrin T. Minh-ha, and Cornel West. New York: New Museum of Contemporary Art; Cambridge: MIT Press. 19–36.

Wittgenstein, Ludwig. 1980. *Remarks on the Philosophy of Psychology: Volume II*. Chicago: University of Chicago Press.

– 1958. *Philosophical Investigations*. Trans. G.E.M. Anscombe. Oxford: Basil Blackwell and Mott, Ltd.

World Health Assembly [WHO]. 1980. *International Classification of Impairments, Disabilities and Handicaps [ICIDH]: A Manual of Classification Relating to the Consequences of Disease*. Geneva: World Health Organization of the 29th World Health Assembly.

Young, Iris Marion. 1990. *Throwing like a Girl and Other Essays in Feminist Philosophy and Social Theory*. Bloomington: Indiana University Press.

Zarb, Gerry. 1997. 'Researching Disabling Barriers.' In *Doing Disability Research*. Ed. Colin Barnes and Geof Mercer. Leeds: The Disability Press. 49–66.

Zenit News Agency, 2004. 'Quality of Society's Life Gauged by Care of Disabled, Says Pope "Rights Cannot Be Only the Prerogative of the Healthy."' Zenit.org: ZE04010805. 8 Jan.

Zola, Irving Kenneth. 1982. *Missing Pieces: A Chronicle of Living with a Disability*. Philadelphia: Temple University Press.

– 1977. 'Healthism and Disabling Medicalization.' In *Disabling Professions*. Ed. I. Illich. London: Marion Boyars Publishers Ltd.

Index

ability and disability, binary of, 194, 200, 210
ability and non-ability, 199
ability/disability, relationship, 193
abled-disabled individual: as desiring normalcy, 151, 176; as new type of disabled person, 148; 'overcoming stories' of, 177–207; popular press stories of, 181–2; as solution to disability, 159–65, 177
able-ism, demand for, 192
able-ist sameness, normative values of, 191
abnormalcy, 96–8, 102, 159, 168; condition of, 152–4
abnormality, 89, 91–2, 168; in births, 29; disability as, 68; of fetus, 79, 82–6, 90, 93–4, 136; in medical context, 133–6, 158. *See also* normal
Aboriginal Peoples Survey (APS), 53, 59, 153
aboriginal population, 47, 167
accidents, media reports of, 6
activist slogans, 195

Advancing the Inclusion of Persons with Disabilities, 47–8, 50–1, 146–8; statistics from, 60
advertisements for cures, 15
age, as form of difference, 8
Alderson, Priscilla, 136
alterity: devalued, 216n19; diminishment of, 137; effacing, 209; ethics of, 143, 145; grappling with, 211; inherent in embodiment, 199; inserting into world, 25; meaning of, 8; 'overcoming stories,' 179, 204; potential of, 37; as productive force, 192, 195, 201; and recognizing disability, 180; relation to, 210
amniocentesis test, 28, 80, 82, 89, 91, 215n11
amputation, 188–90
anthropology of infirmity, 108–9
anti-depressants, 58
antiquated beliefs, 45
appearance as enactment, 17–21, 23, 33–6, 40–6, 60
Arendt, Hannah: on appearances, 22–3; attention to lan-

guage, 81; constraint and
creativity, 115; humans as
interpretative beings, 35; on
need to understand, 120
artificial limbs, 188
Asenjo, F.G., 99
assistive devices, 141
audience, positioned as non-
disabled, 182
Auslander, Philip, 182
author's voice, displacement of,
86

backward attitudes, 45
Bakhtin, M.M., 26
Barnes, Colin, 156, 181
Bauman, Zygmunt, 152, 157
Bhabha, Homi, 36–7
binary of ability and disability,
194, 200, 210
biological-matter-gone-wrong,
154
biological mistake, 90
biomedically based discourses,
145, 151
bio-politics of population, 165
biotechnology industry, 218n27
birth, textual enactment of, 28–31
births, abnormal. See under
abnormality
blind: people, 15, 39, 158, 178–9;
use of metaphor in language,
9, 196
bodily impairment as fate worse
than death, 114
body: as asocial object, 187; as
difficulty, 72–5; as gone wrong,
103; as limit and possibility,
115–16; as machine, 165; as
mechanical, 56; modalities of,

128; as obstacle, 187; perception of, 127; as problem, 122–3,
189; as response, 130; as social
entity, 126; subject/object, 13;
as unessential, 185; as a way of
being, 130–1. See also embodiment
Bonner, Kieran, 37
Bordo, Susan, 175, 184
braces, as symbol of disability,
198
Braidotti, Rosi, 91–2
building code, 165, 170
burden, 97
bureaucracy: disability through,
14; discursive practices of, 145;
hierarchy of, 24, 27–30, 101;
language practices of, 141;
management of disability, 145,
148, 177–8; medical, 31; solution of, 152. See also government
Butler, Judith: Bodies That Matter,
18, 66; on categories, 129; concept of performativity, 18; conditions of emergence, 82; on
gender, 197–8; Giving an
Account of Oneself, 18; to 'matter,' 150; non-viable life, 106–7;
power forming subject vs. of
subject, 31; The Psychic Life of
Power, 21; on recognition, 6, 8,
177, 179, 193; risk of destruction, 190; taking human for
granted, 61–2; unassimilable
remainder, 126; Undoing Gender, 6, 18, 177

Canadian census, 49, 59–60, 66–8,
70–6, 80, 99, 153

Canadian government texts: documenting of disability, 48–9; focus on, 142; language in, 51; responding to community, 64. *See also* government; *In Unison*; problem, disability as

'can do' values, 184

Canguilhem, Georges, 156

capitalism, late, 179, 205

'Cares and Woes.' *See* 'Of Human Bondage'

caring, 39

Casper, Monica, 216n14

census filter questions, 67–8, 70–1, 214n6. *See also* Canadian census

cerebral palsy, 182

charity, 39, 182, 193–5

children, disabled, 47, 83–4

Chronicle Herald, 15

Cicourel, Aaron, 19

citizen, 148, 162, 173–4

civic participation, lack of, 168–9

Cixous, Hélène, 204–6

claiming to know disability, 40

class, 7

clinical description, 79. *See also* medicalization of disability

CNN coverage, Hurricane Katrina, 3. *See also* mass media

Coalition of Injured Workers, 15

Cohen, Jeffrey, 115

collective: consciousness, 77; imagination, 203; life, 203–4; politics, 75

community, 62–6

community of readers. *See* readers, community of

conceptions of disability, 77. *See also* disability

conduct of conduct, 151

conformity, 171–4

confronting culture, 104

consumer culture, 30, 42

contemporary culture, meaning of disability, 12

control, modalities of, 133

Cook, Kay, 29

Corker, Mairian, 36

countable population, 155

cripple, use of term, 195–7, 202–6

critical condition, 181

Crossley, Adela, 80, 92–4, 96–7, 100–1

Crossley, Francine, 80, 92, 95–7, 100–1

Crossley, Jason, 80, 92, 97

cultural: interpretations, 93; model of disability, 213n5

culture, 18, 93, 104

cure for disability, 15–16, 106, 110–13

dated facts, 60

Davis, Lennard, 39, 123

death: connection with disability, 109–12; recommendation of, 113

designing ourselves, 137

desire, 33

desired status of disability, 6

devalued life, 103

devaluing alterity, 216n19. *See also* alterity

deviations from normalcy, 97. *See also* normal

diagnostic breakthroughs, 91

difference: forms of, 8; as needed, 6; outside humanity, 191

Diprose, Rosalyn, 209

disability: as a caused entity, 133; as condition of activity reduction, 73–4; as countable thing, 54; as critical condition, 181; definition of, 12, 38, 46, 77; discourse, 5; documenting people with, 158; as exceptional circumstance, 181; as fluke condition, 91; as individual problem, 66; as loss, 133; low income of people with, 51; measuring barriers, 55; mediating, 65; as metaphor, 5–7, 9; models of, 213n5, 214n5; narration of, 19, 161; as negation, 125–6; as not, 129; as obstacle, 181, 192, 204; as other, 197; participation in society and, 51–2; people with as oppressed minority group, 51; as productive force, 8; relationship with ability, 193; in relation to people, 105; silencing of, 175; studies, 37; symbols of, 198; terminology, 12; as thing, 133. *See also* abled-disabled individual; embodiment; meaning; medicalization of disability; problem, disability as
Disability and Social Policy in Canada, 48–9
disability-as-negation logic, 134
Disability Tax Credit, 166
disabled population, Canadian, 47
discourse: biomedically based, 151; disability, 5; effect of, 23; genetic, 136–7
discrimination, 24, 51
discursive action, 7

discursive practices, key, 6
disgust in stories, 179
distinct biological condition, 156
distinct population, 154
dividing practices of medicine, 89–90. *See also* medicalization of disability
doctor, as textual enactment of medicine, 88
Down syndrome, 89
Dreyfus, Herbert, and Stuart Dreyfus, 117
drug companies, 112
dual consciousness, 154
dyslexia, 9, 13, 109, 116

easy read, 117
economic contribution, 168–9
economic relations, 157
eliminating disability, 106, 135–6
embodied existence: as changing, 60, 70; as encounters, 130; functionality of, 74; meanings of, 12
embodiment: alterity inherent in, 199; bureaucratic governance of, 148–52; community materializing of, 66; in context of citizenship, 168; cultural organization of, 11, 114, 143; exclusions through views of, 162, 176; identity politics and, 16; in inquiry into disability, 40; as lived, 17; the meaning of, 12–13, 111; in medical context, 44, 83–4, 87–9, 133–4, 192; race and, 201; seen as lack, 166; as social phenomenon, 4, 15; as taken for granted, 20; as text mediated, 7, 9; textual enact-

ment of, 177–84, 194; tied up with focus, 200–1; worry about, 108–9, 132. *See also* text
employment, 152, 168–9
empty life, disability as, 204
enactment. *See* appearance as enactment; textual enactment
encounters, 130
Enlightenment values, 136
enunciation, 23–4
environment: conception of, 74; exclusionary features, 56; role of, 75
erasing disability, 175
ethics of alterity, 143, 145. *See also* alterity
ethnicity, 8
eugenics, 44, 106, 131, 218n27
excludable type, 5, 137, 149–51, 159, 165
excluded, made to matter as, 150–1
exclusion: based on identity issues, 72; causing, 150; current practices of, 151; disability as sense-making device for, 159; historical basis, 150; and inclusion, 6, 37, 149–52; *In Unison*, 151; and the law, 174; as main problem of disabled, 142, 149; in mainstream textbooks, 78; noticing, 5; from society, 149
exclusionary features, 56
existence: ambiguity of, 203; assigning sense to, 19; defined by situation, 128; questionable, 44; as questionable, 113
experience: of disability, 9, 13; how known, 37

facts, power of, 61
fact-text: features of, 54–5; god trick, 46; *In Unison*, 49–62, 152–3; as reality, 55; reliance on tacit understandings, 57; separate status of, 47–8
family status, 8
fate worse than death, 114
feminine, as lack, 128–9
feminism: media texts, 38; theory, 8, 18
fetal abnormality, 29, 79, 82–6, 90, 93–4, 102; testing for, 136
Finkelstein, Vic, 116
focus, 200–1
form of text, 81, 98, 120–1
Foucault, Michel: bio-politics of the population, 165–6; discursive practices, 151; governmentality, 83, 149, 151; on government counting practices, 155; normalizing society, 168; sociology of illness, 217n21; truth game, 56
Frank, Arthur, 217n21
freak, the, 182
funding rules, 160
Future Directions, 146, 169

Garcia-Tolson, Rudy, 188–9
gender: on census, 67; gendered throw, 139; intersecting with depictions of impairment, 15, 51; population categories, 155; positions of writers and readers, 64; trilogy of gender, race, and class, 7. *See also* sexuality
genes: deformed, as departure from humanity, 94; disability at level of, 215n12; discovery

of, 135; faulty, cost/benefit analysis, 90

genetic: discourse, 136–7; engineering, 142; media reports of testing, 6; research on curing disability, 15; testing, 136

genome, mapping of, 136, 218n27

genomic industry, 137

Globe and Mail, 80, 82

'Globe Focus,' 82

god trick, 32–5, 46, 57–9, 61, 88

governance, modalities of, 133

government: attention to disability, 59; definition of disability, 45; documents, 43, 46–57, 155; funding, 49; goal of inclusion, 51; inclusionary practices of, 142; posters of wheelchair users, 14–15; production of programs, 154; solution to disability, 152; texts on community, 62–6; vision, 51, 169–70

governmentality, 83, 149, 151

government documents: *Disability and Social Policy in Canada,* 48–9; *Future Directions,* 146, 169; *National Strategy,* 48; *New Approach to Disability Data, A,* 46, 50, 66–74; *Obstacles,* 48; Participation and Activity Limitation Survey (PALS), 50, 60–1; Statistics Canada, 67–8; statistics justifying action, 57; *Strategic Plan 2002–2007,* 48; Survey of Labour and Income Dynamics (SLID), 59; 'Vision of Full Citizenship, The' (extract), 172; *Will to Act,* 48. *See also Advancing the Inclusion of Persons with Disabilities; In Unison*

Grosz, Elizabeth, 8, 214n9

groups, 132, 135

Haber, Honi, 25

Haraway, Donna, 32

hardship, hopeless, 181

Health and Activity Limitation Survey (HALS): difference from PALS, 59–61; PALS, name change to, 68–70; questions from, 70–1; reliance upon of *In Unison* document, 49–50; statistics from, 153–4, 166

hearing aids, as symbol of disability, 198

hearing impairment, point of view, 158

hermeneutics, 102

Hubbard, Ruth, 215n13

Hughes, Bill, 115, 123

human genome, mapping of, 136, 218n27

humanity, disability removed from, 75

human rights laws, 170

humans as interpretative beings, 35

Hunt, Paul, 65, 181

Hurricane Katrina, 3–5

Husserl, Edmund, 19

ICF (International Classification of Functioning, Disability and Health), 68

ICIDH model (International Classification of Impairment, Disability and Handicap), 69

identity: forging of, 3; issues and exclusion, 72; politics, 8, 16; treated as enactment, 23 image evaluation, 24

impairment: depictions of, 15; fate worse than death, 114; not human, 180

inclusion: best practices for, 154–5; bureaucratic management of, 143, 159; conflict with exclusion, 6; empowering, 150; ethics of, 145; full citizenship as, 172–4; goal of inclusion, 51; language practices, 141; as mechanism, 148; noticing, 5; relation with exclusion, 149–52; securing inclusion, 142; as solution, 142; via participation, 148

independent living movement, 84

individual betterment, focus on, 163

individual citizens with disabilities, 151

individual issue, disability as, 56

individuality, 157

inspirational overcomer, 182

institutions, 62–3

integration, kind of, 174–5

interactionist sociology, 195

interrelation of disabled and non-disabled, 38

interrelation of readers and writers, 39

intersectionality: concept of, 3–4; contradictions in the meaning of people, 5–6; in depictions of impairments, 15; with forms of difference, 8; with institutions, 155; in popular press, 82, 94; in reading and text, 115, 118; in science and technology, 83

In Unison documents (1998 and 2000): characteristic movements of life, 164–5, 168, 171; chronology of, 146; citizenship central to disability issues, 148; disability as distinct biological condition, 154; exclusion in, 151; inclusion in, 148; problem of disability, 148, 150, 152; problem of exclusion, 151; as vision papers, 148

In Unison 1998: as blueprint, 152; chronology, 146; vision paper, 152

In Unison 2000: analysis of text, 46–78; as blueprint, 49; chronology, 146; community as solution, 63; disability as problem condition, 62; 'Disability Facts and Figures,' 52–7; excerpt, 53; as fact-text, 49; geared to general readership, 49; goal of inclusion, 51, 154–5; individual stories in, 56, 160–3; narrative structure, 163–4; problem of disability, 51; reliance on HALS data, 49; as report, 152; statistics, need for, 59; statistics, use of, 52, 54, 153

Iser, Wolfgang, 69

journalism, conventions of, 84

Kahakwisthaw First Nation Reserve, 161

Kidzworld, 186–9

knowledge: commodification of, 82; of disability, 40; how experienced, 37

'Label Jars, Not People!' (slogan), 195–6
labelling people, 195–6
labour market, non-participation in, 167
lack: belonging to individuals, 188; body as, 168; causing desire, 33; of civic participation, 168; of data, 59; feminine as, 94; of participation, causing disability, 150; responding to, 185
lack, disability as: and abnormality, 88; biological, 96; condition of limit, 83–4, 87, 130; defined as, 8; imagined as, 180
lack of functionality: difficulties in activities, 74; disability, identification as, 58; disability no longer regarded as, 68–9; government questions about, 62, 166
lack of participation, 52, 150, 152
language: bureaucratic, 141; cleaning up English, 6, 11; of community, 63–4; disability in social justice, 51; games of, 54, 83; medicalization of disability, 81, 83, 87, 133; metaphors of disability, 5–7, 9; person-first, 195–6; sign, 178
Law, John, 12
learning disabilities, 9, 13, 109, 116, 118
legitimacy, establishing, 86
levels of disability, 51, 158
Lewis, Jerry, 206
liberalism, 179
liberal orientation to disability, 84

life: in disability, 183; disability as incompatible with, 95–6, 98, 137; not worth living, 106; textual renderings of, 27; without possibility, 119
limit: asocial conception of, 72; of body, 115–16; and possibility, 205, 211; of reading, 116–18
limit, disability as: condition of lack and limit, 75–6; possibility, 115–16; without possibility, 44, 111, 115, 119–20, 123, 137
Lindenburg, Mark, 182–4, 192–7, 199–204, 206
Linton, Simi, 6
literacy, as normative condition, 26
literate culture, 82, 117–18
living death, 142
Lock, Margaret, 61
lone individual, myth of, 184
looking, as social act, 87

Maclean's, 182
mainstream textbooks, exclusion in, 78
management issue, disability as, 194, 196–7
marginalization, 150, 170
mass media: on genetic breakthroughs, 91; intersectionality in popular press, 82, 94; link with illness and injury, 111; magazines, 28; medicalization of disability, 83–6; news about disabled in, 64; 'overcoming stories,' 142, 181; popular representations of disability, 43; problem of disability in, 142; as sensationalized, 98–102; ste-

reotypes, 202–3; text of newspapers, 80–1; text written for and by disabled, 38; treatment of disability in, 4–6, 9, 14, 26, 76–8, 120–7, 210

meaning: between text and reader, 118; created by government, 168; of disability, 6, 12, 19; of embodiment, 5–7; layers of, 98–9; noticed, 25; of people, 3, 13, 16

meaning-making: defined, 12; as way to read, 7

measuring disability barriers, 55

media reports. See mass media

mediating disability, examples of, 65

medicalization of disability: authority of doctor in, 87–92; consequences of, 43–4, 104–7, 134–6; explaining disability, 132–3; how it works, 43, 79, 81; media's role in, 83–6; objectification in, 92–5, 103–4; as process of enactment, 43–4; role of language in, 87, 95–8; as way of defining body, 46

medicalized condition of limit, 75–6

medicalized discursive regime, 79

medical texts, 28, 96

medicine: authority of, 84–91, 133; conception of disability, 43; discourse of, 102; discursive practice, 134; object of, 79; social vocation of, 90; solutions through, 141

memento mori, disability as, 123

Merleau-Ponty, Maurice: on language, 118; living through world, 115; on ontologies, 102; on perception, 22; on releasing type, 131; on words, 20

metaphor for problems, disability as, 6, 9. See also language

Michalko, Rod: disability and suffering, 59, 214n5; disability as needed difference, 7; life with author, 13; look as social act, 87; thinking about normalcy, 164

Mitchell, David, 5, 20, 171

mobility, 75, 156

Mol, Annemarie, 12

Mollow, Anna, 8

movements of life: In Unison, 158, 164–5, 168, 171; population statistics, 155; textual rendering of, 27

MS Society, 15

name as interpretation, 69

narration of disability, 19, 150, 161

Natanson, Maurice, 16

national consensus, 152

National Post, 64

National Strategy, 48

negation, disability as, 125–6

negative ontology, 44, 96, 105, 124, 126

neo-liberalism, 141, 179, 192, 205

New Approach to Disability Data, A, 46, 50, 66–74. See also government documents

new eugenics. See eugenics

New Orleans, 3

news: depictions of disability, 5; end product of process, 85;

headlines in newspapers, 120–7; reading of newspapers, 117; text of newspapers, 80–1. *See also* mass media

New York Times, 3

non-conformity, 156

non-participants in society, 167–8

non-viable way of being, 111

normal: abnormal births, 29; abnormality, 89, 92; departure from, 105; deviations from, 97; of normalcy, 98, 124; normalizing society, 168; order, 163–4; as real, 159; tyranny of, 155–6. *See also* abnormality

noticing disability, as social act, 24

objectifying disability, 46

objectivity, 22, 133

obstacle, disability as, 181, 192, 204

Obstacles, 48

'Of Human Bondage,' 80–101. *See also* mass media

'Only Case in the World, The' (article), 110. *See also* mass media

oppressive social practice, 40

Orphan Drug Act (U.S.), 113

'overcome!': demand to, 205

overcoming: assumption of good of, 143; disability as needing, 66; expected assumption, 142; sample headlines, 178–9; strategy for dealing with disability, 180; as textual representation, 177

overcoming self, 189

'overcoming stories': alterity, 179, 204; compartmentalized reality, 201; consistent narrative structure, 190; defining features, 184; form of forgetfulness, 203; functions of, 198; as human interest story, 181; illustrating values, 190; pleasure from, 192; repetitive genre, 180; scripts, 182; service to Western culture, 181–2

Paralympics, 189

parenting magazines, 28

parents with disabled children, 100

Participation and Activity Limitation Survey (PALS), 50, 60–1

participatory citizenship, lack of, 152

Paterson, Kevin, 115, 123

perceiving, 123, 210

perception: of bodies, 22; of body, 127; as closely woven fabric, 22; mistaken, 196; of others, 201–2

perceptual fields, 19

perfectability, belief in, 92, 106

person-first language codes, 196

person-first slogans, 195–6

personhood, 169

personhood, split from disability, 93

Philp, Margaret: birth of disabled children, 96–8, 100–1; liberal orientation to disability, 84–6; narration of disability, 89–90; narration of fetal abnormality, 82, 92

physician-assisted suicide, media reports of, 6

'Piss on Pity' (slogan), 195
pity: acceptance of, 185; attitudes of, 202; call for, 199; commodification of, 206; as common practice, 39, 182; disability as plea for, 193–4; issue of, 197; model of, 195; no time for, 160–1; overcoming, 195, 200; providers, 197–8, 205–6; resisters, 198; response to overcoming story, 191; as something to do, 132
political phenomenon, 38
Pope, the, 123, 126
Popken, Courtney, 110–14
popular press industry, 82. See also mass media
population, disabled as, 154–5, 158
population categories, 156
population of disabled, as problem, 43
population of disabled children, 100
pregnancy, medical view of, 28
pregnancy magazines, 28. See also mass media
prenatal: classes, 29; screening, 136; surgery, 216n4
Price, Janet, 91
print media depictions of disability, 9. See also mass media
problem: of doing, 73; meaning of, 13; population, 43
problem, disability as: culture's conception of, 70; functional, 55; how we conceive of, 43; In Unison 2000, 55; medical, 43, 45, 84; needing solution, 9, 52; ongoing constitution of, 38;

only interesting as, 52; repetitive constitution of, 76; solutions to fix, 141; textual enactment of, 50, 60; tragic, 177; understood as, 122. See also disability
problem-body, 122–3, 189
processes of life, 168
productive force, alterity as, 192, 195, 201. See also alterity
Pronger, Brian, 180; Body Fascism, 145
proper conduct, 162
prosthetic devices, 188–90

quadriplegia, 160–3
questionable existence, 44

race: embodiment and, 201; Hurricane Katrina, 3–4; intersecting with depictions of impairment, 15, 51; in media texts, 38; trilogy of gender, race, and class, 7–8; of writers and readers, 64; writing about, 38
rare as common, 112
rare diseases, 112–14
readers: assumptions required, 114; community of, 38, 63–6, 76–8, 81, 97, 104; positioned as non-disabled, 181; seduction of, 83; signs to, 98
reading: about disability, 22; competence, 23; conventions of, 84; disability differently, 6; disgust with, 114; as embodied activity, 119; limits of, 116–18; and text, 115; and writing as social acts, 16

recognition, 193, 201
reflexive perception, 123
remedial programs, 149–50
'respond!': demand to, 187–9,
    194, 201
responsibility, shift to individual,
    179
retelling disability, 131–2
Rezanoff, Melissa, 160–3
Rose, Nikolas, 89, 133

Sandahl, Carrie, 182
science and technology, intersec-
    tion of, 83. *See also* intersection-
    ality
scientific industrial structures,
    137
scientific reasoning, objectivity
    of, 104
Scott, Joan, 23–4
scrutinizing, 16
separation of self and disability,
    197
sexuality, 7–8, 38
Shildrick, Margrit, 91
short-changed life, 89–91, 95–8
Silvers, Anita, 155
Smith, Dorothy: capture of the
    reader, 46, 103, 116; *The Concep-
    tual Practices of Power*, 79; on
    social world, 27; text as social
    action, 31–2; texts in time and
    space, 33–4, 56; writing as dia-
    logic, 20; *Writing the Social*, 27,
    116
Snyder, Sharon, 5, 20, 171
Sobchack, Vivian, 185
social: accomplishment, 12; act of
    recognition, 6; character of
    knowledge, 35; class and

wealth, 214n6; conceptions of
    disability, 158; identity, 75;
    inquiry, 36; interaction enact-
    ing disability, 25; life unre-
    lated to disability, 76; model of
    disability, 213n5; phenomenon,
    38; relational concept of dis-
    ability, 126; significance of dis-
    ability, 11; theory, 36; world, 27
sociological tradition of inquiry,
    35–6
solution to disability, abled-dis-
    abled individual, 159–65
speech synthesizers, as symbol of
    disability, 198
Stabile, Carol, 213n4
statistics: disability rates, 47–8,
    54–6; justifying action, 57; use
    to make disability a problem,
    52
Statistics Canada, 67–8
status, removal from disability,
    74
status of disability, 83, 92, 129
Stiker, Henri-Jacques: on enlarg-
    ing understanding, 19; existen-
    tial understanding, 131; *A
    History of Disability*, 108; inte-
    gration into conformity, 171–2,
    174; social workings of disabil-
    ity, 149; on society and disabil-
    ity, 77; speaking of disabled,
    135; words for disability, 124–
    5; worry about embodiment,
    132
stories of overcoming. *See* 'over-
    coming stories'
storms, 3–6
Strategic Plan 2002–2007, 48
strength of individual, 157

study of disability, 37
subjectivism, 22
subjectivity, 98
suffering, 58–9
survey methodology, 61, 68
Survey of Labour and Income Dynamics (SLID), 59
survey questions, 76–7
sweet innocent, 182
symbolic manifestation of disability, 198
symbols of culture, no unity in, 36

Taylor, Mark, 125
teaching disability studies, 9
technological solutions, 141
technology, aid of, 165
technology-produced injuries, 170
telethon depiction of disability, 183, 194, 202
text: activity of meaning-making, 46; as cultural object, 103; daily production of disability through, 14, 210; disability enacted through, 25–8, 52, 199–201; as disabling, 56; as encounter with disability, 209; intersecting with reading, 115, 124–6; as metaphor for society, 26; objective presentation of, 32–5; as site for study of power relations, 27; as social action, 21, 27, 31, 55, 81, 106, 116–19. See also embodiment; language
textual enactment: of birth, 28–31; of disability, 16–17, 31–2, 50, 60, 76–9, 194; encounters with disability, 11, 14; in medi-
cal context, 88; stereotype and, 205
textured life of disability, 17
Thomas, Carol, 126
Thomas, W.I., 12
throwing like a girl, concept, 127–31
Titchkosky, Tanya, 9, 13, 35–7, 214n5
title shifts, 81, 83–4
Toronto Star, 15
translation, name change as, 69
transportation systems, exclusionary, 170
Trisomy-18, 80, 95–6
truth game, 56. See also language
truth of disability, 18
type, 131
typifications, 130

ultrasound: authoritative image of, 85; explanation of technology, 215n10; images from, 28; media reports of, 6; as social action, 87; used in text as agent, 82; use in god trick, 88
understand, need to, 120
understanding of disability, change in, 70
unemployed, 51, 167
United States of Shame, 3
unsafe work environments, 6

variation, opposed to difference, 191
victim, meaning of, 84–5, 95–100
'Victims of Love,' 83–4. See also 'Of Human Bondage'
view of disability, updated, 68–9
vision impairment, 156

'Vision of Full Citizenship, The' (extract), 172
vulnerability, 4, 116

war, media reports of, 6. *See also* mass media
weakness, exemplar of, 123
Weber, Max: concept of oriented action, 20
webs of interpretation, 102
Weiss, Gail, 19, 25, 115
West, Cornel, 45
wheelchairs: becoming a user of, 163; depictions of users of, 4–5, 15, 112–13, 122–3, 186, 188–9; perceptions of, 198; point of view of user of, 163; as symbols of disability, 198; the use of, 165
white canes, as symbol of disability, 198
Will to Act, 48
woman-as-problem, 101
woman's right to choose, 102, 136

women: delaying childbearing, 100; and disability, 93, 99; excessive subjectivity of, 98–104; made into problems, 83–4; natural ignorance of, 104; separated from bodies, 86–7, 90; separated from pregnancy, 213n4; in sexist society, 128
word as label of reality, 195
words for disability, 124–5
work-produced injuries, 170
work rates, difference in, 167
World Health Organization (WHO), 69, 133, 153
world view of negation, 125
worry, 108–9, 132
writing disability differently, 6

Young, Iris Marion: *Throwing like a Girl*, 127–31

Zola, Irving, 86, 98, 109, 171